THE GREEN PARADISE

by the same author
from the same publishers

The Distant Lands
(*a novel*)

Paris
(*essays — bilingual*)

South
(*a play*)

The Apprentice Writer
(*essays*)

JULIAN GREEN

THE GREEN PARADISE

Autobiography
Volume I (1900–1916)

Translated by
Anne and Julian Green

With a Preface by
Julian Green

Marion Boyars
New York · London

First published in this enlarged edition in
the United States and Great Britain in 1993
by Marion Boyars Publishers
237 East 39th Street, New York, N.Y. 10016
24 Lacy Road, London, SW15 1NL

Distributed in Australia by
Peribo Pty Ltd., 26 Tepko Road, Terrey Hills, NSW 2084

Enlarged edition previously published in France under the title
Partir Avant le Jour in 1984 by Editions du Seuil
© Editions du Seuil 1984
© this translation Julian Green 1993

Library of Congress Cataloging-in-Publication Data

Green, Julian, 1900—
    [Partir avant le jour. English]
    The green paradise : an autobiography / Julian Green ; translated
by Anne and Julian Green ; with a new introduction by Julian Green.

    1. Green, Julian, 1900–   —Biography.   2. Authors, French—20th
century—Biography.   3. Authors, American—20th century—Biography.
I. Title.
PQ2613.R2Z52513   1992
843'.912—dc20
[B]   92—18637

British Library Cataloguing in Publication Data

Green, Julian
    Green Paradise: Autobiography. — Vol.1
    I. Title   II. Green, Anne
    843.912

ISBN 0-7145-2955-9 Cloth

Printed and bound in Great Britain by
Biddles Ltd, Guildford and King's Lynn

About the Author

Born in 1900 of American parents living in Paris, Julian Green has spent most of his extraordinary literary career there, writing now in French for a wide and enthusiastic readership. He has published over sixty books in France: novels, essays, plays, a four-volume autobiography (of which this is the first), and, so far, fourteen volumes of his Journal. Initially writing in English, he published a number of celebrated books in England and the United States before writing almost exclusively in French.

As an American, Julian Green is the only foreign member of the Académie Française. He is also a member of the American Academy of Arts and Letters, winner of the Harper Prize, the Prix Marcel Proust, the Prix France-Amérique, the Prix Cavour and numerous other international awards. He is also one of the few living authors to have their collected works published in the prestigious Gallimard Pléiade series.

Julian Green's epic novel of the antebellum South *The Distant Lands* was published in 1991, simultaneously with his play *South* which is set on the eve of the Civil War. The sequel to *The Distant Lands*, set during the Civil War, will be published in 1993.

His book of essays about Paris with a selection of the author's own photographs of his favorite city is available from the same publishers. His early writings in English under the title *The Apprentice Writer* will also be published in 1993.

Julian Green lives in Paris.

Preface

Memory . . . I've sometimes been told, after the first publication of 'Partir avant le Jour' in 1963, that I had to have a good memory so as to remind myself of so many things. In that there is an element of illusion. My memory could be much better. It has its peculiar side which is a visual memory rather than an auditory one—except for music, a bit like a painter's memory. I wanted to be a painter, in fact, and to a certain extent I remained one. The words I call back are very rare, but those I do, I have in some manner recorded definitively. I don't remember twenty phrases my mother ever said to me. In another sense, there are numerous 'blanks' in the first volume of this autobiography, and quite as many also in the second. I am continually compelled to say that I don't remember anymore . . . But put end to end, these recollections form a kind of continuity which can provide a false scent. For what I remember nearly always has an almost photographic clarity, but once again these are isolated moments and separated by intervals which I don't succeed in filling in. I have compared this to a museum gallery where the pictures are hung some distance from each other.

I have not tried to flesh out long conversations, where I have retained only a few words. One often finds these conversations in *Memoirs* and I recognize that they often convey the sound of truth, but they can't be literally exact and I love the truth to be *literal*. I have been told that there lies a characteristic trait of the Protestant. And it is possible that my early education, which was Protestant, has marked me in this manner.

Why have I written these books? I've said in the first volume what I intended to do. This applies to the entire autobiography. I wanted, in fact, to re-discover the driving force which dominated my life. I've spoken of God's progression in the human heart. First in childhood, then in adolescence (in the second volume), then in early manhood (in the third and fourth). This progression is not always easy to follow. This very thing is the greatest mystery in our lives, this progression of God. Often one does not see it except after the event. I believe one does not see it clearly until many years later, when life is drawing to its close. That is why one needs to wait before writing down one's recollections if one would try to understand the direction of the journey one has made on this earth. I'm not sure, moreover, that one understands anything really important in it. One glimpses rather than actually seeing. In my case, it seems that I have been protected during all the early part of my youth by some kind of invincible ignorance. Protected from what? From a carnal experience where one's faith would perhaps be lost, as often happens. The experience came at a moment when the danger it presented was not at its most serious. It seemed clear to me that the single fact of announcing that I had a religious vocation (even if I was wrong) created a kind of forbidden zone around me. I didn't doubt it for a moment.

When did I really understand? I understood it fully when I had written these volumes of my authobiography. It's a strange business. I've had to reach the age I am today so as to realize the meaning of certain facts, small as well as large, which have set their mark on my childhood and my youth. I don't say that I've understood everything. But what strikes me is the vigilance of God who, according to the words of the psalm, neither slumbers nor sleeps, but guards each of us as if he was alone in the world, so long as he offers no resistance . . . In the matters whch concerned me, the most serious mistakes occurred much later.

There has been talk of impeaching the young man I used to be. In fact I've said that this book was *a bit* like an impeachment, but one should not go too far in that direction. I would find it alarming if a man, whom God could pardon, could not then pardon himself. However, souls do exist who hang onto their guilt as if it were a treasure. This is not the case with me.

I've also been asked about possible connections between this autobiography and psychoanalytic methods. I suppose that the man who entrusts himself to a psychiatist, in other words a doctor of the soul, feels the need of a cure. Curing is not my purpose. Curing what? I only wanted to see clearly. Curing the child and the adolescent? What preoccupied me was to understand the child and the adolescent I used to be. And besides, I am almost completely ignorant about psychoanalysis. Perhaps I have a certain defiance in that respect. It doesn't seem good for us to know too much about what is going on inside ourselves because that leads to one losing the taste and the sense of mystery. But what really matters is to give speech to the child which has never stopped inhabiting our heart.

Julian Green
1970
Translated by Arthur Boyars

The Child is Father of the Man . . .
                              Wordsworth

Just anything . . .

To write just anything is perhaps the best way of dealing with really important subjects, of taking the shortest road to their heart of hearts. Very simply to say what passes through your mind, as memory fancies. Memory brings up everything confusedly at all times of the day. This confusion will be faithfully repeated. No precise itinerary exists for the exploration of our past, and that is the way I see things today, November 20, 1959.

I am writing this as the afternoon ends. A good time to glance over my shoulder at the day before night falls, because night is another world. When daylight fails, the stars will shine. The dark sky will then say what it has to say. At present the sun still gleams over my paper and it occurs to me that my first memory is one of physical pain. I am being looked after, something hurts me.

Next comes the moment when I am lying on my mother's knee, naked, flat on my stomach, swimming motionless toward snowy curtains and the light that filters through them. I am filled with a vague happiness, a happiness so often experienced later, whereas the pain I have just mentioned (was it previous to that day, or the same day, or a few minutes before?) is mingled with fear and a kind of horror.

We lived at that time in a low-roofed house at the bottom of a garden closed by iron gates. I believe the house still stands at the foot of the Rue Raynouard. In the garden was a summerhouse surrounded by bushes, and if all that no longer exists, I would rather not know it.

We were poor. The houses on either side of the garden were

3

occupied by people seemingly no richer than we were. There was Madame Soret and there were also the Atalayas, a Spanish family whose children played with my sisters. Sometimes Madame Atalaya would go to the window and, both hands on the railing, tilted backward, she gave tongue, called her son and daughter: Jesus and Aurora. It seems as though I still hear her. There she is, at the dawn of the century, calling for all she is worth:

"Hayssooss! Aoorrorra!"

My mother sometimes gave me a sou with which to buy myself a cake, in a bakery on the Rue Raynouard, near Madame Soret's laundry where the white blouses hanging around the ceiling gently waved their sleeves when you opened the door.

I had to pass through the garden and walk a few steps up the street to reach the bakery, panting, and repeat what my mother had told me to say, in her foreigner's French: *"Un sou* cake." People laughed and gave me a piece of shortbread or a Breton girdlecake. I had no idea why they laughed, but I laughed with them.

A little farther along the street, at the dairy, I roused the owner's mirth by singing what our maid, Jeanne Lepêcheur, sang: "In an evening of love . . ." These are the only words I can remember. I scarcely knew how to talk. Jeanne Lepêcheur was young and very likely pretty. She was at any rate attractive. I think she must have been very fond of me and I can still hear the sound of her soft, rather hoarse voice: "Now then, come along, Joujou. Come along, my Joujou." She called me Joujou and the name stuck to me until I was fifteen or sixteen. During those happy times of the Rue Raynouard, when asked my name, I answered at a breath: "Joujou Guitte." Guitte, because I could not pronounce Green. Everyone burst out laughing and Jeanne took my hand and led me away: "Now then, come along, Joujou."

4

She wore a red satin ribbon around her neck and in her drawling, plebeian voice hummed songs that had a great deal to say about midnight. "Midnight is the gangster's hour." I listened anxiously. The words sounded mysterious, but there was something sinister about the tune, particularly when heard at dusk. I would have liked Jeanne to sing me something else, but she had a decided taste for gloom which did not, however, exclude wanton love and patriotic ditties. Her store of melodies comprised one about the Tragic Year (1870) and without knowing what the Tragic Year might be, I snuggled closer to the woman as she howled dismally in the twilight. "Now then, come along," she would say to comfort me and we would sometimes go down to the Seine, which was not far distant.

People talked to Jeanne, I know it, I am certain of it. Men talked to her and whispered conversations took place, a yard above my head. I understood none of it. Mouth half open, my everlasting biscuit in my fist, I looked up at the speaker as one looks up at a tower, then Jeanne would draw me away by the hand: "Now then, come along, Joujou." I think that if I have always been so fond of the working classes, it is due to her. I was in love with Jeanne.

At home, my parents and sisters passed to and fro like shadows, came in, went out, returned, talking an unknown tongue. I have no definite recollection of them in connection with the Rue Raynouard.

In September 1904, we left the Rue Raynouard for the Rue de Passy. Bedel's big vans moved our furniture to the top of the Rue de Boulainvilliers, strange furniture that amazed our French friends. At 93 Rue de Passy, we were to spend six happy years, interspersed with a certain number of frightful nights, to be mentioned later. Here I am, in a setting of which not a detail has escaped my memory, with my parents and five sisters. My brother Charles has been in America for a long time. At home, I am the only boy, but a boy with six mothers.

The apartment is not enormous and doors open unceasingly. That is my first memory of the Rue de Passy. The girls come in and go out, as though they were playing a game that I cannot understand; their mother is in a constant state of anxiety because the linen must be washed, or dried, the children's hair combed, and the housekeeping accounts added up.

Of the four rooms that give on the street, Mary's is the first. It is always untidy, but this untidiness is established, accepted once and for all, an untidiness that is both changeless and justified: Mary being one of my eldest sisters and a most unruly one. Her curling pins strew the mantelpiece and her stockings hang over the straight-backed chairs. On her bed are the cards with which she has told her fortune, on the floor, her breakfast tray. A hatbox is stuffed with the programs of all the plays she has been to. She domineers over us, she goes out a lot, she moves in society. . . .

In the center of the flat was the dining room with its big square table where the children did their homework in a great lake of light shed by the gas chandelier. Here, no one was frightened. The pages of books turned in silence and the maid who watched over us sniffled quietly as she hemmed linen. She was a bouncing Alsatian called Josephine. Rosy-cheeked, she stole a little, lied a little, and stammered when she was found out. My mother's exhortations, all for Josephine's good, were answered by a mysterious: "Tsch!" That was her usual comment. You could interpret it as you pleased. Did she approve? Did she disapprove? Tsch! We all knew that she had trysts with a policeman called Arthur at the corner of the Rue de Passy and the Rue de la Pompe and that she finally married him.

Each morning she soaped me in my tub and this took her a long time, for she was slow. One day my mother appeared suddenly in the dark bathroom.

"From now on, I'll wash him," she said.

6

"Tsch!"

Josephine, who was down on her knees before me, got up and left the room. My mother was fonder of me than of her other children, because I was the youngest, and watched over me with wary tenderness. I did not yet know her thoroughly.

But I am going too fast. I have not yet spoken of the bathroom that stood in a zone of horror between Anne's room, where someone imagined having seen what looked very much like a severed head on top of the little white-painted cupboard, and Eleanor's room, where a faceless woman sometimes appeared. In the daytime none of this was perceptible, but when it grew dark the bathroom became a crossroad of terrors.

It should be explained that Anne's room gave on the Rue de Passy and that, even when her candle had been blown out, the place was lit by *Cacao Bensdorf,* the gas sign gracing the front of a neighboring grocery. The murky, yellow light that came through the net curtains lent a melancholy aspect to the room. The corner farthest from the window was piled with shadows, not to be dispelled even by a lighted candle. Generally speaking, the gallant little flame neither improved things nor made them more reassuring by tilting ceilingward great banks of darkness that swooped down silently behind the footsteps of an anxious child. You were not to feel frightened. Mamma said there was nothing, but there was something, just the same. There was something in Anne's room and in the bathroom, there was something in Eleanor's room that looked out on the landlord's garden, something in the room where I slept with my parents.

The flat was like a forest with clearings. Nothing to fear in the dining room, nothing in Mary's room, any more than in the kitchen. Everything seemed to come, alas, from the room where I spent the greater part of my time; I grew up and developed within the walls of this room between the ages of four and ten. It was a large, square, peaceful room. On entering it through the hall, you faced a window through which showed chestnut trees that belonged to Monsieur Cassagnade, our landlord. To the right, a mantelpiece topped by a mirror. To the left, my parents' big brass bed, then the door of Eleanor's room and, on its right, in a corner, my little iron bedstead. I can recall this modest, commonplace setting far more clearly than many other rooms where I have since lived. I played on the floor, and in a formless tongue of my own invention, talked to myself or to someone whom I thought I saw.

In the course of these dim years, I can remember a minute of intense delight, such as I have never experienced since. Should such things be told, or should they be kept secret? There came a moment in this room when, looking up at the windowpane, I saw the dark sky and a few stars shining in it. What words can be used to express what is beyond speech? That minute was perhaps the most important one of my life and I do not know what to say about it. I was alone in the unlighted room and, my eyes raised toward the sky, I had what I can only call an outburst of love. I have loved on this earth, but never as I did during that short time, and I did not know whom I loved. Yet I knew that he was there and that, seeing me, he loved me too. How did the thought dawn on me? I do not know. I was certain that someone was there and talked to me without words. Having said this, I have said everything. Why must I write that no human speech has ever given me what I felt then for a moment just long enough to count up to ten, at a time when I was incapable of putting together a few intelligible words and did not even realize that I existed? Why must I write that I forgot that minute for years, that the stream of days and nights all but wiped it out of my consciousness? If only I had preserved it in times of trial! Why is it given back to me now? What does it all mean?

At night, someone turned the handle of the door near my bed and the sound woke me, but I went back to sleep immediately.

This was not the case with my parents, or with my sisters Eleanor and Lucy, who slept in the next room and were greatly disturbed by the noise. The following morning, everyone avoided talking about it before me, except by allusions. "They were dreadful last night" was a sentence that sometimes recurred without enlightening me much, but, by dint of its being repeated, it ended by making sense and thrusting a way to my brain. I do not know when it was that the full horror of the business burst upon me: rather late, I think, but I will deal with the matter in due time.

My terrors were of another kind. People tell me that when I was barely five years old I used to point to a corner of the room and talk to someone in an inarticulate tongue. My sisters, attracted by the strangeness of my soliloquy, would listen for a while and then, suddenly panic-stricken, would hustle each other from the room, but their fears were no doubt groundless. For I have always thought that children, like animals, probably see a whole world of harmless beings that escape the notice of grownups. Whence the elves, trolls, and fairies with which primitive humanity has peopled its tales, at a time when this very humanity was so close to childhood. However this may be, my fears did not come from such regions. It was only in growing up that I discovered all the terror contained in the closet where my mother kept the family's clothes.

The event must have taken place around 1907, for who could have spoken to me about the devil before then? All I knew about the devil was what the Scriptures related; my mother read the Bible to us every day and I was just becoming accustomed to its English. What idea did I have of the fallen angel? I do not know, but, some days, seized with an ungovernable curiosity, I suddenly opened the door of the clothes closet that was in my parents' room and, with a beating heart, called the devil. For I imagined that he lived there.

Nothing happened at first. The inside of the closet was dark;

9

the long line of clothes, squeezed close one to another like a flat-tened, headless crowd, could only be seen dimly. I had to call once more; I was aware of that at least and also knew that two calls would not be enough. Three calls were necessary, were exacted. So I called a third time and the unforgettable thing happened. The clothes moved. They parted gently to allow someone to pass. I am sorry today not to have had the heart to wait instead of rushing away, howling.

My mother, to whose arms I flew for protection, could make nothing of my cries, but Eleanor and Mary, specialists in the occult, raised their eyebrows and simply remarked: "He must have seen something again." Now, I had seen nothing, except that the clothes moved and parted, but at the time I write this I can remember the inexpressible horror caused by that dark, scarcely suspected presence. There is no doubt in my mind that there was "something," but what? I can only ask. With years I have found out that it is useless to call the devil, for he never leaves us for a minute.

I might be told that all this took place in my imagination and it may be so, but I can only say what I believe to be true. Peer-ing into this semidarkness, I see small events that have nothing to do with the invisible world, but whose repercussion over my life has been too powerful for me to pass them by honestly. So here are the crude facts and their tragicomical consequences.

Every evening, I was in bed by seven. The door of my room stayed open, and the drawing-room door as well; a dim but reassuring light reached me, across the dark hall, and from time to time the hum of voices and my mother's charming laugh. I think that she must have remembered the agonies she went through as a child, in the Savannah house where she was born, a haunted house if there ever was one. However, there was another reason for leaving my door open. For young though I was, my mother watched me closely, having a horror of certain misbehaviors such as I have never met in anyone else, and when she could not spy on me herself, my sister Mary took over.

Of course, I knew nothing of these schemes. I was innocence itself and remained so for a long time, but it is beyond doubt that, lying on my back in bed, I took pleasure in touching a body of which I was hardly conscious as forming part of myself. How old could I have been? Five, perhaps. It was probably before the clothes-closet business. At any rate, I did not understand English very well, as will be seen by what follows.

All of a sudden one evening, my sister Mary stood by my bed. I had not heard her come in, but anyway, why should I have hidden, not feeling guilty? With an emphatic gesture, she pulled back the blankets to my feet, shrieked, and called my mother, who ran in, holding a candlestick. I appeared in the light, just as I was, not understanding what it was all about, smiling perhaps, my hands on the forbidden regions. There were exclamations, my mother put down the candlestick, left the room, and returned armed with a long, saw-toothed knife, used for cutting bread. At that moment, hearing the commotion, the cook appeared at the door. Lina Ranoux was her name and I will have the opportunity of discussing her later. "I'll cut it off!" cried my mother, brandishing the bread-knife. I could not understand what she said. In fact, I understood nothing of all this agitation around me. Lina burst out laughing, but I melted into tears at the sight of my mother's indignant face. Then my sister murmured something, covered me up, and kissed me. The candle was extinguished, everyone left, and I went to sleep. In all likelihood, I would have forgotten the scene completely if I had not been reminded of it a little later. As to the traces it left in me, I cannot but think them to have been very deep. Mother, you who never in your life really struck me but once—and even then by mistake—you who loved me so much, who loved me almost too much, you who feared continually for me, what could I understand about that brandished knife and

11

about your voice, that despairing voice? Was I not obliged to wait till I was twenty before guessing why you had uttered that strange sentence? You have been gone for almost half a century. What would you think of your son? "I will go to you, but you will not come to me." So spoke the black book that you read us every day.

I do not quite know why Jeanne Lepêcheur did not follow us to the Rue de Passy. Lina Ranoux took her place as our maid. She came from Périgord and was born in the village of Badefol d'Anse, in the land of the Dore and Dogne rivers. Lina was a ruddy-cheeked peasant with a sharp tongue. She had a turned-up nose with spreading nostrils, swung heavy hips as she walked, and although she had none of Jeanne's sweetness, she was not a bad sort, if rough. In the morning, my sisters went to the kitchen door for their shoes, thrown merrily at their heads by Lina: "Here, catch your boots, you minxes!" she cried. My mother was kept in ignorance of this detail. With me, Lina spoke less brusquely but, to enjoy my bewilderment, would say all kinds of things in patois and then laugh, hands on hips. Her voice rang through the kitchen, where I sometimes went—as a great favor, it seems—to help her wipe the plates. *"Alcotétof!"* she would say, seizing the bread-knife, in fits of gaiety. Although not knowing what she meant, I recognized the words and my mother's gesture and that is why I have remembered them.

I led my little secret life in the big room full of mysteries. Before the horror of the closet was revealed to me, I lived in an inexpressible happiness not entirely forgotten. Love was in and around me, like the air I breathed, but when I was about five, a sort of disaster must have occurred, the meaning of which escapes me. It certainly happened after the minute when, raising my face toward the sky, I had the feeling of an immense and affectionate presence. Months went by perhaps and, at a moment that I cannot determine, seated in front of the window, I was suddenly conscious of existing.

Every man has known the peculiar instant when one feels sharply divided from the rest of the world, by the fact of being one's own self and not part of what surrounds us. I leave it to specialists to explain things that, I must admit, are not very clear to me. So far as I am concerned, all I know is that I left a paradise at that moment. It was the melancholy hour when the first person singular put in an appearance in human life to occupy the center of the stage and stay there jealously till the last gasp. Of course I was happy later, but not as I used to be in the Eden from which we are chased by the fiery angel called Me.

Perhaps an attempt should be made to straighten out these recollections a little, but I do not feel up to it. I have the impression that all these memories float up simultaneously, in great confusion, and where does chronology find its place? I now return to a period when all I saw of grownups was their feet. That was long before the closet affair. I had to stand, my head thrown back to catch sight of their faces, somewhere on a level with the ceiling. I got everybody mixed up, for we were eight in the flat, and the comings and goings confused me. In the middle of the day and toward the end of the afternoon, I recognized big shiny shoes, legs in gray trousers, and a deep, calm voice that rang out above the others like a somewhat muffled bell. Then I cried: "Papa!" as my sisters did and the bell answered: "Hello, Beaver!" They called me Beaver because I was always on the floor, busy with spools, boxes, pencils, and anything else I could lay my hands on.

When I was alone with someone who spoke to me gently in a tongue that I could not understand, I knew I was with the one who loved me most. As I then lived in a kind of twilight, my mother's presence gradually acquired a magical quality and now, with a whole lifetime behind me, I still remember her voice with a beating heart. When she came to kiss me good night, I would stand up in bed and put my arms around her neck. At an age when I could barely talk, we used to say the Lord's Prayer together in English. My head on her shoulder, I repeated the words she spoke gravely, slowly in a room with no other light but that which reached us from the drawing room: "Our Father . . ."—"Our Father . . ."—". . . which art in heaven . . ."—". . . which art in heaven . . ."—". . . hallowed be Thy name . . ."—". . . hallowed be Thy name. . . ." These words I mangled, because I could not understand them, yet something passed from my mother to myself, through this murmur. The main part of what I believe today was given to me then, in that shadowy room, where spoke the greatest of all loves.

While it is sometimes so sad to see the years fly by, I do not know why the happiness I feel in going back to my childhood contains no trace of melancholy. Death did not yet exist. It seemed as though we were all together for good. To die . . . what did that mean? I had not the least idea.

My mother was in the habit of going to and fro, from one room to the other, looking very intent, and I sometimes followed her to the kitchen, where she washed the children's clothes with a big piece of white soap, her wedding ring laid on the edge of the sink. I was really only happy with her. She talked gently to me in her own tongue, a tongue still mysterious to me, as she soaped our little shirts, and I would give anything to know what she said. But there were also gloomy days when she lay in her big brass bed. The curtains were drawn, my mother would say a few words to me in a faraway, suffering voice.

I understood that I should leave the room and went to Lina. She was a fitful woman and often changed moods. When she was well disposed and had nothing better to do, she would say: "I'll show you how it's danced in my country." And hands on hips, she lifted one foot, then the other, as she sang in patois. Not a word could I catch, and after a while, her cheeks scarlet, she would burst out laughing.

I was torn between fear and delight, for with Lina I found myself in a very different world from ours. She did not laugh as we did, there was something rough and almost savage about her voice that fell on the ear like a slap. She would sometimes throw herself on me and give me a deafening kiss.

There was a kind of violence in her teasing as, for instance, when she sat me on a table, forbade me to move and washed the kitchen's tiled floor. The thundering of water as it filled the iron bucket, the broom swaddled in a washcloth lunging in all directions—and I thought more particularly in mine—by a woman who, in my eyes, turned into a warrior and laughed at my fears, all that is strangely actual to me now.

Once she baked some little cakes, gave me one, taught me a short song, and led me to my mother's room. The curtains were drawn, it was very dark, but outlined by the white pillow I could see a pallid face in a great dusky stream of hair. Cake in hand, I began to sing:

> "I like cakes,
> There's butter in them,
> When they're baked right,
> There's butter in them,
> Butter in them, butter in them,
> Butter!"

My mother asked one of my sisters who was with her: "What is he saying?"

I held out the cake, as Lina had told me to. Mamma then murmured something in a voice full of pain and that saddened me because it was not her real voice, and Lina took me back to the kitchen.

I played with a legless, armless papier-mâché doll which I loved madly. I do not know why the doll was called Agathe. I

15

used to hug her to me passionately, I took her for a person, and a person who loved me.

Later, a year later perhaps, I was given a little table and a little wooden armchair painted pink. Settling down in front of the window in my parents' room, I drew before knowing how to read or write, and perhaps the greatest difficulties that I have ever encountered took birth in the formless scrawls that kept me quiet for hours.

At this point, darkness closes in once more. I realize that I do not quite know who I was then. The bread-knife incident recedes into the past and although Lina cried: *"Alcotétof!"* when she saw me run to the toilet, I did not understand. The truth is that I hardly understood anything. I was deep in dreams that seemed to me never ending, but, since I have mentioned the toilet, the time has come to talk about the blind man on the Saint-Cloud bridge. For I imagined that the blind man on the Saint-Cloud bridge hid in the tiny space between the wooden cover of the seat I had to lift and the wall. I must explain that the blind man, like Agathe, had neither arms nor legs and that, seated on the sidewalk, he showed passersby two empty sockets of a horrifying pink. It was useless, on the Saint-Cloud bridge, to bury my face in Lina's white apron, I could not help looking at the man. He sang. People threw pennies into his tin bowl. And what did he sing? Can I ever forget it? A love song of which I remember the opening lines:

> "Oh, my pretty one,
> Don't go away,
> Stay with me,
> I beseech you!"

Why did I imagine, when I sat down in the place just mentioned, why the devil did I imagine he was behind me? Whence do the nightmares of childhood arise? Out of what depths?

I remember that my mother read the Bible to us in English, in her room. She sat by the window and my sisters settled down around her. My sisters, that is Anne, Retta, and Lucy. Eleanor and Mary, being over twenty, were elsewhere. As for me, still too young to understand, but loath to leave Mamma, I was simply told to be good. So I played silently at my mother's feet, listening no doubt to the voice above my head, the quiet sound of those mysterious sentences. For one day, by a sort of revelation that came to me as a shock, I discovered that I could grasp the meaning of certain words. Which ones? If I only knew, they would maybe enlighten the darkness where I grope, but the fact remains that something in my brain opened. I remember nothing else, except that the discovery suddenly moved me; I got up, wanted to speak, but was told to hush.

This must have been in 1906. Months went by, a year, perhaps. I then knew a little English. One night in bed, I began to cry and my mother, hearing me from the drawing room, ran in: "What's the matter?" I stood up, put my arms around her neck and asked, sobbing: "Mamma, am I saved?" Time will never be able to wrest that minute from me. My mother hugged me and said firmly: "Listen to me. You believe that Jesus is God. You have faith. You are saved." She added in a softer voice: "Now, go to sleep." And she kissed me. I believe my question must have struck her, for she mentioned it to my father.

I do not remember her ever telling me that she loved me, although she proved it in so many ways, every day. As for me, I seized all opportunities to display my fondness. I pursued her with my "I love you"s. Sometimes she made me sit with her in a large, low armchair and, wrapping me in the big, gray shawl which enveloped her, she hugged me silently.

From time to time, Lina took me to the puppet show in the Muette gardens, about five minutes from home. The little theater stood near the railroad station and the pretty statue of La Fontaine, so stupidly destroyed by the Germans during the occupation. The fabulist looked smilingly at the animals that, thanks to him, spoke such pure French, but Lina and I did not linger around La Fontaine. Crossing the avenue that bordered the railroad track, we planted ourselves in front of the tiny stage, along with other children and their nurses. After waiting a little while, the curtain, no bigger than a napkin, rolled up suddenly and that in itself was startling enough. Then began a drama that made everybody laugh, but of which I understood nothing, except that at the end, amid shrieks from the audience, appeared a puppet dressed in black and more sinister than the others; in its stiff little arms it held a homicidal bat and brought it down once, twice, once again on a defenseless victim. The latter, whose back was turned on its aggressor, folded up and dropped on the edge of the stage. Open-mouthed, dumb with horror, I recognized, so to speak, the clothes closet's atmosphere. Children laughed around me, but I was frightened of the squeaky voice that rose from the back of the stage, because it was not a human voice and the sound of those blows made me dreadfully uneasy. I remained motionless, but thought I saw the door of the closet open and the devil appear in the guise of that tiny little puppet which suddenly became immense. The rest took place in the greatest confusion. I cannot say that I had lost the thread of the play, never having held it, but my lasting impression of the show was that of a miniature nightmare that suddenly escaped from the theater to spread into the air.

Lina was extremely pleased: "They've beaten up the police," she said in her brassy voice. I remember that her walk was slow and prudent, the tips of her black boots carefully turned outward.

◇ ◇ ◇

Such terrifying moments had little effect on me then. I was the happiest of children, but I had no friends. I played alone at games the memory of which baffles me now, for do not such strange amusements show me some of the most powerful tendencies that have ruled my life?

My mother sometimes lent me a Bible for children, profusely illustrated. I could not understand much of the text, but looked at the pictures with passionate interest. One had an extraordinary effect on me and all but caused a minor tragedy. For I wanted to be the High Priest in person, offering the Almighty a burnt offering. The engraving that represented the sacrifice was admirably precise, and I attempted to reproduce it in a spirit of servile imitation, realistically. The High Priest's robe was provided by my mother's red dressing gown and I girded my loins with a Turkish towel. I made a sort of turban out of another towel and then turned my attention to the high altar, for there had to be one. The problem was quickly solved by perching the cover of our sewing machine on my little pink table. As the cover was rectangular and all of its surfaces were flat, it corresponded exactly to the use I had in mind. My father's hairbrushes took the place of the shewbreads.

At this point, all that remained was for me to walk to and fro in front of the altar giving a kind of reverent bellow. One detail, however, saddened me a little: the engraving showed a smoking victim on the altar. There should be a victim, if not a calf or a sheep, something that was at least valuable and of consequence.

After thinking this over for an instant, I ran to the hall. There, on one of the clothes-rack pegs, my father's top hat gleamed softly. He wore that hat only on Sundays, or on ceremonious occasions, and I remember what care he took of it, smoothing it delicately with a small brown velvet cushion, before putting it on his head: not a speck of dust was allowed to

sully that shining topper. I hesitated, probably a little scared by
the sacrilegious boldness of my plan. Then, suddenly making
up my mind, I decided to offer the Almighty Papa's top hat.

Climbing on a chair, I seized the venerable object and, a
minute later, it lay between the two shewbreads. My liturgy
was a trifle at fault and I had confused several engravings one
with the other. Be it as it may, I thought that the hat looked
wonderfully well, waved my sleeves, and, bellowing louder and
louder, went off in search of a matchbox, for the engraving clearly showed a victim swallowed up in flames.

Had I been less noisy, my enterprise would probably have
succeeded, but such exaltation made both my mother and
sisters run in to see what I was at. "What's all this?" asked my
mother. I immediately replied: "A burnt offering."—"A burnt
offering!" repeated my mother with a smile. Nevertheless, she
punished me, but with a light hand.

To finish with my father's top hat, I must relate what happened one Sunday morning at the Protestant church on the Rue
Cortambert, although this painful incident really took place two
years later, in 1907. That Sunday, my mother said to my father: "We're bringing up our children like heathens. They don't
go to church often enough. As I'm not feeling well, you ought
to take them there today." For she was in bed, the curtains
drawn, always a bad sign, a sign of pain and sadness. "It's too
late to take them to the Avenue de l'Alma church," said my father, "but we can go to the one on the Rue Cortambert."

I do not know what Mamma replied. She had brought us up
as Episcopalians. My father was born a Presbyterian, he who
was so little of one! But he had been brought up in that
denomination and remembered the teachings of his childhood.

However, a moment later, he put on his tail coat and the top
hat that Anne had carefully smoothed with the brown velvet
cushion, took his stick, and away we went, the three girls and
the boy!

The way was simple enough. On leaving the Rue de Passy, we took the Rue Guichard, crossed the Place Possoz, and walked up the Rue Cortambert. The singing had begun when we entered the church and my father pushed us like a herd of animals toward a long, well-waxed bench where we sat, Indian file. Papa first, then myself, then Lucy, Retta, and Anne.

"Oh, Canaan, land divine,
And our celestial home!"

The church was vast and bare, without ornaments or stained-glass windows, most severe. Such iciness made me feel shy and I regretted the church on the Avenue de l'Alma, which I will talk about later, but then it was curious to be here, among people who sang hymns in French. That seemed particularly strange. My mother's religion was English, and consequently all religion should be English.

My father placed his top hat between himself and me, that is, on his left. Not knowing what to do with my big straw sailor hat, I placed it on my left, like my father. Papa held a hymnbook and tried to follow the singing. We children kept our mouths tightly shut. My sisters, like myself, had a curious feeling of embarrassment on hearing God addressed in French, because, in our little Anglo-Saxon world, that was not the way He was spoken to.

As the hymn was about to end, a gentleman who had come in even later than we stood at the end of our bench and asked us to be obliging enough to make room for him. We began by looking at each other rather vacantly, like people who do not quite know what to do, but my father, having understood the situation, waved his hymnbook as a signal for us to move closer to him. At the same time, he exchanged a smile and a bow with the newcomer.

At the end of the hymn, we all sat down and the clergyman began his sermon. Everything was quiet. His voice rang out

21

and hit the walls. No one budged. Glancing sideways at Lucy, I saw her look at the preacher with the rather grumpy air she had when she was bored, and noticed that she had my big straw sailor hat on her knees. She was right. As for me, I was almost dead with fright. For, during the last few seconds, I slowly realized that I was sitting on something hard that was giving way under me and that this something was my father's top hat. The latter, however, had no idea of what had happened and listened with interest to what the clergyman said. He was still happy in his ignorance. Everyone was happy, except myself. But what to do?

I do not know when Lucy discovered the disaster. She asked me, giggling, what had become of Papa's top hat (Lucy was a little cruel, as we all were) and then, seized by uncontrollable laughter, she rolled a handkerchief into a ball and stuffed it in her mouth, attempting to conquer her horrible mirth. Retta and Anne, who had not heard the news, began to laugh on seeing Lucy's faces. My father glared at them and I suppose that they calmed down, after a time. But I, at any rate, remained wonderfully serious.

What happened next? I have rather forgotten. We left the church and, on reaching the Rue de la Tour, my father took my hand to make me walk faster, for he was in a hurry to go home. Bareheaded, stick in hand, he strode at such a pace that his coattails waved behind him. Unable to go so fast, but held by a very firm hand, I skipped and flew along, much against my will, and breathless, while the three girls followed as best they could, giving terrible whoops of uncontrollable hilarity.

On reaching home, without the least hesitation, I ran to my mother's room and, not wasting a minute on explanations, slipped under the bed. Anyway, the explanation was to follow, the explanation burst into the room in the shape of an angry gentleman who demanded where I was. I could see his feet and the tip of his cane as it thumped the floor furiously to punctuate his questions:

"Where's that boy? Where is he? I insist on knowing!"

My father and mother then exchanged words that sounded like the Ogre's conversation with his wife in the fairy tale. Mamma wanted to know what I had done that was so wrong. My father hit the floor with the end of his stick and insisted that I was hidden somewhere in the room. I have completely forgotten what happened afterward, except that I was punished, but I have no recollection of my father spanking me.

Sometimes at nightfall, in winter, we all sat around a wood fire. Behind us lay the room's vast darkness, but the logs burning on the hearth lit up our youthful features and my mother's beautiful, pensive face, and we thought we saw the imperial eagle on the iron fireback beat its wings beyond the flaming wood. I imagined the bird to be a live one and asked absurd questions. Then my mother, not quite understanding what I meant, would hug me. Wrapped to the feet in a long gray shawl, she stretched her hands toward the fire, a gesture I can still see. No one felt the cold more than she did and she wanted everyone to be warm, for she came from Savannah, where roses bloom in the heart of winter. At times she would nod, smile a little mischievously, look at us, and say: "Believe me, children, it's freezing in hell." She had a horror of cold. I think that she saw it as a picture of despair.

She often talked to us about that faraway land, the South where she spent her youth, and with her we walked down avenues lined with gigantic magnolias, where everything smelled good and the air was pleasantly warm at Christmas. I would catch a word here and there and felt happy with my cheek on the gray shawl and my mother's arm around my shoulder. In the firelight, I saw the whole family's stockings and socks dry-

23

ing on a towel rack, along with the flannels and, less and less attentive, listened to sentences that unfurled above my head like scrolls. The phrase that recurred most often was "over there," sometimes spoken with a sigh, sometimes with sudden exaltation. I wondered what it all meant. Soon the imperial eagle's wings beat more feebly, my mother's voice receded into the distance, and through some magic trick I found myself in bed.

Is it not strange that I should understand her thoroughly only at present, now that I have lived a greater number of years than she spent on earth? She made her sons and daughters the children of a country that no longer exists, but that lived in her heart. She caused the shadow of a tragedy to hover above our heads, saddening the brightest hours. We were forever defeated but unresigned and, to use one of her favorite terms, we were rebels. On one of the drawing-room walls, framed in gold, hung a water color displaying the Southern flag, a large St. Andrew's cross spangled with thirteen stars on a background of blue. "That's your flag," Mamma would tell me, "remember. That one and no other." And then, talking to my sisters, she explained things that I could not grasp. I scarcely knew what a flag was and what the word "war" signified.

Writing this, I still question the weighty legacy of sadness that our mother bequeathed us and wonder if it is wise to teach children history, to make them vainglorious or hopeless beforehand, under the burden of victories or surrenders. History has destroyed the South's borders, but my mother used her principles, which admitted of no weakness, her ideal, her austere religion to restore them in us. "We did not fight for slavery. . . ." How many times have I heard that said! "The Negroes' freedom would have come of itself. . . . Your grandparents had no slaves, except as servants, and these were anxious to stay with us. . . ." "Then why did it happen?" asked my sisters. My

24

mother patiently resumed her explanations: "We were prosperous. . . . The others were jealous of us. . . . And then, we were proud. . . ." She seemed so sad that I felt like crying, but the bitterness of her memories never turned her into a fanatic. Years later, she once showed me the photograph of a bearded man: "He was against us," she said, "but he was a great, a very good man. You must remember his name. He was called Abraham Lincoln. He was killed by a madman. That was the most crushing blow ever dealt the South."

I knew my mother's face then. I could perhaps describe it, but something in it would escape me. You can tell the color of an eye, say it is gray shaded with blue, but a loving expression cannot be put into words. Now, my mother's love was what I yearned for. It seems to me that our most important business on earth is to love, the rest matters very little. My mother did not spoil me, but she kept me by her more often than she did her other children. She talked gently to me and I did not quite understand what she said. Yet her voice fashioned my mind, much as hands would fashion clay, in the dark. Sometimes she was annoyed to find me so slow in learning her tongue. At other moments, she would laugh and call me her little Frenchman.

I can see her once more, sitting by the window in our room, the Bible on her knee, and in writing about such things I rediscover her, behind the words. "And Jesus said . . . Then Jesus answered and said . . ." Little by little, I grasped fragments of parables or, troubled by all the sadness contained in my mother's voice, a few details of the Lord's Passion. It was impossible for me to understand why, being so good, He was so badly treated. Sometimes, whole verses found their way to me, like a sudden light breaking through a dark sky: the dreadful crown set on the holy head, the purple robe.

Sometimes, she repeated: "My little children, love one another." And I can see her leaning slightly toward us, over the book. She often showed me a reproduction of one of Murillo's pictures that represented Mary holding her child in her arms. There was nothing around them but clouds and the Virgin had large dark eyes that fixed one's attention.

The drawing room must have been a strange place. When I think of it, I am there, I am six years old, running between the furniture, but it is not easy to convey the impression all that made. It was part of the forest, with its rather mysterious light, its shadows, its slightly disquieting regions. The room was large, with a single window that did not give it enough light. Drawn up around a carpet, like trees around a lake, were chairs and armchairs, and a child wandering about on all fours saw nothing of them but their legs. I crawled thus from the piano, which stood quite near the door, to a couple of black wood bookcases on either side of the window. Now, the door had this peculiarity: instead of being flat, like most doors, it was curved in such a manner that, by opening it wide, it was not in contact with the wall, but provided a small rounded cavity that was one of my hiding places. There I waited for my father's return and jumped at his legs with the idea that I was a wild animal, but my little roars were answered by a quiet voice that fell from upper regions: "Why, it's Beaver. Good evening, Beaver, aren't you in bed yet?"

In the daytime there were moments when my sister Mary sat down at the piano and played tunes that I recognized only much later, but which have followed me throughout my life. Seated on the carpet, I glued my ear to the smooth wooden surface and felt caught in a storm of sound that threw me into an extraordinary state where joy verging on exaltation mingled with an agreeable fright. I wished this could last, that a dizziness wrought by the crash of chords would never cease. I watched the pianist's feet, sometimes pressing one pedal, sometimes the other, and recollect the dress she wore: it was russet-colored and flapped around her heels. At other times I would sit at some distance from the piano and what I heard was different. All these tunes made you happy, but in a peculiar manner, for in listening to them, you felt a sadness that melted, I cannot tell how, into perfect bliss. And suddenly came the painful moment when my sister would get up in the middle of a phrase and leave the room, in her usual capricious fashion. So I remained on the carpet, horribly disillusioned and my head still buzzing. The simplest of certain melodies are still fixed in my memory, where I think that nothing will ever dislodge them, and I used to sing them to myself, when I thought I was alone, to recall some of that lost delight. "Do you hear what he's singing?" Mary asked Eleanor one day. I looked at them, astounded. "Sing that little tune again! Sing, Joujou!" I began again obediently. They threw themselves on me, kissed me, and I screamed.

What I heard—I know it now—were Mozart's sonatas. They have given me what very few things in this world have given me, and given it to me at the best time possible. Twenty-five or thirty years later, I heard celebrated pianists play those same sonatas and have sometimes remarked to Anne, whose memories are the same as mine: "Very fine, but Mary played them differently." "You're right. They don't play them like Mary." The years are still going by and great pianists step into each other's shoes. Slowly, I began to have my doubts. Mary had her own way of playing Mozart, which was not necessarily the best. I say it a little sadly, as though I were betraying something or someone.

Every morning, I went with my sisters Retta and Lucy to the Cours Sainte-Cécile, only eight or ten minutes from the house, but for me the walk was both adventurous and fascinating, for we had to go first to the Place de Passy, where two yellow omnibuses always stood waiting with their large-rumped draft horses, and coachmen whose voices were raised to a bawl in order to be heard above the rumbling carriages. There, it seemed to me that everybody screamed and walked faster than anywhere else, that it was a rough-and-tumble place: women laden with baskets, delivery boys, people hurrying to go right, people hurrying to go left, all this in an atmosphere of jollity and danger, under the wide-open eyes of old houses which looked down impassive, squaring their shoulders in the sky.

Next came the short Rue Duban and the fantastic store cram-full of toys to its darkest recesses, but in front of which I was not to linger, because you should always run to school, then the Place Chopin and its post office at the bottom of a pretty garden full of trees: like a frontier between noise and silence. The Rue Singer, which came next, was almost always empty.

Pushing open an iron gate, you found yourself in a little yard beyond which were two rockwork stairs, like rounded arms that encircled a grotto. Right or left, according to fancy, you walked toward a long garden where bushes and trees concealed whitewashed walls. I found myself there alone, one autumn morning. Why, I do not know, but of all the mornings in my life, this is the one that I remember most clearly. The air was fresh, and for a moment I stood motionless, listening to the noise of someone beating a carpet in the neighborhood. At the same instant, coming from another direction, the sound of a piano playing one of my sister Mary's favorite tunes. (Much later, I recognized Mozart's "Turkish March.") I listened, probably open-mouthed through attentiveness or surprise.

Talking of these things, it seems as though time is destroyed and that I am there once more, in a garden that no longer exists. I could feel the fresh air on my cheeks and a thought that I was unable to express was fixed in my brain. The sound of someone beating a carpet and a music that was brisk, and yet a little saddening as it rang out in the distance, all that is so present to my mind and how strange it was—yes, that is exactly what I felt and could not determine—how strange it was to be in that garden with the earth under your feet, that freshness on your face and in your heart something secret, the joy of living, at a time when you did not yet know what living meant.

In Carmelite cells there is a notice with the following words: "What made you come here, Daughter?" The question God asks the souls of nuns, He also puts in His own way, with all the sweetness and delicacy of love, to the soul of a child who understands the question only later, and whose cell is the world.

God speaks to children with extreme gentleness, and what He has to say to them He often says without words. Creation provides Him with the vocabulary He needs, leaves, clouds, running water, a patch of light. It is the secret language that books cannot teach you and which children know very well. That is why they are seen to stop suddenly in the midst of their pursuits. People then say that they are absent-minded or dreamy. Education corrects all that in us by making us forget it. Children can be compared to a vast multitude who have received an uncommunicable secret and who gradually forget the secret, the multitude's fate being taken in hand by so-called civilized nations. Such or such a man laden with absurd honors dies crushed under the weight of years, his head full of futile learning, having forgotten the main thing which he knew by intuition at the age of five. As for me, I have known what children know, and all the reasoning in the world has not been able completely to tear away from me that unutterable something. Words cannot describe it. It stands on the threshold of speech and, on this earth, remains mute.

I was scarcely able to utter so much as ten words when the enemy cast his shadow over me. As I have said, right and left of the drawing-room window were two bookcases and the one on the left contained large picture books. I was not forbidden to look at them. What harm could there be in these engravings? At the most, it could have occurred to a grownup that some of these pictures might frighten me, but I was supposed to be too young to understand. Seated on the floor, eyes wide with surprise and a curiosity whose nature I did not suspect, I examined the splendid, tormented bodies with which Gustave Doré peopled Dante's *Inferno*. Fear together with admiration made me so attentive that every detail found its place in my memory, adding mystery to mystery.

One day, marveling suddenly at this avalanche of nudes, I picked up a pencil and, with strokes as bold as they were awkward, went over the lines of the body I judged to be the most beautiful. If I had dreamed what I have just written, a doubt might remain in my mind, but under my very eyes is the album with the engraving. The pencil has left a sort of furrow in the paper without tearing it, and my unpracticed hand most clumsily followed the contours of a perfect shape that determined my tastes once and for ever.

Here I can only pause and lose myself once more in endless conjectures, as I have always done in thinking over these things. I was only seven and very innocent. Where was my guilt? What ancestors guided my hand and fixed my choice? For minutes on end, I reveled in the magic vision that I wished to seize and possess by surrounding it with a thick black stroke —a fruitless, violent caress that has never ceased to scorch me. All that will be weighed later in the faultless scales, but under the eyes of Love.

Is it not strange that in 1960 a man can wonder if he dares make the confession of a child of six? But we who wish to speak to the generation succeeding ours often talk like the generation before us, with all its legacy of words, fears, and interdicts. Be it as it may, a truthful confession brings to light far more than the author thinks. The fact is that the author is of no importance, for he is nothing, or almost nothing. The important thing is to attempt to seize and faithfully recall the passage of God in a man's life, and that is how I am gradually beginning to glimpse the meaning of this book. I have to write it to understand and know all it contains, but on beginning a fresh page, I hesitate. Why not admit it?

My mother sometimes took us to the Luxembourg Museum; it no longer exists and its statues and pictures have been dispersed. It was housed in a pink stone building on the edge of the gardens. You first crossed a gallery cluttered with marble statues that I thought very tiresome. Mamma always stopped in front of the statue of a young nun with clasped hands, in a habit of gray marble. The work was called "Far from the World," and my mother each time remarked in a compassionate voice: "How sad!" I asked her what it meant and why it was sad, but do not remember her answer. We then passed on to the paintings, some of which linger in my mind: Cormon's "Cain," Bonnat's "Job," a picture I thought repulsive. There was also the "Lady with the Glove," by Carolus Duran, and then, at some time or other, we found ourselves in a smaller gallery; there, a certain picture held my mother's attention, because, she said, you could understand the feelings of an indignant pharaoh who had just killed with his own hand two slaves, the bearers of evil tidings. Fuming with rage, he lay on his couch with his victims dying at his feet. A long, bloodstained sword told the story in its own way.

"Yes," Mamma would say, with a gay little laugh, "I can understand the man." And turning to her daughters, she added: "Now please don't take what I say literally. You're so foolish!" As a rule, her sarcastic remarks were addressed to my sisters, not to me, either because she thought me to young to understand, or because she loved me a little more than the others. Alas, she had no idea of what she was doing, for the enemy lent me a terrible lucidity when I looked at that picture. I do not know when it first struck my eye. Probably not before I was six. After the age of eleven, I never saw it again, but between six

31

and eleven I was very often shown it, with devastating effects.

I am not expressing myself too strongly. Were it not for that picture my life would not perhaps have turned out as it did. I imagine that my first sight of it only moved me faintly, but how can I tell? Is it not possible, on the contrary, that I was then given a violent and determinative shock? In any case, there came a day when, with all the pain a man is capable of bearing, I felt the torment of unappeased hunger. I remember very clearly that under a kind of hallucination, I fancied that one of the great brown bodies struck down by death really lay under my very eyes, and it seemed as though my whole being, soul and flesh, threw itself on him. At the same time, I knew this to be an impossibility. Such painful frustration is not to be described. It left a deep mark on me forever. All that life could teach me about the *durus amor,* I learned in the space of a few seconds and at an age when I could not understand its signifi- cance. All I knew was that I felt unhappy, and unhappy for the first time in my life, without having the least idea why. It never occurred to me that the slave in question was very closely con- nected to the lost soul in *The Divine Comedy.* I only entered into such considerations much later.

So far as I can remember, my torment ceased at once on leaving the museum. All that remained in me was a dim sad- ness, or, more precisely, a sort of languor that kept me from wanting to play that day. Then a tune performed by my sister Mary, or one of my mother's jokes, drove all that away. I think I can say that I was exceptionally innocent. Or should I say ig- norant? But innocence and ignorance are closely associated, and it is remarkable that, at the age of six, the word "purity"— a word I had heard enunciated among so many others—stuck in my mind and began to have a meaning. What meaning? That, I could not have told. I loved something, the nature of which I did not know. And on that account, what I am about to write will appear peculiar. I most distinctly remember that one day, between the end of lunch and the moment when Josephine was to take me to school, I sat at my little table, drawing and so absorbed in my work that I did not hear one of my cousins come in and stand behind me. Sarah, for that was her name, was sixteen or seventeen and had come to stay with us for a time, as I will have the opportunity of mentioning later. Leaning over my head, she gave a little scream: "Why, what on earth are you drawing? It's fantastic!"

Being perfectly unconscious of doing anything wrong, I did not dream of hiding, but my cousin's scandalized astonishment struck me and for that reason I can see that drawing as though it lay under my eyes. It showed naked people, men and women being hounded and whipped before him by a cruel torturer. In the perspective given by time, I wonder if the drawing was not inspired by a recollection of Doré, but I think a strange idea lurked in my mind: the people were being punished for being naked. Their crime lay in not wearing clothes.

I took the greatest pains over drawing these bodies; it seems to me that I threw myself wholeheartedly into my work and that, through some sort of hallucination, I became what I drew, formed part of it, with such a savage joy that I bit my tongue. Fundamentally, any explanation I gave myself about hell turned on the problem of nakedness, with the inevitable consequence of also turning on the problem of purity. However that may be, the drawing was taken away from me, but what is certain is that my mother was not told of it, for she never mentioned the matter to me. She knew that a pencil and a piece of paper kept me quiet and that was enough for her.

Rather, but not too, often, my sister Eleanor allowed me to pay her little visits. Her room was next to the one where I slept with my parents, and the door was close to my bed. At night, I sometimes heard the knob of the door turn one way, then the other, but went back to sleep at once, as I have already said.

Eleanor shared her room with Lucy, the youngest of my sisters, who slept on a couch while my eldest sister had a bed at the far end of the room. In the daytime, my sister Eleanor's room was charming. What a pleasure it is to be taken there once more by memory! There, I stood in a very different world from mine and was sensitive to the change from my usual surroundings. No doubt my sister's presence transformed everything to an indescribable degree: the simplest objects, the furniture, and, in a certain way, the light. For Eleanor was radiantly beautiful and, without knowing it, I felt the effects of this enchanting royalty. Twenty years my senior, she always greeted me with a smile so good-natured that I laughed with delight and looked at her in wonder and admiration. She would sit me down in a corner and tell me to be good; then, sitting at her dressing table, she would let down, to my utter amazement, a heavy stream of burnished copper-colored hair that covered her back and shoulders. As she ran a caressing comb through a reddish mass of hair, both dark and golden, she hummed tunes from operas that I never hear without sadness, remembering her pure, light voice, the mysterious sentences that traveled through the stillness.

I have often been told that Eleanor had an exceptionally beautiful voice and know that she would have liked to be a singer. However that may be, I listened with delight to the harmonious murmur that turned the little room into an enchanted spot. As I write, it seems as though I can see the Japanese fans on the mantelpiece, the branches of honesty in a vase and, on the wall, a photograph of Emma Calvé as a nun in *La Carmélite*. Farther on was the photograph of a picture that greatly intrigued me. "Why do they look so sad?" I asked. A man stood with his back turned, playing the violin behind a pianist, and all around them, on low couches, people listened, some with their faces buried in their hands as though in great pain, others with their fingers clasped under their knees and gazing into space. I learned later that the picture was called "Beethoven" and had been painted by Balestrieri. Eleanor, who was all sweetness, in spite of her hastiness and red hair, would then explain that these people seemed sad because they were listening to fine music and, all of a sudden she would add: "Now, little boy, you must run along."

In Eleanor's room was a plaster crucifix. I could not understand the significance of an object that I examined with interest and asked my sister the meaning of the inscription above the Savior's head: "INRI." "INRI!" she repeated smiling, but without an explanation. She was a recent Catholic, converted by an Irishwoman, a friend of my mother's, and here many questions rise in my mind. What did my mother think of this conversion? I have never been able to discover. Eleanor was the only Catholic in the family, and I do not remember anyone talking about Catholicism when I was a child. I only remember that Mamma said to Eleanor: "Since you are a Catholic, I want you to be a good one." And she saw to it that her converted daughter never missed going to mass on Sunday.

For my part, I had no idea what mass could be. With Anne, Retta, and Lucy (but not Mary), I used to go with my parents to the big American church on the Avenue de l'Alma. In that vast building of the purest neo-Gothic style, the Protestant service was performed very nearly as it is in the Anglican church. As for all American families in Paris, an oak pew was reserved for us and each of us sat, wonderful to say, on a big red velvet cushion. Kneeling was just as pleasant, for you also sank down into velvet, and when I prayed I buried my face in my hands, like Papa, without feeling any religious emotion. I did not know what was asked of me. The sermon, almost always inordinately long, bored me to death, because I could not understand a tenth of it, but I woke to the psalms and hymns. That mighty volume of voices carried me along like a river. Although I held a hymnbook, I was too shy to sing, particularly in English,

35

but I liked inviting the sun, the moon, the stars, the rain, the snow, even the hail, and the sea, not forgetting the monsters of the deep, then the trees, the fruits, the old men, the young men to praise the Almighty, although the meaning of the words escaped me ("Praise Him and magnify Him for ever"—magnify was what baffled me for I only knew the words "magnifying glass," no help to me whatever in this case). And then, my ideas about the Almighty were confused. What I dimly understood about this chanting was that it concerned something serious, since you were not to move or talk, and that it all took place in English. I had been told that I was in the house of God, and God spoke English. He spoke English in the Bible that our mother read to us, and when you spoke to God, as I did every night on Mamma's shoulder, it had to be in English.

Something brooded over Lucy, my youngest sister, and already darkened her life. Out of her round camellia-white face, immense green eyes looked at the world seriously, inquiringly. It seemed as though back of that sea-colored gaze lay a question never to be put into words. I think that a sorrow was concealed at the bottom of her generous, tender heart, a sorrow caused by a secret injustice of which she felt a victim, although she never spoke of it. Maybe, as a child, she was scarcely aware of it. She seldom talked and usually retreated into a silence that sheltered her like a fortress, but sang softly to herself when she was alone. Sometimes great fits of gaiety made her burst out laughing, and she would turn to me, as the one she felt closest to. Little by little, by groping blindly, she discovered that she was not quite like the others, that certain things escaped her and, though so young, anxiety already marked her features. She loved our mother blindly, totally, but was deeply attached to Papa, who, through an obscure desire to re-establish some sort of balance, called her his favorite daughter. It was no doubt because Papa suspected that it grieved her to be less pretty than her sisters. However, it was impossible to know what went on in her mind. She silently took stock of everything around her, drew her own conclusions from all she saw, and kept them to herself. In my presence, twenty years later, she threw a copybook into the fire, probably a kind of secret diary. After gazing sorrowfully at the little holocaust, she left the room, and on a bit of paper that the flames had spared I read this short sentence, so sad and so weighty: "It's not that I'm complaining, I'm only stating facts. . . ."

Even at the age of ten, everything wounded her, everything that she could not understand, and that made her hang her head and cry silently. I think that with me, she had a feeling of security because I was five years younger than she was. She would say: "Draw something for me, Joujou." So I would make little sketches framed in pencil, with a caption of my own invention, often an episode from a long story, like those told by the colored sheets of drawings that I was so fond of. No sooner finished than the paper was snatched from me by a frowning Lucy to be examined with severe, attentive eyes. This hardly took a minute, then Lucy said at once, commandingly: "Draw something else!" I obeyed. The second sketch was subjected to the same curious scrutiny and dropped on the floor. Then she absentmindedly clapped her hands and left the room, singing softly to herself. I remember that one of her favorite tunes was "On the Road to Mandalay."

I can only very vaguely remember the scrawls I showed my sister, but feel sure that none of them had the peculiar character of those I drew when alone, that I drew for myself and, without being aware of it, for the *other one*.

If Lucy seemed mysterious to me, what would I say of my sister Retta, a year her senior? That extra year was just what separated her from me. Retta's place was with the older girls and their secrets, their own particular language, while a sort of silent complicity existed between Lucy and myself that lasted until her death. I was fond of Retta without understanding her, but who understood her? Although she belonged to the big girls' clan, something about her isolated her from the world. First of all, she was perfect. There was nothing to blame in her, she always told the truth, she was grave and beautiful with black hair, black eyes, pink cheeks, she loved us all without saying so and did her homework like an angel. Angel—the word leapt to your lips on seeing her. We have kept her copybooks, illustrated with little maps, that made people cry out with admiration and surprise. She faithfully reproduced what she saw in her atlas in different colored inks. Brown strokes shaped like caterpillars featured the mountains. She embroidered collars and handkerchiefs with a patience and skill that made grownups wag their heads. The tip of her tongue sticking out between her teeth, she turned out papers on French literature in a copperplate hand. I remember that she wore her hair down her back; a big round comb like Alice in Wonderland's kept it tidy and bared a smooth white brow. Whether she was reading her Bible or playing the piano, she did everything with a gravity bordering on a sort of fanaticism. It was useless to tell us to pattern ourselves on her, she surpassed us too easily in all ways and seemingly without knowing it, for no one could be more modest, take a back seat more artlessly, but she was secretive to an unimaginable degree. You would have thought that all the blood inherited from our Scottish ancestors flowed in the veins of this astonishing little girl. The passing years only made her more beautiful in our eyes, then came the day when she stood before us with all the serenity of an empress while an incredible piece of news spread through the house: she had been expelled from the Lycée Molière.

Mamma was sent for; she went to the headmistress's office to be shown letters that had been submitted to an expert graphologist. These letters, addressed to a Left Bank department store, contained orders of all kinds, ranging from sets of kitchen utensils to sheets and towels, from table services to office supplies, all these goods being distributed among different lycée teachers who, faced by such massive deliveries, could only throw up their hands in horror. The latter were shown the letters justifying the orders, letters that were, of course, forged by Retta. She had carried out her plan with all the care and imaginative subtlety she exerted in everything she did. Among the articles delivered, some were strange, others ridiculous, but Retta had done her best to avoid anything commonplace, and the choice of certain objects showed a purpose and even a touch of ferociousness of which she would have seemed incapable. Thus it was that a blameless spinster professor received mountains of baby clothes. A bathtub was sent to a teacher whose ideas of cleanliness were not sufficiently clear. But the department store could not provide for everything. Because Retta did not fancy another spinster's looks, a coffin was carried to the latter's door. That perhaps was the darkest, the most Scottish touch of all. Without tears as without regrets, without being in the least upset, Retta confessed everything, admitted everything, but preserved a deep silence when questioned about her motives. She was not scolded. That would have been useless. One look at her inscrutable and rather sternly beautiful face, and all threats died on the harshest lips. Retta quietly left the Lycée Molière and completed her education at a private school.

I was baptized at Christ Church, a small Anglican church no longer in existence, situated at Neuilly, 81 Boulevard Bineau. I scarcely know anything about the circumstances of my baptism, except that my godmother was an Irish Catholic, Agnes Farley. She once said to my mother: "You'll never make a Protestant of your son." Most unfortunately and much to my regret, my mother's answer has not come down to me, for if I had known it, I would know things that might clear up a mystery.

I had none of the feelings that I should have had at the American church on the Avenue de l'Alma. To speak plainly, I was bored there, save when sun, moon, stars, rain, snow, and men were asked to magnify the Almighty (or to enlarge Him with a magnifying glass, according to my private interpretation). I sometimes plucked my mother's sleeve, whispering that one of the stained-glass windows had been put in upside down, and she ordered me to hush. In the Avenue de l'Alma, after the service, I asked questions about the incriminated widow, and my mother, who could not make heads or tails of my story, brushed me aside, as you would drive away a mosquito; but years after her death I realized that the stained glass pictured St. Peter's martyrdom, he who was crucified head downward. I examined that window with all the attention lent by boredom, and that is all I remember of the church, except my great admiration for the red velvet cushions on which we knelt; I would have liked to take mine home with me.

My behavior at the English church on the Rue Auguste-Vacquerie was quite different. We used to attend service there once in a while. I am not very sure what it looked like, but I do remember that when the Reverend Mr. Cardew knelt before the altar and in a quavering voice, but with an unmistakably sincere tone, struck up a hymn immediately taken up by the congregation, I was filled with indescribable emotion. It was because of that man that I loved God. I did not know it, and the Reverend Mr. Cardew did not either. Recently, I was told by a Catholic priest that Mr. Cardew had left behind him the memory of a spotless life, after having long been chaplain to the *Folies-Bergères* girls.

In the center of the 93 Rue de Passy "forest" stood the dining room. Certain winter days come back to me, without saddening me in the least. Once more, I am at table with the others: everybody is there, no one is absent, no one has died and, to all appearance, all are happy, my father and mother, my five sisters and Roselys, a girl from Philadelphia whose gaiety and charming little grimaces amuse us. My father stands carving a big roast of beef, he frowns and bites his lip during this delicate operation. "Nice, thin slices, Edward," says my mother. "You'll have lace, Madam," he replies, flourishing his long knife. Everybody laughs, I do too, without quite knowing why. The garnet-colored glass decanters that my grandfather brought from Bohemia shine like rubies in the light; snow-white rice smokes in a silver dish. Lina comes in with a platter of fritters such as I have never tasted since, corn fritters, and Roselys claps her hands and cries: "I *love* corn fritters!" She laughs and talks like an old colored man to amuse us. You cannot help loving her. Even though she comes from the North. ("Not a word about the War, children," Mamma had said before lunch.) It is Christmas. The table is set with our very best, a damask tablecloth, heavy family silver, everything that our parents had clung to during hard times, because all that came from over there, from their fabulous native land that wrenched so many sighs from Mamma when she thought of it, the South, struck off the list of nations. How nice and warm it is in that Parisian dining room. The porcelain stove gives out an intoxicating warmth and long before the dessert, alas, I dimly hear Papa murmur: "Look, Beaver is going to sleep."

I sometimes think of myself as a blind man trying to remember the light. I asked my mother why God had created the world, but I no longer know what she answered. Then I asked her when God had begun, and she told me that He had existed before all things. And what was there before then? Before the time when He had begun to exist? "He Himself." And before that *before*? Before *before*? He Himself. He was before all possible befores. For Him, there were no befores. And when would He end? Never. For a few seconds I felt as though I were falling into an abyss. I must have been six and truth was clearing a path to my mind, with a kind of violence that frightened me and that I have not forgotten. My emotion was so strong, even, that it afterward left its mark on all the ideas I could form about the Creator. I can very well understand the Jews calling Him the Everlasting, and from this notion of eternity proceeds the notion that fear is the beginning of all wisdom. Even now, it seems to me difficult to think without trembling of the love unsparingly lavished by the One who has neither beginning nor end. My mother, I think, also experienced that curious inner dizziness given by the idea that in God, time is abolished. For her, as for me, the words "never" and "always" had a magical resonance.

I was beginning to speak a little English when she made me learn Psalm XXIII, in the matchless King James version. Such simple sentences, childlike sentences, clung easily to my memory, and though their meaning was so mysterious, it never occurred to me to question anything: no more my head being anointed with oil than the table prepared for me in the presence of my enemies. I believed what my mother believed and as far as I remember she explained nothing; she made me repeat each verse after her, then the whole psalm, and all that formed wonderful pictures in my mind that, I may say, intoxicated me. I saw the shepherd, I saw the valley of the shadow of death, I saw the table prepared for me. At that age, I needed nothing more. Something took place in me that will have no end, something was given me and I realize today that I do not know much more than I did at a time when I first pronounced such majestically familiar words. As I said them, although in a still halting voice, I felt as though I were following someone step by step and advancing with him toward a vast palace bathed in light which I was never to leave, but first I had to cross the dark valley without trembling. That was the Gospel in miniature. How often, in times of anguish, have I not remembered the comforting rod and staff that keep us from all danger! Every day, I recited the prophetic little poem whose riches I shall never be able to exhaust. However, my mother did not stop there. She also made me learn Psalm I; I liked it on account of the tree planted by the rivers of water, whose leaf shall not wither, but my difficulties began with the following psalm because I could not understand why the heathen raged against the Lord's anointed. I preferred another text that she wished me to memorize, St. Paul's famous thirteenth chapter on Charity. It took me a few minutes to learn and many a year to probe its full meaning, nor do I think I will succeed in doing so before my death.

I had reached the age of reasoning and my mother undertook to begin my religious instruction. With this purpose in mind, she made me learn the Creed in English as it is said, approximately, in all Christian churches. I had some difficulty in understanding what I recited, but it was out of the question to ask about things that I would not even have known how to formulate. It all seemed to me very obscure, and yet it all seemed true, since my mother believed it.

There ended my religious education. Nothing else, except a daily reading of the Bible. My sisters' instruction had been far different; they all learned the Church of England catechism by heart and were, one by one, confirmed at the Avenue de l'Alma church. For my part, I can say that Protestantism scarcely touched me. What took place in my mother's mind? I shall probably never know in this world, and can only catch a glimpse of the truth. I remember her once saying to me in an extraordinarily solemn voice: "When you grow up, you will probably see men who will try to persuade you that the Lord Jesus is not God. Lots of men say so, in this country. Don't you believe them, don't you believe them!" She stood facing me, looking at me with such a sad, earnest expression that I remained speechless and, so far as I can remember, she did not say another word.

Sundays followed one another without her taking us to church as she used to, but not an evening passed without her making me repeat the Lord's Prayer. She had faith, beyond all doubt she loved Christ; she talked to me about Jesus in such a manner that, when I was five or six, I imagined she had known Him and it grieved me to know that He was dead; I could see how distressed she was each time she read the last chapters of the Gospel to me.

I realize that there are gaps in this narrative. Too many events have eluded me and the main things perhaps remain concealed from me. What is certain is that I put endless questions to a mother who spoke for God, always the same questions: "What is there, after Eternity?"—"Nothing."—"And before Eternity?"—"Nothing."—"How can there be nothing? What is nothing?"—"There was no beginning and there will be no end." I stood, open-mouthed. Intellectually, I still feel so before the two chasms of before and after, which exist only for us prisoners of time.

When my mother talked about religion and said certain things, an immense silence surrounded her. One day she said: "Now, listen. If you were ever to do something wrong, I would rather see you dead. Dead at my feet." She did not watch over me very closely. She had too many children for that and also, strange as it may seem, she who would have died for us was not at all maternal, in the usual sense of the word. She loved us with all her heart, but one had to know it and her sole outbursts of tenderness were reserved to me, it seems. She gave me her father's name, as you would hand someone your most cherished possession. Her irony was exerted on my sisters, not on me. I saw her come and go, full of cares. Yet she burst out laughing sometimes when talking to my father and more often still with my godmother Agnes.

Agnes was tall and portly, a watch chain around her neck, and had such an agreeable voice that you listened with pleasure to what she had to say, even without understanding it, which was often my case. When she came to see us, it seemed to me that the whole flat shook, for her step was quick and heavy. She had light eyes, and when she laughed, she laughed immoderately. She never talked to me as one talks to a child. Scattered snatches of conversation return to my mind. Joined end to end, they would sound a little like this: "What do you think of politics, Julian? Not much. I can see that from your expression. Do you like Louis XI?" I knew that Louis XI hanged his enemies in orchards. "It's perfectly true," said Agnes. "I've always adored that man. You shall have a book on Louis XI. Show me your drawings." I showed her those specially intended for her. "What are all those people in helmets?" —"Romans."—"I see. Unfortunately, I hate the Romans because they remind me of the English. Couldn't you draw something else for me?"—"Oh, I could draw you a picture of hell." —"All right, a picture of hell will do. You can show it to me the next time I come." She turned to Mamma: "Mary, you black Prot, are you the one who talks to him about hell?" But my mother seldom mentioned hell to us. "Of course not, Agnes. I try not to think about hell. Judas is probably there—and perhaps Napoleon Bonaparte—but I hope that God will forgive them in the end."

The business of Judas worried my mother greatly, and the questions my sisters asked on the subject contributed to her anxiety. "Mamma, as it had to happen, as there had to be a traitor, why is he damned?"—"I know, I know. There's something in it that's hard to understand. Anyway, he ought not to have hanged himself."

I remember that the drawing of hell was carried out with exceptional care. What Agnes thought of it, I no longer recollect, but what is still very present to me is a remark made by another

45

friend of the family, a sarcastic Englishwoman whose tough appearance concealed the kindest of hearts, when she glanced at my masterpiece through her lorgnette. She first congratulated me, then burst out laughing as she turned to my mother and said: "That's exactly the way my room looks when I'm packing!"

My mother spoke French with a supreme contempt for all rules of grammar and applied genders in a hit-or-miss fashion. She thought it arbitrary that a chair should be feminine and an armchair masculine, but devoured French books, with a marked fondness for Maupassant. I think that one should mentally go back to the dawn of the century to grasp what appears a little surprising in the choice of such an author by a woman so deeply religious. In the view of many Anglo-Saxons, around 1906, Maupassant was scarcely to be mentioned; he embodied the real or alleged immorality of the French race, whereas Anglo-Saxon immorality was simply hidden to observers. My mother saw these things in her own way. And thus, she felt more touched by the writer's pity for mankind than bothered by his unbelief. As to his risqué situations, they made her smile, I might say more precisely that they made her burst into peals of laughter. Without dreaming of concealment, she and Papa read *Le Rire* before us, an illustrated weekly that we were forbidden to look at, but in all this lay a sort of innocence that I will not attempt to explain. It was probably due to the period. I remember that *Le Rire* went too far one day and was suppressed. The front page of the following number showed a drawing of Adam and Eve, both of them naked. However, around Adam's waist was a large handkerchief marked with an *A*. "Adam," said Eve, "lend me your handkerchief."—"I can't," replied Adam, "*Le Rire* would be suppressed." Great merriment on my mother's part. "The French are so funny!"

She was the opposite of a fanatic and I cannot help thinking that I sometimes perplexed her. This is only an impression, no doubt, but such a strong one that after fifty years I am unable to forget it. Between us was the bond of faith, and she was conscious of it when she talked to me, she guessed what lay closer to my heart than anything else. Hence the rather strange seriousness of tone and expression in dealing with her last-born child. With me, she was not quite the same as with the others, and the difference is not easy to define. I appreciated the way she treated me and thought no more about it.

Years after her death, I was told of something that spoke volumes for her idea of true charity. She and my father were at the Café de la Paix, where they had had supper after the theater. It must have been around 1912, when the family was a little more prosperous. As they went toward the door to reach the boulevard, my mother passed a woman who was obviously a prostitute and quickly slipped a gold piece into her hand. "Why did you do that?" my father asked gently a moment later. "She wasn't as pretty as the others and nobody noticed her: she had no customers. . . ."

My sisters kissed me all the time. They ran after me, hugged me, showered me with kisses. I ran away from them to complain to my mother: "The girls kiss me all day long!" And I added, using one of Mamma's favorite expressions: "They make my life a burden!"

In the afternoon, each in turn, one of my sisters took me to the Bois or sometimes downtown. From time to time I accompanied lovely Eleanor on one of her slow peregrinations through the old streets of Passy. For she walked very slowly, stopping at every shop window and only quickening her pace before the black den where lived the embroideress who might pop out suddenly to demand the money owed her for months and months by my sister Mary.

47

The Rue Bois-le-Vent, the Place de Passy, the Rue de l'Annonciation were as familiar to me as my parents' room. Sometimes we ventured as far as Notre-Dame de Grâce de Passy and went in for a moment. At that period it was a big country church that dated back to the First Empire. Now that it has been enlarged, much of its charm has gone for me, but around 1906 it delighted me. Dark and a little mysterious, I thought of it as an enchanted spot, for no sooner did you go into the church than you left behind you everything that was commonplace, everything that you saw daily. I hardly knew where I was. Eleanor simply told me to remove my hat, I saw her genuflect and cross herself, but asked no questions. The golden ornaments on the altar shone in the duskiness, and at the very end of the church, in a dark corner, was a grotto made of real rocks above which the statue of a woman in white stood like a ghost. At her feet burned tapers of different lengths, some straight, others a little awry, with small orange flames that fluttered in the drafty air. There my sister stopped and I stopped with her to look at the lady whose eyes were raised toward the vaulted roof. I have not the faintest recollection of a religious emotion, but a keen one of dim admiration. The grotto, the statue, the lights—what could all that mean? The fact of not understanding increased the strange pleasure I felt in being there. Eleanor gave me no explanation. Was she waiting for someone or something? Not at all. After a while, she once more made the curious gesture that went from face to shoulders, and that worried me a little, because, after all, she was my sister Eleanor and at home she never waved her hand in that manner. However, I asked no questions and in the street she was once more the smiling, beautiful person whom I loved.

The furniture in the midst of which I saw my mother come and go surrounds me; she leaned against this table, sat in this big rocking chair. If she came back, she would no doubt recognize *home,* the setting she had grown to like, but she is not here and all that remains to me of her, with a lock of hair and her little memorandum books, is her Bible in which so many pages are missing and, as too many children read and learned psalms, whole leaves have been torn away by their fingers. I ask questions of the book where she has underlined passages that helped her to live, try to arrive at some conclusion, but in vain. There came a moment when she escaped us. Long before her death, she was wrapped in silence. Young as I was, I knew her faith to be deep, but there was a time when she scarcely ever talked about what lay nearest her heart. No doubt I am going too fast, for during the happy days in the Rue de Passy, everything was still in place, we were all very close to my mother. Happiness was possible, we counted on it, but knowing what followed, I cannot help seeing the first shadows brush my mother's anxious head. In the little memorandum books I have just mentioned, a big asterisk marked the days when she lay suffering in a room carefully darkened by drawn curtains, then, the signs recurring too often, she found it simpler to note the days when she felt well. As to the small events in her daily life, they varied little: "Took the children to the Luxembourg on top of the bus. . . . Washed Lucy's hair. . . . Washed Retta's hair. . . . Agnes had tea with me. . . . Paid the coalman's bill. . . ." Nothing else. The little notebooks give no further information about such a thoughtful, good and secretive woman.

I feel at times that I am not living, that I am dreaming that I am alive and all of my past life appears like a kind of vision from which I wake each day and that continues each day. For death will perhaps be our great awakening. Then we will understand why we moved among shadows, but behind all that was God, as lights quivering behind the veil that hides the sky from us.

What about my father? Papa, as far as can be known, was not introspective. In the morning, full-dressed and smelling of Cologne water, he knelt at the foot of his bed, buried his face in his hands, and said his prayers. My parents' room served as a passage. My sisters went through it in slippers, light-footed as sylphs. In vain did my mother attempt to drive them into other regions. "Children, be quiet! Your father is saying his prayers," she said in a whisper that traveled to the hall. Papa groaned and clapped his brown hands to his ears. Then Mamma closed the doors and no one came in.

My father simply believed what the Gospel said, but he believed it to the bottom of his heart and without the ghost of a theological complication. He prayed to God like a child. I have never known a man more upright or more simple in his life, as in his faith. How glad I am to be able to tell myself today that I never once disobeyed him, any more than I remember ever having disobeyed my mother, although taking little credit for it, because in my eyes they were perfect and perhaps they really were. What surprises me, having had such parents, are the inconsistencies of my life. There must have been grandparents and, above all, great-grandparents of whose secret life I am ignorant (the famous "Grandpa the Pirate," who was really a corsair in the British navy), but between them and me, between them and all of us children, rose a kind of spiritual barrier formed by my father and mother. They stood between us and evil, between us and misfortune. We knew, and my mother knew it as we did, that when my father was there, nothing wrong could happen to us, that the walls around us were twice as solid and the light twice as beautiful.

Yet it sometimes happened that a storm burst in the middle of a meal, either because of the Dreyfus affair, or because of a difference of opinion over the Civil War. My mother's head was full of first-class arguments, for she came of a family of lawyers, and the discussion quickly turned into a verbal battle royal.

"There they go again!" said my sisters, delighted. Two or three times a year, the dreadful thing occurred: my father got up suddenly and, flinging his napkin in the midst of the dishes, left the room. Then my mother ran after him and soothed him as you would soothe a bear: "Please, Edward, please!" I can hear her now. Papa stamped his foot, but he always came back and everyone was happy once more.

I had moments of inexplicable sadness mingled with strange pleasure. Can you feel happy to be a little unhappy? Particularly when you do not know why you feel unhappy . . . Toward seven in the evening, in the big kitchen, when night fell softly and the sound of muffled voices in the vicinity floated through the open window, I had a strange warning that the minute was coming and, sure enough, there occurred a sudden silence. That silence invariably took place, although it was short. Lina was silent. It seemed to me that the whole earth was silent. It was then that my heart sank. I congratulated myself on being in the kitchen and not alone in my parents' room. Lina's presence comforted me, whereas, over there in a room where the light wavered ominously, someone or something unknown came out of the walls and whispers circulated through the haunted room; but in the kitchen, it was different. Sadness dropped down from the sky. You had nothing to fear, but there was that gentle impression of misfortune, and I received my share of it without understanding what it was. When I heard my mother read us the account of Creation: "And the evening and the morning were . . ." the word "evening" resounded in me with magic power. I imagined that God had created the world at seven in the evening, and even now, that moment in the day is of a religious nature for me, particularly on fine April afternoons when the light is slowly shipwrecked through the trees and the distress of being mortal is allied to the joy of living.

At the age of six or more, I had a horror of darkness that cannot be described. If I have ever known fear, it certainly originated there. The most wonderful thing in the world, when I lay abed, in the dark, was the appearance of a candle lighting up my mother's face. "What! Aren't you asleep yet?"—"Oh yes, I am, Mamma." And closing my eyes on a sort of blaze that I saw through my lashes, I slipped with a peaceful heart into the depths of the abyss.

If I could once more see the child I was at eight and observe him carefully, I could better understand the man I have become, but the veil woven between us and our past probably has its reason. If we could recall everything, certain moments of a rarer quality would lose their significance by disappearing into a body of memories. Oblivion is a selection, only allowing essential things to subsist.

In 1908, at the lycée, I was in Monsieur Soyer's class. Monsieur Soyer wore a frock coat, had a red beard, and his sudden and capricious fits of anger were terrifying. I do not know why I recollect a sentence he once uttered concerning diseases: "It's useless to talk to you about the horrors that lie in store for us all. Your kidneys are in wonderful condition. . . ." I did not understand what he meant, but the sentence stuck in my mind while almost all the rest of his teaching has left it. If this forms part of the "selection," it is, I admit, mysterious.

I can remember only two of my schoolmates in Monsieur Soyer's class. One was called Lantin. He had the gentle face of an artist or of a martyr, with long, straight hair, a starched collar turned down over a loosely tied bow, and, what made me shudder with disgust, gray teeth. The other was called Brissaud. He was a jolly, cocky boy who came up to me and confided, in fits of laughter, that his father, a cavalry officer, whipped him when he had bad marks. And because I often did the opposite of what I really wished, I kept away from Brissaud and sought Lantin's company—Lantin, who inspired a

52

sort of horror in me. I talked to Lantin, listened to Lantin, and avoided Brissaud. Why? I could not have said, but long since then I have acted in the same way.

That same year, on a June afternoon, something happened in me that remains in my memory as one of the most singular moments of my whole life. I was sitting in the classroom by an open window from whence I could see a small tin roof that covered a gallery with little iron columns. At a short distance beyond stood a long brown brick building, and I could also see branches of plane trees with their fresh new leaves, but I particularly recollect the metal roof, because it was when I looked at it that I was suddenly torn away from myself. For a few minutes I felt certain that a world existed other than the one I saw around me and that this other world was the real one. The happiness I felt was such that I will not attempt to describe it, for I believe it to be beyond all the resources of human speech. Any agreeable sensations I had had previously were nothing in comparison. It was not the same thing, it was not of the same order, it was not in the same country. . . . A moment later, I was once more with my schoolmates and with Monsieur Soyer's voice passing above our heads, as though in a dream of boredom. Sad and bewildered, I became conscious again of what is called reality. Many a time have I pondered over that extraordinary minute when it seemed that everything stood still, that time had ceased to exist and I thought of nothing, neither about myself nor others, nor God. Simply, I was, though the word "I" is perhaps one too many in this affair, but the more I talk about it the less it seems possible to express. When I understood that it was over, I felt like crying. How gloomy the classroom, the walls, the boys' faces, the light itself, and I had the impression that we were all cramped together, as though in a prison.

And perhaps that was all I was to know in this world about the invisible universe. That was the second great minute in my life, the first being situated around my fifth year, or earlier, when, raising my eyes in my parents' room, I saw the night sky through the top pane of the window. Thus was I given the feeling of the soul's immense adventure on this earth.

The Rue de Passy flat was a world that I was never to see again. We left it in October 1910 for the Rue de la Pompe to live in a modern building with, marvelous to relate, electric light. My father's situation had improved.

You crossed a large, dull courtyard, sad in cloudy weather, sinister when the sun shone in a blue sky, for the neighboring houses then seemed black. Not a trace of vegetation. Stone and silence, but a silence that appeared horrible to me, accustomed as I was to the Rue de Passy's gay uproar. Here the slightest noise was banished, like an impious element that disturbed the bourgeois peace. It was not the deep and living silence of monasteries, but an arrogant, cantankerous silence, the silence of the rich. We were going to live among the rich. The only noise I remember, in thinking of the place, is the sound of footsteps crossing the lifeless courtyard. You glanced out of the window and felt like committing suicide.

A magnificent, intimidating staircase uncoiled its great disdainful spirals to the second floor, where we lived. Then, how shabby I thought the Rue de Passy staircase with its mean curves and narrow landings: it was there that a young sex maniac, pursuing two terrified little girls, my sisters Retta and Lucy, had had time enough to expose himself before being chased away with a broom by the janitress.

Nothing of the sort could have happened on the Rue de la Pompe staircase, nothing so scandalous, nothing so interesting. By that I mean that there was nothing human about this staircase, and that it lacked atmosphere. It was noble and stupid, rejecting the very idea of an extreme gesture or disorderly attire, whereas the Rue de Passy staircase, with its timid lighting, encouraged passionate impulses. The shock to Retta was not very serious, for she was very well balanced, but I have always thought that it must have affected poor Lucy in a determinative and disastrous manner.

However, when the door of our flat on the Rue de la Pompe opened, it was home, the magic place where my mother and sisters went in and out, gossiping and laughing in a setting made familiar to me by our furniture and where my father's presence gave us all a feeling of security. Although he was a head taller than anybody else and wore a brigand's mustache, his majesty remained that of a baby, which is saying a great deal. Standing in the middle of the drawing room, it seemed as though he had only to smile to ward off ruin, rain, revolutions, death, everything that will always threaten us.

I must say that, in spite of its disheartening 1905 façade, our new flat spelt happiness as soon as you entered it. The large, bright rooms excluded any possibility of ghosts, like those harbored by the Rue de Passy. Mary, who thought herself an expert in such matters, declared that they would follow us, that sometime or other they would discover our new address. In Eleanor's opinion, this would take them several years. "And what if they had come here with our furniture, eh? If they were here already?" I listened. After glancing at me, my mother would lay a finger on her lips.

Through the drawing-room window you saw the Avenue Montespan and its trees running down to the Avenue Victor-Hugo. That was the place to stand in summer when the sun was setting. Was it the mirage of childhood? The visible world has never appeared to me under a more strangely attractive aspect than through these Parisian windows when strips of emerald barred a pale gold sky. By dreaming over these gloriously colored clouds, you ended by seeing them in such a manner that they seemed great islands lost in an ocean of light, but a few minutes more and night swept over the miraculous vision in a huge, black flood. Marveling and disappointed, I watched the vanishing of a paradise that seemed to have been pocketed by dusk. To my mind, the home of the elect could not offer a more supremely radiant aspect, for the day would come when we would be in heaven forever. My mother had told me so, I counted on it, and I still count on it at times, although the enchanting landscapes then offered to my faith have given way to a different conception.

In a corner of the drawing room, I sometimes saw my mother, wearing the big gray shawl that came from Scotland, curled up in the hollow of a vast armchair, holding a book—a novel by Hardy or Maupassant—and sooner or later the book would slip from her fingers and she slept, looking very earnest. As I write, how easily I recall her delicate profile against the flowered slip cover. I wonder what dreams lie behind a brow still so smooth. She looks as though she were thinking. She must not be wakened, she is asleep. She does not know that she has almost come to the end of her life and that our world is about to disappear.

Too many memories return for me to wish to set them in order. I mean that strict chronology would destroy all spontaneity. I prefer telling things just as they come into my mind.

Beyond the drawing room were my sisters' rooms. Two beds in each room, which made four, Eleanor being somewhere else. I will return later to that side of the house. In the part I am now speaking of, there was also a bathroom. Long and narrow, its window was so high in the wall that all you could see was the sky in a frame of honeysuckle. For many reasons which I cannot forget, a room where a voice did not have the same ring as elsewhere, a room where there was something furtive and reticent about the light that filtered into it. This was sometimes the setting for a very strange scene, the meaning of which I missed completely.

My mother bathed me herself, running a heavy cake of yellow soap over my shoulders and down my back, a soap that she never lost the habit of using. This operation over, she got up and, moving away from the bathtub, looked at me disapprovingly. At this point, words might betray me, and others should be invented to describe what took place in the eyes of a woman I loved so much. I felt that she was both displeased and attentive. "The neck," she said, "and then the ears and behind the ears." I obeyed. "And now the body . . . Under the arms and then the front . . ." She said the word "body" in such a way that until I was fifteen or sixteen, I hesitated to use it, as though it referred to something shameful.

In a silence scarcely broken by the splashing of water, a mysterious thought passed from my mother to me, a thought that fixed itself I cannot tell where, to reappear in my consciousness many years later. Because of the way she looked at me, lovingly to be sure, but with an indefinable mistrust, I now understand that human nakedness aroused her suspicion. A sentence once escaped her that I remembered precisely because it was incomprehensible to me and at the same time it had such a strange sound that it was impossible for me ever to forget it. I lay in the warm water and, a few steps away, my mother was drying her hands with a worried air when suddenly she glanced down at a very precise part of my person. As though she were talking to herself, she murmured: "Oh, how ugly that is!" And she turned her head with a kind of shiver. I said nothing, but felt myself blush without knowing why. Something in me had been affected in an incomprehensible manner. I must have been eleven and profoundly innocent. My mother looked at me sadly, as one would look at a culprit too much loved to be punished, and once I was dressed, she hugged me.

It took me years to discover the secret of what I can only call a phobia. Before dying, my mother revealed part of it to me, as I will tell later, but she had not the least idea of its meaning or, above all, of its never-ending consequences. I myself, half a century after all this, am I really sure of seeing things clearly? This woman, who was so human and so tenderhearted, how anxious she was that nothing wrong should happen to me, how much she longed for my salvation! I did not always understand her. She seemed to me both mysterious and wonderful. I would not like anyone to think of her as a puritan. The very word would have horrified her, but the way she spoke to my sisters was not the way she spoke to me. I knew that she loved me with the same rather fanatical love that I myself had for her. Around her, perhaps unknowingly, she erected terrible interdicts. The idea of purity that she formed in my brain, proceeded from her misgivings.

That idea has sometimes harmed me, sometimes protected me, and I am still indebted to it on many scores, for it will probably stay with me until I die. The body was the enemy, but it was also the soul's visible fortress and chiefly the temple of the Holy Ghost. Everything pertaining to the flesh became both dangerous and sacred. The flesh was to remain spotless. On that account, the least threat alarmed my mother to an unimaginable degree, the moment I was concerned. The integrity of the body was linked to the integrity of the soul. One should remain unsullied.

After a whole lifetime, I cannot recall these things again without emotion. I remember that one day, as she was bathing me, she suddenly moved back and cried: "Those red spots! What can they be?" Clasping her head in her hands, she fell on her knees by the bathtub: "Leprosy!" she said.

That was the disease so often spoken of in the Scriptures. I kept a horrified silence and, all of a sudden, my mother threw her arms around my body, as though to protect it. "I won't leave you," she said through her tears, "I'll go with you to Molokai." With a beating heart, I asked what Molokai was. "An island. You don't know. Soldiers force you to march before them with their guns. . . ."

The name of Molokai, which could mean nothing to a Parisian, had great meaning for a woman brought up in the Southern States, but she was really thinking of something that was not Molokai. The nightmare lay elsewhere, the nightmare was something else. There was something in my mother's memory that she could not forget. I wept with her, all naked and all dripping, on her shoulder.

An hour later, Doctor Brégi appeared. He was an old gentleman with a most venerable air and a white beard that made him look like Coligny. We were all of us fond of him on account of his gentleness and great good sense. He examined me from head to foot and, turning to my mother, asked what I had eaten the day before. "Yesterday? I don't remember. Oh, yes, mussels." —"This evening, Madame, you must make him drink one or two cups of camomile tea" (his great remedy) "and in the future, no more mussels."

Papa and my sisters made pitiless fun of her: "You are always so dramatic!" She laughed heartily with us all, and the next day all traces of leprosy had left my body, but I could not forget my mother's terror.

I slept in my parents' room, which looked out on the vast and sinister courtyard. Their beds stood at the far end of the long, badly lit room. Mine was next to the window, and at the foot of the bed was my little table. It was there, through some perplexing mystery, that I reveled in the strange drawings, more and more precise and more and more complicated, of which I was the innocent author. These nudes, which I colored in pink, absorbed me to such a point that I no longer knew what was going on around me. I must say that no one watched me much. I was so good! I wish to specify, however, that many of my drawings represented historical scenes, battles, riots, coronations, and massacres, everything that could inflame my imagination, and to give them a more ancient and more authentic touch, I tore them up and patched them together again with strips of transparent adhesive tape.

For there were two very distinct tendencies in my tastes as a draftsman, one that could be openly acknowledged, the other not. I was getting on to eleven and beginning to realize that those which were not acknowledgeable should not be shown. I was perhaps being secretive, but am not very sure of it. I believe, however, that it was around this period that a terrifying idea of purity shaped itself in me. Where did it come from? From my mother? But how? I am unable to see clearly on this point. "Pure" and "impure" were words that had no part in our daily vocabulary. I met them only in the Bible, but there, they stood out to an extraordinary degree and bordered on the sacred. That perhaps was at the origin of the peculiar theology I worked out in my head. The Bible was in itself sacred. A book, no doubt, but a book on which it was not permissible to place another book. So thought my mother, and we took it literally. You could lay a Bible on top of another Bible, but nothing else. Every one of its pages, every one of its sentences, every one of its words contained the truth. The Bible was religion. Now "pure" and "impure" recurred there unceasingly, like torches around a burnt offering, and in my mind "pure" was everything that was acknowledgeable, that could be shown, "impure" everything that was hidden. What tortuous deductions led me to such a conclusion? I cannot answer, but I know that with time, the ramifications of these two ideas extended further and further. I finally imagined two incompatible worlds. You could leave one to enter the other in the twinkling of an eye.

My pink nudes (of a toothpaste pink) were, in my own judgment, impure. In the same way, Dante's *Inferno* and the picture at the Luxembourg. All that formed part of an interdict, together with a great many other things. For instance, the horses harnessed to the delivery wagons of the Louvre department store. They were so beautiful, so shiny, so round . . . Impure! This went so far that the sound of horses trotting in the Rue de la Pompe—which could be heard from my room—roused the colossal ghost of the Impure in my imagination. I tried to draw these animals but most distinctly remember that my heart thumped and my emotion grew so overwhelming that I took fright and abandoned the idea. Something disquieting stole into me. I felt my head spin. All that should be hidden. The impure should be hidden and I tore the drawing into tiny pieces.

What was wrong in all this? That is what I cannot make out, even at present. I was perfectly unconscious of doing anything wrong. Remorse never troubled me. I had no idea what remorse could be. I never disobeyed my parents and there was seldom any reason to punish me. All I knew was that in drawing naked people instead of, say, a military review with bands and flags, I passed from an everyday world to a secret one, mine, the one I bore in my head and wanted to see on paper. So, the tip of my tongue sticking out between my teeth, I grasped the colored pencil with all my might as it traveled slowly over the paper. I was happy and my happiness was strange and immeasurable. In a manner that I cannot understand, I identified myself with what I drew with frenzied attention, and at the same time, I possessed it. I did not feel alone at such moments. There was someone with me, of that I am certain. In drawing these contours, I appeased a mysterious covetousness. No one ever came in on me unexpectedly. Since the day when my cousin Sarah leaned over my shoulder to see what I was doing, no one ever thought of glancing at the deed of darkness to which I applied myself with such passionate diligence. Yet it would have been easy to discover the whole thing. The door stayed open and I was too much absorbed to be on the watch and, first of all, I would have had to feel guilty, which was not the case. I was bewitched, I swam about in a sort of diabolical enchantment, and something always warned me when I should turn over my drawing, whether fit to be seen or not, for in that lay the wily trick of the one who abetted my efforts. I was never caught. "Are you still drawing?" someone absently inquired at times. "Yes, you'll see, it will be a surprise." That was the answer that had been suggested to me, the one that could reassure everybody, if anyone had been uneasy, but no one was. The surprise arrived in due time, was taken to my mother, then to each of my sisters, to my father when he returned from the office, and even to the cook, the housemaid, and, when she happened to be there, as far as Sidonie, a seamstress who worked for us by the day. I needed compliments and admiration. "How does he think up such things? Just look at these ladies and gentlemen waltzing. . . . And the tenants who live on the floor above complaining. . . . And the concierge in her lodge. . . ." My parents laughed heartily with the innocence of parents. My sisters smothered me with kisses, I ran off with my drawing: "You kiss me too much! Life isn't worth living!"

One night, around 1911, I was awakened by a murmur of voices as my father and mother chatted from one bed to the other and I understood that they were talking about me. "He draws all the time," said my father. "Have you noticed how he sticks his tongue out when he's busy? What a funny little fellow he is! I think he's gifted."—"He's a good child," said my mother.—"Yes, but he gets horrible marks in arithmetic. Do you realize he doesn't even know how to add?" I do not remember what they said next and fell asleep again.

Did my mother have any suspicions? I think not, yet she must have watched out for the enemy, for one day, in explaining the parable of the talents, she let fall a singular sentence that I have not forgotten. "The gifts that come to us from God can be put to very different uses. For instance, if Julian put his gift for drawing to a bad use, God would take it away from him." I did not understand this very well, but the words stuck in my mind. What bothered me was the ambiguity of the word "talent." To

bury your talent in the ground . . . How so? It never occurred to me that my mother suspected me of drawing im-
purities. Perhaps she had an intuition of it and brushed it aside.

Regarding sexual life, my ignorance was complete. I knew
nothing whatever about relations between men and women. Not
a word was breathed on the subject at home, and in the Bible,
when I came across a sentence concerning something of the
kind, I asked my mother what it meant. Such or such a patriarch
knew his wife. I imagined greetings and low bows, but that was
not quite enough for me. "Ask your father," said Mamma. On
consulting my father, he looked embarrassed and said: "Your
mother will explain that to you." I returned to my mother. "Oh,
you'll understand these things later," she answered evasively.
And then she added: "Anyway, you don't need to know about
it."

The question was settled. As I did not need to know, it could
not be interesting. My mother could not be mistaken. I
was very happy. On the strength of what my mother once said
to me, in peals of laughter, I believed that all my sisters had
been bought at the Galeries Lafayette, whereas I came from the
Grande Maison de Blanc. "A bargain!" cried my mother as she
hugged me.

I return to the drawings mentioned a while ago to say once
more that the idea of a possible link between them and evil
never crossed my mind; I return to it because I believe it was
then that a sort of siege was laid to my heart. This secret world
was for me a source of prodigious joys, and at the same time it
fed desires never to be gratified, for they surpassed human pos-
sibilities. That was the body's dream. There was a monstrous
hunger in me, the nature of which I failed to understand. I did
not know what I wanted, nor what these drawings signified. All
I knew was that they should be hidden and destroyed, even
though they were to be repeated again and again. As to touch-

ing my body as I did when I was four or five, that was out of the question, I never dreamt of it for an instant. I never looked at myself, and I must say that until I was fourteen it did not occur to me to do so.

The crime lay in not wearing clothes, the crime lay in going naked. And so the men I drew were criminals. In the streets and at home, men and women were dressed. Everyone was dressed from head to foot, always. Boys wore stockings, or such long socks that only their knees were bare. I alone was naked, in my bath, under my mother's eyes, and I did not look at myself, for the thing to do was to get dressed as quickly as possible, cease to be naked. What was naked, apart from hands and face, could only be indecent. The word began to have, if not a meaning, at least a certain value in my mind. Another word that struck me was "virgin." "Virgin" was closely related to "pure," "pure" was closely related to "clean," and "clean," through a sort of mad logic, meant "virgin." One day, a few minutes before lunch, I asked my sister Eleanor if she had washed her hands. "Why no," she answered, amused, "they don't need washing at the moment, at least I hope not." I gave her a little pat. "You're not a virgin!" I cried. This made her laugh all the more since she had been married for a rather short time. The general merriment made me laugh too. I had said something funny and, very proud of myself, I repeated: "She's not a virgin! Eleanor is not a virgin!"

From time to time, my mother took us to the Louvre, occasionally dragging us through the sculpture galleries. She little knew what she was doing. She could not suspect that I left the place in a kind of sexual intoxication that made me suffer all the more since the precise cause of my torture was hidden from me. Nakedness, criminal nakedness, why was it allowed to be seen: exalted, supreme, perched on pedestals and seemingly trampling us underfoot? "These are works of art," explained Mamma, "statues of false gods, gods that have never

64

existed. Now, come along. Don't stay here. We're taking the Passy—Hôtel-de-Ville to go home. If there's room, we ride on top of the bus."

Why are children taken to museums?

I did not understand. These words would discredit me in the minds of a great many men of the present day, yet I am continually obliged to use them in order to describe the confusion in which I grew up. Nevertheless, I was happy as few children have ever been. If there were moments in my life of a darker joy, I think I may say that I then had little part in it. An irresistible force took me under its wing and guided my hand toward a sheet of white paper. This did not happen very frequently. There were intervals, seemingly well planned, that allowed me to see what *progress* I had been able to make. I add, to have done with the subject, that there was not a trace of obscenity in these drawings. I did not know what obscenity could be, I knew nothing about the gestures that lead you to perdition, and evil forced its way into me by far more subtle means. So much so that I wonder if, after all, my mother did not chance on one of these drawings (for I was so deeply absorbed that I talked to myself as I drew). And what is singular about the naked people I depicted is that none of them had a sex.

I would like to find the gossamer thread that passes through my life from birth to death, the one that guides, binds, explains. Was I very different from children of my own age? I was certainly more ignorant of life, less conscious and surely less wise, less knowing than my schoolmates. Yet I longed to be like them, do as they did, look like them, and in spite of this I remained alone. What I said amused no one, held no one's attention. I broke silence only to say things that apparently had no sense, and the scoffing smiles I then saw made me burn with mortification. I was both proud and bewildered.

At school, everything that had the slightest bearing on the

sciences or even on plain arithmetic threw me into an uneasiness that quickly turned into anxiety, for I found it impossible to grasp what it was all about, or why it was necessary to cover the blackboard with figures. What could be the reason? History, on the other hand, fascinated me. Riots, wars, revolutions, the great high-flown sentences that issued from famous men's lips, weird clothes, attitudes, what a number of subjects for drawings! I learned foreign tongues with an ease that surprised my professors. Above all, I loved the beauty of words. Poetry exerted a magic influence over me, comparable to that of melody over a savage. I understood or did not understand the meaning of all the words and that was of no importance. Something was communicated to me and I listened with parted lips.

The lycée world was very different from ours at home. At home, I was in my parents' country. At the lycée, I was in France, a miniature France crossed by currents of ideas that seemed strange to me. As you climbed from the eighth to the sixth form and from the sixth to the third, antipathies became more precise and more vicious. A hatred of the Jews took shape. Foreigners were disparagingly called *métèques*. Religion was absent. A love of country occupied the empty space, and this love caught me, filled my heart.

If I did not continually keep a sharp lookout, this book would lapse into an autobiography, pure and simple. Now, what I wish to do is quite different. I intend to look where my eyes have never turned, except by chance, I want to see more clearly into that part of conscience that so often remains obscure as we move away from our childhood. The good seed that God sowed so bountifully, the bad seed sowed by the devil—how did all that grow?

In the sixth form, I was twelve years old. I remember that we were so numerous in the big classroom that looked out on the street that we had to crowd together on the benches. Lost in a never-ending dream, I saw nothing of what went on around me. Perhaps nothing went on, but I remember that some of my schoolmates were angels of purity in my eyes while others seemed the incarnation of evil.

Two boys were known for their piety. I heard it said that at chapel, where I never set foot, being a Protestant, they remained for minutes on end, heads buried in hands, lost in prayer. They never spoke to me, but I regarded them as superior beings. The word "Catholic," which I heard mentioned in reference to them, did not have much meaning for me, in spite of Eleanor's conversion. The same applied to the "first communion," which was also talked about. I did not know what it was; my mother did not speak of it. All I understood was that these two boys lived in a mysterious world that was not ours. Nevertheless, the idea that they were chosen and set apart stuck in my mind, I saw them in a kind of luminous cloud, and what is certain is that I thought them to be in communication with God. Something was given to me by them, something that I cannot manage to determine, perhaps a feeling of what is divine in the heart of man. Yet how vague all this is! I would have liked to talk to them, but dared not. They were rather ugly, particularly the one who wore spectacles, and both stood at the top of the class in every subject. I passed them like a ghost, hoping they would say something to me—but they said nothing. . . .

Very different was a boy I shall call B., although I have so little fondness for initials. He was a Jew, brown-faced, wonderfully handsome, and his green eyes were intelligent and hard —far more so than one who had not seen them could believe. His conquering smile displayed perfect teeth, and everything in him, even the dimples in his round cheeks, everything in him breathed insolence and something more than insolence: he was aggressive. One could not look at him without irritation, but in spite of this, one looked at him. He went by, giving blows right and left, and his high, arrogant voice distributed insults.

Short but well built, strapping, lively, he was dressed with an elegance that rather cowed those among us who were less prosperous than he. However that may be, one day, when we were in the classroom waiting for the teacher, he stood near the professor's desk and, with a smile on his lips and sparkling eyes, he ripped his trousers open and exposed himself to us.

Some of us were not seated. How could I forget the details of this scene? We chattered together in small groups, and B., having placed himself between the desk and the street, could be seen by many of us, but not by our professor when the latter came in. Words cannot express the enormous happiness I saw in the boy's face, nor his extreme self-conceit. That struck me far more than the rest, of which I had only a glimpse, for I turned away my head violently and felt myself blush to the ears. Even at present, my mind's eye shows me the domineering look he cast at us and the kind of diabolical glee that radiated from his whole person. This impression remains so strong that I wonder if I have ever seen evil more perfectly incarnated in a human being with everything brutal and scornful that pride can give. Two or three seconds later, the professor put in his appearance, everything returned to the commonplaceness of daily life, but my heart thumped under the navy blue jersey that fitted my body so tightly. I had seen what should not be seen, what my drawings never showed. What seems to me more astonishing than the rest is the ease with which the scene was wiped from my memory. It had frightened me, but I forgot it, and forgot it for years.

Weeks went by, months perhaps, I am not very sure. I can see myself once more in the fifth form, sitting in an almost empty classroom. It is probably almost time for the summer holidays. My neighbor is a boy whose name is too well known for me to write it without changing the course of this narrative. He is what is termed a brilliant scholar. Bent over his desk, he twirls his pen in the inkstand while speaking to me under his breath. A rather prominent eye, a lock of hair sweeping over the brow, a moist, fleshy mouth and large, flat cheek, everything about him shows a taste for facility and pleasure. His chubby hand continues twirling the pen and he whispers: "Do you want me to tell you the secret of your birth?" I do not understand, but feel uneasy. A secret? I do not reply and my neighbor is silent for an instant. It seems as though something in or around me prevents people from wanting to talk to me. Finally, the voice whispers again: "You were born inside your mother and then taken out." I do not answer, I bend over my book as though I have not heard, I want to go away, never to see that boy again. What he said had scarcely any meaning in my mind, and then it is coarse, but something cries out to me that it is true, otherwise, why should I be so moved? And yet, no. My mother . . . it is not possible. Not my mother, not me. Such a violently impure thing could not have happened when I was born. To be taken out of one's mother's insides . . . My neighbor sniffles. He always sniffles, even in summer. Throwing aside his pen, he adds: "I'll tell you the rest another time."

I have the impression of looking at my past life through a telescope. The picture is small but clear. The classroom and its tall windows of frosted glass that prevent a sight of the street, its transoms opened every hour to chase away any germs floating about in the air! Why could they not also chase away the hatred that weighed heavily on our heart. . . . I say it sadly: it was at the lycée that I obediently learnt to hate my neighbor. The hatred of Germans came first. It had an almost official character. It was the lining of patriotism. You could not love France if you did not hate Germany. Everything that came from beyond the Rhine was open to suspicion. I know all that could be said about Germany's policy and the results it produced in '14 and '39, but nevertheless it is true that hatred is a sad and petty sentiment and that a child's soul can be poisoned by it. The shadow of 1870 extended over us, covering us like a vast and sinister cloud. Almost all our professors had lived through the great defeat and religiously handed down to us gloomy childhood memories which they seemed to treasure. The German class was held in such a manner that Alsace, decked in mourning, always stood among us. Daudet's story *"La Dernière classe"* was sometimes read to us, drawing tears of anger and sadness from one and all, and that included me. Yet I had my own personal tragic year named 1865 and marking the end of the Civil War, but with ill-stifled sighs of rage, I also welcomed 1870. I wished simply and purely that the German Empire would disappear, particularly, I must confess, when I had to learn declensions printed in Gothic lettering.

Next came, alas, the hatred of Jews. That was not peculiar to any one class, but was breathed in on all sides. The Jews were numerous at the lycée: Didisheim, Calmann, Cohen, Bloch, and so many others! . . . Almost all of them flaunted, under our eyes, signs of an aggressive prosperity. How can I forget that while we slaved over our papers, a cheap nib in our fingers, they, with a disdainful hand, guided an Onoto fountain pen, such as only the rich possessed, for all this happened a very long time ago. On Saturdays, striking nonchalant attitudes, they watched us writing, and if a thoughtless professor asked suddenly: "Now then, Cohen, aren't you taking notes?" Cohen's answer put him in his place: "No, sir, I am Jewish."

I never talked to Jews. The fact is that I spoke to no one, or almost no one. Among all these noisy, quarrelsome boys, I found none of the affectionate sweetness that waited for me at home. At the lycée, as I was most often silent, it seemed as though a forbidden zone surrounded me that few wished to cross. I did not suffer much from this, but somewhat regretted not being able to mix with the others. Unfortunately, I did not understand the rules of their games and never knew what to say in order to amuse my schoolmates or, if necessary, to make them shut up.

Where Jews were concerned, my feelings were peculiar. On seeing them, I was conscious of being less well dressed than they and, above all, less sure of myself. I think they did not even notice me when they happened to come across me, for in their eyes I did not exist. Sometimes, a cry of "Dirty Jew!" rose from one corner or another of the playground, followed by pitched battles. I so often heard the cursed epithet coupled with the name "Jew" that I ended by finding it natural. And thus the poison crept into me. I understood that you had to hate a Jew as much as you hated a German, otherwise you were not French, and I wanted to be French. At home, I returned to another world that was Mamma's, a world that existed only thanks to foreign words, to memories, to allusions, whereas at the lycée I was right in the heart of France, a turbulent, combative France that I loved but, as I saw only too clearly, did not cherish the chosen people.

My anti-Semitism came to a sudden stop one day as I was crossing the great, ominous courtyard of our house with my mother. Now, our landlady was Jewish. She was called Madame Rothembourg, and my mother, who was holding me by the hand, told me not to make a noise for, she explained, Madame Rothembourg was ill and in great pain. "But, Mamma," I replied, "what does it matter? She's a Jewess." That was the sentence that passed my lips, dictated by the lycée. And the answer thunderstruck me. My mother at once let go my hand and, moving back a few steps, stared at me in silence. I can still see the horrified expression in her gray eyes. Without saying a word, she walked ahead of me and went quickly up the stairs. I followed as I could, with a thumping heart. For the first time in my life I had the feeling of having displeased her, and it was unbearable. That night, when we said our prayers, she made me ask God to forgive me.

❖ ❖ ❖

I had remained very much of a child. Toward the end of
June, in a corner of the fifth form, I cried softly over my copybook, thinking about the country, about Andrésy, where we
spent the holidays. At that very moment, I said to myself, the
meadows were lovely out yonder and the birds were singing in
the Hautil Woods, but I was not there. A glance at the lycée
playground showed me the sun shining on the gravel and the
dark covered court where the boys played fives. Overwhelmed
with sadness, I wanted to be somewhere else. Our ranks were
thinning and, early in July, the classrooms almost empty. Our
schoolmates had gone, some to Cabourg or Trouville, the rich
ones to Biarritz in expresses that tore along, I was told, at a
dizzy speed.

We others, we Greens, went to Andrésy, Seine-et-Oise, in a
train that ran most sedately toward Conflans-Sainte-Honorine
and stopped at every station, but before a journey that threw
me into convulsions of joy there came the school prize-giving.

It took place in the vast auditorium of the old Trocadéro. On
an immense platform, the faculty in black, yellow, and red
robes. Am I dreaming? I do not think so. That was the way it
was. To the right, a long table laden with gilt-edged books and,
above all this, sky-blue draperies on either side of the organ
pipes, intended, so it seems, to suppress the famous echo that
made the auditorium all but unserviceable. Now, the echo,
chased away from one corner, took refuge somewhere else, repeating hymns and speeches with unfailing accuracy. You had
to pretend not to hear.

I do not know how, but in spite of the untimely departure
of so many pupils, the auditorium was full, or almost. We all
wore white cotton gloves. A military band played the "Marseil-
laise," everyone stood up, then some political minister or other
came forward on the platform and the first of the speeches began. "Ladies and gentlemen . . ." and with jovial condescen-

72

sion: ". . . my young friends." I did not understand a word
of the speeches. Neither did my mother, who was with
me. Then, after some other deadly orations, came the glorious
list of good pupils. The echo repeated each name, like that of a
victory, and you could see the boys climb the red velvet steps
and come down again, their brows wreathed with gilt, silvered,
or green laurels according to the merits of the elect whose arms
were heavy with glittering red books. And what about me? And
what about me? My heart beat fast. Then came my form. I
looked at my mother, who looked back at me with a waggish
little smile, for my name was never called. And yet it was! One
day, my name was thrown to the echo, which tossed it back into
giddy space. An honorable mention, I had an honorable mention! "Go get your honorable mention," said Jean S., inspired
by some playful demon. I believed what Jean S. said, he was
one of the hardest workers among my schoolmates and fond of
me. Anyway, his own name had been called several times and
I had only to follow him to the top of the red velvet steps. How
thick that velvet felt under my feet! I trembled with emotion.
For the first time, I had wangled a prize. My mother could not
believe her ears. Her son's name had been called. . . . An
honorable mention in French . . . She had let me walk off
with a little approving gesture: "Of course, you little silly, go
up, as you're told to!" She had no idea of what an honorable
mention could be. At last, I stood on the platform and repeated
my name to the professor in charge of the awards. "Did you say
Julian Green?"—"Yes." And I added: "It's a foreign name."
—"Wait until I attend to the others." The others, sure enough,
were given their prizes. Jean S. received an ample store of them
together with a laurel wreath that made him look like a pig
about to be sacrificed, for he was fat and pink. "So you said
Julian . . . Julian who?"—"Green."—"I don't see that name.
What prize have you obtained?"—"An honorable mention in
French."—"Are you making fun of me? Prizes are not given

for honorable mentions." I turned the color of the carpet and walked down the steps. At that moment, the military band struck up an air from *Carmen*. I returned to my seat to the tune of "To-ré-a-dor," in a great victorious din that broke my heart. Pride bled. My mother said nothing, but gently squeezed my arm and, once the ceremony over, took me to the other side of the Place du Trocadéro. There I was to be comforted at a cake shop called Doidy. A *baba* first, then an *éclair,* on condition that I eat my meat and vegetables at lunchtime. As to the honorable mention . . . "Never mind," she said, "we won't tell anyone about it, will we? Such things do happen. . . . That's life. . . . You'll see. . . . Were the cakes good?"

Every year we rented a different villa at Andrésy. The first in 1909, 36 Boulevard de la Seine. It was a small furnished house, furnished chiefly with knickknacks, I thought, for they were everywhere, in glass cases, on brackets, hanging on the walls, but none of them were to be touched. The rooms were dark and a long garden separated us from the boulevard, where carriages seldom went by. You crossed the road, walked a short distance under a double row of lindens, and a small grassy slope ran down to the bank of the Seine, which I looked at, marveling. What a fascination there was for me in those quiet, powerful waters, green shading into black and sometimes reflecting the sky so faithfully that they seemed to bear along a cargo of clouds. I gazed for a long time at the Seine, as though some sort of affinity existed between itself and me. While the sea disturbs and upsets me, I love the river that has flowed through my life. I must say that there was something dangerous about it to my mind and I was sensitive to that something. Simply by taking one step forward, you fell into those unfeeling depths and you died. For I did not know how to swim. "Not too near the edge," said my mother. And she added in the dreamy voice induced by the magic presence of water: "If you could see the big rivers we have at home . . . Over there, I wonder if this one would even have a name."—"Are they wider than this one?"—"Yes, you can hardly see the other bank." And the thought of distant lands she would never see again made her sad.

From the bank where we stood, I could see a long island magnificently decked with great trees. And from time to time, there passed little steamboats filled with passengers who gaily waved their hands at us. At other moments, a plaintive bellow heralded a tug. Even now, I cannot hear the sound without a pang. You waited a few minutes, then the tug finally appeared with its long trail of black smoke and, as the lock was not far, it gave a hollow melancholy hoot, one for each of the barges it had in tow. In my imagination, the call became the voice of an ogress, but a good ogress counting her children. And we too counted, in strict time: "Two, three, four . . . five!" Then at the end of a cable came the wonderful flat-bottomed boats, bearing mysterious and charming names on their keels: the *Marie-Jeanne,* the *Daughter of the North,* the *Girl from Saint-Malo,* the *Louise.* I felt as though part of me sprang on board those vast, black barges gliding noiselessly over the dark water. I was going somewhere abroad, to unknown countries, and a sort of blissful languor came over me as I watched the low, wide sterns move away. And on the last barge, there was almost always an ill-tempered little dog that ran barking from one side of the deck to the other.

It was in that little house on the banks of the Seine that I heard of my sister Eleanor's marriage. At Mombasa, British East Africa, she had married a young engineer whose first name was Kenneth. The news made no impression on me. To tell the truth, I wonder what did interest me at Andrésy. I was so happy that I lived, it seems to me, in a kind of rapture. You had to take me by the hand and shake me slightly to obtain something like attention. I used to laugh to myself when alone. One day—that was a strange moment—I was in our maid's room. Why? I have no idea. By her bedside, on a small table, I saw a thick book in a glossy paper cover adorned with such a strange picture that I have never been able to forget it: a blonde and perfectly beautiful young woman roped to a cross. She wore a white chemise and did not seem to be in any pain. Roses stuck in her hair gave a festive air to this pseudo-torture, but nevertheless, its victim rolled her eyes like a martyr. I asked the maid what it was and she replied—I cannot visualize her, but I can hear her voice and remember the languid attitude she immediately adopted—: "It's called *Fausta's Surrender*." And she repeated the title with indefinable complacency. Of course I could make nothing of this, but merely noticed in a corner, under Fausta's feet, in the middle of a circle, the price of the volume: sixty-five centimes. No more has remained in my mind except that I left, knowing my mother did not wish me to talk to the maid. Yet, was it in this room or somewhere else in the house that a most unusual thing happened to me? I cannot manage to recall all the circumstances, but this much is in my memory: I am standing by a wall painted a light yellow and, looking at this wall, am suddenly overcome by an unutterable happiness that wrests me out of myself to the point of not realizing where I am. Not the happiness of being at Andrésy for the holidays, or even the happiness of childhood, it is a causeless happiness, coming from nobody knows where and that sweeps through souls as the wind sweeps through trees. How long did it last? I have no idea, but it made a powerful impression on me.

The maid I mentioned was called Berthe. Even though she took a languorous pose when talking of Fausta, she was a tall, rough girl. She was often seen to bound from her kitchen clutching a broom, in pursuit of a black dog called Pyramus who had just lifted his leg to the beans in the vegetable garden. Berthe's formidable strides crushed the vegetables under her heels and the dog ran away limping to the Boulevard de la Seine, where

76

he met his friends. I think he belonged to Monsieur Nicole, the restaurant-keeper who showed movies during weekends in a room usually reserved for banquets, but I will talk of this another time.

Lord, to return to the spring, to drink fresh water, to live over the days when one never really sinned . . . Paradise on earth in the strange little universe I had made for myself was at a time when desire did not prevail. Flesh meant anarchy, meant the horror that darkened every face. Even now, how I loathe that inexorable force that reduces men to slavery by its all-powerful whims! But at Andrésy, I *knew* nothing. I had forgotten what my schoolmate had told me about the way I was born. I probably thought it was not true, that it was a dirty story invented by a boy whose sniffling made me sick. At Andrésy, I was so happy that my teeth ached. By that I mean certain moments when the joy of living swooped down on me, causing a horrible and delightful tickling in my molars that I have never been able to explain. I would roll on the ground like a lunatic. I could not walk a few steps down a country road without skipping about and singing.

Two or three times a month there was a movie show at Nicole's, and the whole family attended it. The room was pitch dark, and from the far end came little screams and giggling, the meaning of which was lost on me. For the village youth occupied these remote regions, while we sat far nearer the screen, and the first thing one saw was something that looked like black rain. Then a man's voice gave the title of the film and, as things progressed, made comments intended to throw some light on the action. You saw, for instance, men rolling pumpkins from the top of a very steep street and then rushing down after them. "Catch as catch can," observed the commentator gravely. I could not see very clearly, I understood very little, but everyone laughed, and at the bottom of the

77

room people laughed too loud. There followed another film, either termed dramatic or touching, for each title was followed by a descriptive adjective. A woman in a cape appeared at a department store and applied for work. She was taken on approval. She did her work badly and, at the end of the day, was dismissed, but given her pay. "For the first and the last time," said the commentator in an expressionless voice. "I think that's hard on her," said Mamma under her breath. Several people sniffled softly in the room. I did not understand. I felt sleepy.

The show seemed of very little importance to us, but thinking that over now, I am a trifle surprised. Had we no presentiment of seeing something new? I do not think so. None of us could take seriously pictures that moved on a white sheet. After all, we thought, it was not much more than another form of magic lantern, an amusement for children.

However, I remember a movie show that must have taken place around 1911 or '12, in the open air at the Muette, on the lawn behind La Fontaine's statue.

The weather is mild. A screen, which I think immense, is set upright on the grass. I am seated with my mother and sisters in the crowd and the night is deeply still. How strange to be there, and so late! And what are we shown? A horrifying tale: the devil takes the stage. You see him, he is in a drawing room, he wears a frock coat and everything about him denotes the greatest elegance. "Is that what the devil looks like, Mamma?" —"Yes."—"And you can see him like that in drawing rooms?" —"Certainly," replies my mother confidently. "It's perfectly true." I do not remember the following scenes, but all of a sudden a little girl appears, she runs along a river on the bank of which two sinister-looking old washerwomen are beating their linen with a paddle, and as the child goes past them they turn and glare at her in a terrifying manner. The child runs faster, the women get up, I squeeze my mother's arm, I am frightened, the child runs as fast as she can, her hair streaming in the wind, but the old women take huge strides, their gray locks flying on either side of their fiendish faces. Then a smiling lady becomes visible suddenly, she is wearing a long pleated garment with a silk girdle that she unties and throws across the river and behold, the girdle changes into a little wooden bridge; the little girl has just time enough to get to it, for when the pursuing old women are about to set foot on the bridge, it fades away behind the fugitive, a small portion remaining so she can reach the opposite bank in safety.

No one could believe how much these pictures impressed me. They are forever fixed in my memory in all their mystery and incoherence. My mother afterward explained that the lady who appeared was the Blessed Virgin, but I do not remember her talking very much about her. I only knew that she loved her. She sometimes drew my attention to the photograph of a Murillo that hung in a corner of our room: Mary, her feet on a cloud, clasping her little Jewish baby to her, looking anxiously at us with her great, dark eyes.

Too many things come back to me and how can I set them in order? The summer holidays . . . The year following the one spent on the Boulevard de la Seine, we rented a house situated a little farther on, at 5 Grande Rue. How clearly I see the square house and roughcast pink walls, with the garden and terrace overlooking the road that ran by the river. . . . The sun came in our windows, happiness lived under that roof, we sang, we talked without cease, but at night something happened. I went up to my room as early as nine in the evening and fear went up with me. Holding a candlestick, in the black staircase—no electric light or even gas—I looked uneasily at the huge shadows cast over the walls by the little flame, shadows that moved along with me. They accompanied me thus to the top step and I sat down, for there was no question of going farther, going to the place of horror that my room had become.

Setting down the candlestick by me, I would open the little book I carried under my arm in the hope of finding some comfort there against my fright. It was the *Fables* of La Fontaine. My shoulder glued to the wall, I read at random, but the darkness turned the short animal stories into phantasmagoria. The night around me was full of things that moved silently, and my heart thumped.

Sometimes the drawing-room door stood ajar, for I was known to be frightened and Papa said I must be hardened, but my sister Mary was kind enough to cheat a little, in spite of my father's orders, and that is why, one or two evenings a week, by leaning over the banisters, I saw a great luminous streak in the darkness. A reassuring hum of conversation reached my ears. I recognized my mother's voice and felt braver as I turned the leaves of the little volume with the sea-green cover. And there were also evenings when Mary sat down at the piano and played Italian tunes, the music of which she had brought from Naples and Amalfi. I heard *"Torna a Sorriento"* and *"Vedi 'l mare quant è bello, Spira tanto sentimento"* . . . for Mary sang to her own accompaniment.

These languorously sad airs seemed strange to me. I could not make much sense of the words, although I remember them. What I liked best was a little military tune that my sister sometimes struck up with a gaiety that quieted me for a few minutes. *"A Tripoli me ne vado"* . . . I did not know then—and how should I have known?—all the sinister implications concealed by these brisk words nor how many of the breasts that breathed them out were to be riddled with bullets. I was locked inside my small personal nightmares. When Mary stopped and I heard the piano lid come down, my anguish returned. I sometimes heard the pianist cough and blessed a cough that linked me to a world of familiar things. I did not know that my sister, according to a pernicious custom dating back to the nineteenth century, went to Italy to check the first symptoms of tuberculosis. That was a word never to be mentioned. You simply spoke of delicate lungs. Poor Mary! You were the brigand of the family, the bold one. . . . You were fond of us, but found us a trifle bourgeois. It sometimes happened that you could not find your words in French or in English although Italian sentences came quite naturally to your lips. You were the traveler, the go-ahead, the artist. I then preferred you to my other sisters and you knew it, and that was why you left the door ajar. I think of you, poor dear brigand who went through so much suffering. Italy was the country of your choice, as it was for so many Anglo-Saxons in your times. However, there were dreadful evenings when some unknown atavism woke in you and, instead of "Tripoli," you sang us Scottish songs. "Drowned," for instance. It began with funereal chords pounded with such energy that the piano candlesticks rattled. All of a sudden, you found yourself far from Andrésy, by a misty lake in a faraway country where men, bare-legged under their kilts, dragged a girl's body out of the water. Another song from the same album (*Songs of the North*) took us to the heart of a wood where birds sang, but there was a chapel nearby and six braw gentlemen walked toward it, bearing a coffin on their shoulders, Maisie's, so proud in her beauty when she was alive—and beautiful no longer. I listened, my gratification mingled with horror. All things considered, it was not unpleasant, so long as there was a light and I heard all that downstairs, with the family here, there, and everywhere. My difficulties began when I had to go up with my brass candlestick and when these songs came back to me in a nightmarish setting. I waited up there, my soul alive with fright, then at last came the moment when a certain bustle in the drawing room told me that everyone was going to bed. I then ran quickly with my candlestick to my parents' room, where my bed was, and lay down, my breast full of throbs, plunged in the abominable element known to children as the dark, but soon I caught sight through my lashes of the first rays from the lamp my mother held before her and heard the whisper that brought me back to life: "He's asleep, Edward. Don't make a noise." I was not asleep, I had just time enough to realize that happiness was there once more, that the ghosts had gone, and sank like a stone into exorcised night.

During the summer holidays, Sidonie spent a few days with us. That was my mother's idea: she was sorry for the old maid who led a monotonous, difficult life in the garret of one of the blackest houses on the Rue des Archieve. She was small, spare, bent, with frizzled gray hair, a quick, apologetic voice, and a pince-nez on her sharp, inquisitive nose. Sometimes she removed the pince-nez to think things over and used it to scratch her cheek. All I knew of her was that she had lived a long time abroad and had, in her early childhood, seen Paris in flames during the Commune.

When she happened to be at Andrésy on Sunday, she took me to mass with her. Why? That is what I cannot manage to understand. I suppose that in my mother's mind, this could not do me any harm, although I was a Protestant, but there was no Protestant church at Andrésy and, moreover, to be a Protestant in France meant, of course, being a Calvinist, and the very word turned us to ice. So I went to mass with Sidonie. Hand in hand, we walked up the Boulevard de la Seine to the charming village whose little, dark streets preserved a medieval aspect. "It's very old, very old," said Sidonie, throwing her head back to look at the roofs through her pince-nez.

As I remember the church, it was beautiful and venerable. It was built of pale yellow stone, the tops of the columns were very prettily worked, the gold ornaments on the altar shone, the flames of the tapers fluttered, almost invisible in the sunlight. There were lots of people, the singing was in Latin, very loud and any old way, it seemed to me. Then there was that strange silence when a little bell began stammering madly and everybody bowed their heads. I did as Sidonie did, I bent my brow. And a little later, marvelous to relate, a choirboy wearing a bright red robe and a surplice edged with white lace passed around a basket filled with tiny but delicious brioches. Of all the moments in mass that, I humbly admit, seemed to me the most interesting. When the basket paused before me, I lost my head, not knowing how to choose the finest brioche possible in the shortest time. It would have required time and thought. Now, they were all beautiful and almost similar, but how was I to find the biggest? Sidonie finally snapped up a couple in her little wrinkled hand and I saw her make a curious round gesture in front of her face before swallowing her brioche, then, with the other hand, she handed me mine. Apart from a mysterious gesture that I could not understand, I imitated Sidonie's promptness in making the wonderful mouthful of blessed bread disappear, bread that could, I think, hold its own with the Israelites' manna.

On returning home, I took off my straw sailor hat; it had an elastic band that passed under my chin and burned my ears a little. My mother asked the old maid if I had been good. "Very good, Madame," replied Sidonie with a flat little laugh, "very good." What could Joujou understand about mass, isn't that so, Sidonie? And Madame, a Protestant, what could she understand either?

For there was a touch of slyness in Sidonie. She liked us well enough, but she judged us. She could not accept being poor and having to work so hard. Often, she removed her steel-mounted pince-nez and bit the frame with her little gray teeth, much as a parrot angrily bites the perch on which it swings. The rich, the rich! How she hated them in her heart! Yet we were not rich, but, as she used to say, in not too loud a voice and looking anxiously around her, we were comfortably well off and she was not. Life was unfair. Poor Sidonie rebelled against what she called fate. In spite of this, she had a respect for my mother, knowing how good she was.

I wonder what went through my mother's mind when she sent me to mass, and if I come back to the subject it is because I believe that for years she had been going through an inner crisis of which no one was ever aware. The faith of her childhood may perhaps have been impaired, it might be that she was not quite sure that Catholics were not right. Consequently, my religious education remained in suspense. The Bible was put into my hands and the child had to shift for himself, try to understand the mysterious texts, but how I wish those happy days could be given back to me again, days where desire had no place, where the body knew nothing it should not know, where blameless flesh stayed pure without the ghost of an effort, where passions had not devastated the heart, where the enemy had not thrust a foot inside the door, ready to come in with his junk of obsessing phantasmagoria!

What about the drawings? Well, there had been no secret drawings since young B. had exposed himself to us in school. His gesture had put an end to the world of nudes colored a toothpaste pink. And so long as my mother did not take me to the Luxembourg Museum, so long as I did not see the shining delivery horses trotting down the Rue de la Pompe and hear the insolent sound of their little hoofs, my soul was at peace.

Yet there was Marceline Valador.

I do not remember how we met the Valadors. It was at any rate at Andrésy, during the summer holidays. The three of them, father, mother, and daughter, lived in a tiny villa separated from the road by a narrow garden. The father looked like a badger in a straw hat. The mother, a voluptuously corpulent person, kept the queenly attitudes of the beauty she no longer was, alas. Her skin was almost the color of a cigar. All her dignity seemed to have taken refuge in a double chin on which rested a motionless face with eyes ringed in black under heavy lids. This pair, who came from South America, had produced a daughter whose beauty would be a pitfall for many a man, as I realize today. With sensuous innocence, she exposed to all eyes faultlessly round arms and legs, of which the light seemed enamored, for they shone like silk. How old was she? Ten, perhaps eleven. I was very fond of her, I was too fond of her, I went to see her every day. She had a full, fleshy mouth and large eyes of the deepest black; hair like night hung loosely around a dusky, charming face. Under her mother's watchful gaze, I sat by Marceline when she went to the piano, in a little drawing room crowded with armchairs, and she played me the piece she knew best, the overture of Boïeldieu's *Voitures versées*.

"Do you like French history?" she asked suddenly.—"Oh yes, very much!"—"And American history? As you're American . . ."—"It is short but noble," Madame Valador then said politely as she knitted, thirty inches away from us.

I breathed in Marceline. Her arms smelt good, her hair smelt good. When I leaned over to turn a page, the warmth of her cheeks was on mine. I think I was in love with Marceline, without in the least suspecting it since I knew nothing at all.

One day, my sister Mary entered my mother's room looking like a reformer and said in English—but I understood perfectly—: "I don't think Julian should go on seeing that little Marceline. If I were you, I'd beware of her." Marceline, you who probably knew no more about things than I did, I wonder what my sister suspected you of. It must be admitted that you were awfully disturbing. Sometimes we looked at each other, open-mouthed, and then began laughing foolishly, because we found nothing to say. Your mother then reared up behind us like an Aztec wall and suggested a short walk down the road.

I do not quite know what happened afterward. Mamma, always distracted when she was shown the shadow of evil over her son, wrote, I think, a little note to Madame Valador and my visits ceased. I remember how sad I felt every time I passed the horrible little villa where pretty Marceline overturned Boïeldieu's carriages.

One winter, however, I received an invitation from the Valadors, who lived not far from the Gare de l'Est in one of the tragic black houses such as are seen in that quarter of Paris. The flat was badly lighted. In grottolike darkness refreshments were served, with grenadine syrup in high honor. Then a piano concealed behind a portiere bravely struck up a waltz. In a sailor suit with a pleated skirt, and in black stockings, Marceline displayed teeth whiter than rice in a broad smile. With burning cheeks and sparkling eyes, she danced, watched closely by mothers. One boy after the other pressed her waist with a hand gloved in white cotton. Lots of boys and lots of girls swirled with awkward grace over the highly polished floor, triumphant chords sounded above little shrieks and laughter. Alas, I did not know how to dance. "You must stand here," said Mamma, "stay in this corner and keep out of the dancers' way." All I could do was to obey, but how lovely Marceline was! A kind of warmth radiated from her whole person. I wonder if she even recognized me. She swirled about like a fairy, and the boys skipped around her.

When I came back from the country and found myself locked up with twenty or thirty boys of my own age in a big room that smelt of ink and black cotton aprons, I sank into a melancholy that words cannot describe. There were no windows through which you could see the country, as at Andrésy, there were only transoms with long strings for me to stare at in mournful dullness; or my attention centered on my inkstand and I could not take my eyes off it. My sorrow was beyond words. I thought of the way our shrieks of happiness sounded in the wind as we ran across the meadows, my sisters and I, and I could feel a lump in

86

my throat. The professor made me shy. I had nothing to say to anyone. Fortunately, I knew that my mother was waiting for me on the other side of the street, in a flat that gradually became home, a place of refuge where nothing sad could happen.

My mother would take me aside, in the room that looked out on the courtyard's nothingness, and tell me to stay with her. In her hands I recognized a book with a brown cover that did not scare me, because it was she who held it, and she would make me read a page of English. The door was closed. My sisters were not to hear me and make fun of a French accent that I had some trouble in getting rid of. Next came a list of words to learn, and I learned them properly, because my mother spoke to me gently. She was patient with me and her tenderness was perhaps too great, for that tenderness took possession of me and became a necessity.

At other times, she made me read passages from the Bible and, verse by verse, put into my heart sentences that have never left it. I was the sheep that followed the Shepherd. When I was weary, He made me lie down by delectable waters and bathe my face in their freshness. Suddenly, I was a man and He prepared a feast before me in the presence of my enemies, and in front of them I sat triumphantly at a magnificent table! He anointed my head with oil. My mother explained none of these royal incoherencies, and she was right, she handed me the text, she wished me to receive it as she herself had received it. I asked no questions. The Bible was a person not to be too closely questioned, the Bible was a person and books were only books. What was in the Bible was true, because it was God Himself who spoke. What there was in other books was sometimes true, but in another manner, and generally of small importance. Little by little there rose in my mind what I might call a scale of realities. For the Bible said "the fashion of this world passeth away." Everything moved, everything fled away, but in this whirlwind and this phantasmagoria, the words of the Scriptures endured forever. Not a dot on an *i* could be changed. Any more than you could change the place of a star in the dark sky that my mother taught me to look at carefully with her. "Look at the stars," she said simply, and I felt her arm on my shoulder. We stayed so for long minutes without saying a word, and it seemed to me as though I were in another world.

Were there many happy days? I have the impression that there were nothing but happy days. Once or twice a year, my mother took us to the Châtelet, but the performances affected me so violently that it made her rather uneasy, I think. *Around the World in Eighty Days* and *Michel Strogoff* threw me into a sort of fever. I was too completely taken in by what I saw not to be in a state of excitement for several days. The snake grotto where reptiles oscillated in semidarkness drove me frantic. Vainly my mother whispered that it was not true. I stretched my arms toward the stage with a horrified gesture, from the top gallery. In the same way, the sword, heated red-hot and placed before Michel Strogoff's eyes, gave me such a terrible fright that my mother had to reassure me: "Don't worry! Nothing is going to happen." Next day I related the whole play from start to finish to the grocer's wife, Madame Soudry. She was a tall woman, with black hair parted down the middle over an ogival brow, and she wrote with a hand that seemed to do nothing but glide straight along the lines of her big book. Her fingers gathered together closely over a sharp steel pen, thick pointed fingers sticking out of black mittens, she listened with an indulgent smile: "Of course, Monsieur Julian, they did not really burn Michel Strogoff's eyes, otherwise, how could he play his part the next evening?" I shook with impatience: "But that's the way it goes in the story, Madame Soudry! Can't you understand? They did not really burn his eyes."—"Poor actor, I should hope not!" I could not manage to explain what I had in mind, or she pretended not to grasp my meaning, to tease me, and the sharp steel pen sped gently from left to right.

For weeks I was haunted by the magic words: "Look for all you're worth, look hard!" So far as I was concerned this advice was unnecessary: I looked with the attention of a maniac, and long after, the word "Tartar" was enough to re-create the entire performance in my imagination, with all its dances, its chases, its pistol shots that made my mother jump, its hairbreadth escapes from violent deaths—and you wiped your brow—its yells of triumph or of rage, its dialogues I understood all wrong, but that made my heart beat. I was in such a state that I had to be soothed, in attempts to make me understand that the whole thing was false. No one understood that, for me, all that was truer than truth itself. I wanted to be what I saw on the stage and, once at home, I looked sulkily at my room, whose great fault was not to be at St. Petersburg, nor at Irkutsk, nor at Omsk, nor even at Tomsk. In my way, I suffered. All at the same time, I wanted steppes with a pack of wolves panting behind my sledge and the imperial drawing rooms lighted by gigantic chandeliers. All I had was Papa's and Mamma's room, with my bed in a corner.

Usually, I was only allowed to attend matinees, but around 1912 my mother decided that I could go with her to hear *The Chimes of Normandy*. She was not at all musical, she could sing only hymns, but with so much spirit: "Onward, Christian Soldiers!" I do not know why she thought it necessary for me to hear a musical comedy. Yet how could I forget an incident that struck me years later: no sooner had she entered the Gaieté-Lyrique than she suddenly felt faint and was given a chair in the check-taker's office. She lifted her hand to her brow with a look of suffering and was given a dose of pyramidon and a glass of water. I stood by her, bewildered. The thought crossed my mind for the first time that she was unlike anyone else in the world, that she was all alone in the world, on that chair. After a while, she got up and we took our seats in the theater. "It's nothing," murmured someone. For a minute or two, death had pressed a finger on Mamma's brow, but neither she nor I knew it.

Have I mentioned this? Next to my parents' room, where I slept, was the dining room. I went to bed early after kissing everyone good night, a ceremony performed as slowly as possible, because I did not want to go to bed. My father and mother played backgammon and my sisters read or sewed. One evening I came out of my room and, eyes closed, in the deepest silence, walked around the table and then returned to bed. I was told of this much later, as though it were a most usual occurrence to which little meaning should be attached, and I think that was right, but I had small manias far more peculiar, which were reminiscent of rites and which I kept secret. Thus it was that around the age of twelve, I could not possibly have left for school without first touching all the doorknobs in the house. I flew from one room to the other, surreptitiously making the gesture that seemed indispensable to my peace of mind. As we were rather numerous, these eccentricities passed unnoticed. They formed part of a mysterious order that childhood sets up around itself to propitiate fate. Of course, in the street I never put my foot on the lines between the long stones bordering the sidewalk. When running, you had to be careful, otherwise who knows what calamity lie in store for you? I was greatly surprised to hear, later, that all the boys in the world and all the little girls too, I suppose, have acted in the same manner.

More peculiar, I think, was the uneasiness caused me by the contact—even a fleeting or fortuitous one—of anyone but my mother. At the lycée, if a schoolmate touched my knee or elbow, I immediately felt uncomfortable and, why not say so, vaguely disgusted. No one should touch me. That was the law I had made unto myself. If an elder person's hand came near my face to stroke my cheek, I drew back at once. In my eyes, the body was holy, and suffered no physical contact. My body was holy. The idea ruled my mind with such despotism that it ended by affecting my whole being, and I thought that everything I did was right, because it was I. What wrong could I do? None. Others could do wrong, not I. I was pure. That was the word that summed up everything, although I was ignorant of its meaning. Around me lay a sort of self-created forbidden zone, the reality of which finally became perceptible. What part did pride play in all this? Immense or nonexistent. I wanted to go out to others, to all the others, and could not, because, thinking myself alone, I was and remained alone. Sin broke that magic circle, much later. It was through sin that I met humanity.

I do not know why my thoughts return to young B. Ever since he had made that indescribable gesture, he was to me like one of the devils spoken of in the Gospels, the devils who throw people into the fire or into water. In my eyes, there was something inhuman about his handsome saffron-colored face, and I could not go near the boy or rather, see him come up to me, without being seized by a violent emotion that was probably anger. One day he whispered things in my ear that seemed meaningless and I insulted him. I remember only too well what I said: I was still in my anti-Semitic phase. "Dirty Jew!" That wretched piece of abuse . . . We were on the threshold of a schoolroom and about to leave it after the German class. Our professor stood behind us. His name was Koessler. He had been an officer. His elegant figure was dressed in a well-cut frock coat that molded the torso and flared a little at the waist. He always wore a monocle and his often sarcastic speech stung us like a faint whiplash. Hearing what I said to young B., he drew us into the classroom, closed the door, and then simply said: "Have it out." I threw myself with all my might on my opponent, and together we rolled to the foot of the platform. Such fury possessed us both that we never dreamt of crying out and, in the deepest silence, did the best we could to kill each other. Now that I can see these things more lucidly, it is clear that we unwittingly freed ourselves of a kind of amorous rage that assumed the face of hatred. Monsieur Koessler would have been very much astonished if that interpretation of our scuffle had been given him. Standing with his legs wide apart, his hands behind his back, he watched the fight from the platform, or the podium, as he called it, and when he judged we had had it out, he ordered us to get up, which we did with flashing eyes and clothes covered with dust. We did not shake hands, and I ran home to say that I had beaten the little Jew, while he ran home to say that he had beaten the little Christian. My father laughed discreetly, because he sometimes had unpleasant dealings with Jewish businessmen, and my mother, who was pugnacious, burst out laughing as she listened to my tale. "But I have nothing against Jews," she said, by way of settling the matter. Truth compels me to say that I probably had the worst of it, for I remember a thickset little body crushing mine and a burning-hot breath on my face.

Around 1911 or '12, my father told us that he read the paper as he crossed the boulevard, and we could see mounting anxiety in my mother's eyes. An accident was always possible. . . . We heard the case of a gentleman who was run over by an omnibus, yes indeed, and trampled down by the horses. My mother hid her face in her hands with a muffled cry and my father, who was a tease, gave us a wink. The fact remains that you could walk slowly along the sidewalk without being deafened by the roar of cars or sickened by the fumes of engines.

At this time, I often dropped in at a bookstore on the Rue de la Pompe, kept by two single ladies who had taken a liking to me and lent me books. A volume of the Nelson series under my arm, I ran to the Square Lamartine; once there and seated on a bench, I turned the pages of my book with an avidity all the more mysterious since I understood little of what I read, but I understood something and that something delighted me. Dumas *père,* Edmond About, and Victor Cherbuliez were the three authors the Misses Chavanon considered apt to improve my mind without poisoning it. Titles come back to me: *Le Comte Kostia, Miss Rovel, L'Aventure de Ladislas Bolski, Le Nez d'un notaire,* and of course *The Three Musketeers,* with that strange story of Milady, although I could not see what she had done that was so wrong, but her execution interested me. I adored reading a fine account of an execution.

I returned the book in the evening and, if asked what I thought of it, answered that it was very good, but if the subject had been gone into thoroughly, anyone would have experienced great surprise, for the intrigue escaped me invariably and all I remembered were details and sentences, some of which come back to me at times, like little tunes. What astonished me most in these novels was the lovers' desperate eagerness to obtain what was never described. When I saw a lovers' dialogue approaching, I skipped it, I preferred duels, violence, vengeance. I was stirred into a rage without knowing why. Words went to my head, I could hardly stifle my shrieks. All this had a quiet little garden as a setting: the statue of a man seated sideways in an armchair, a dog at his feet, reigned over it. Near me, children patted the sand with their shovels, but I saw none of all that, I was carried away by the book.

At home, from time to time, a wonderful person called on us. I was madly in love with her unknowingly, for unknowingly I was like the men and women I found so tiresome in love stories. She was called Emily Grigsby and came, I think, from Kentucky. She was a friend of my sister Eleanor. My memory of Emily is that of a woman dressed in white lace who talked in a voice that was both soft and broken. I cannot otherwise describe the sounds that left her lips, due, I believe, to some complaint of the throat. I always looked at her open-mouthed. I could not help it. The softness of her skin, the outline of her camellia-white cheeks, and her smile threw me into a sort of stupor: a sight I could not get used to and one that filled me with happiness and despair at the same time, because I wanted to kiss Emily, but I might as well have wished to kiss a cloud. She was remote because she was beautiful. Between herself and me were wide distances. One day, when she had just left, I slipped behind her on the staircase and, seeing her shadow on the wall, glued my lips to it. She knew nothing about it and, going back to my room, I threw myself on my pillow and clasped it in my arms, for I had to love something, a shadow, a pillow, since Emily was gone. I suffered on her account.

On another occasion, but I think it must have been on the Rue de Passy, she arrived, followed by a black servant who went to the kitchen and began preparing some dish or other. I do not know why he was there, with our cook, but I remember looking at him with admiration as, with a spoon, he stirred something in a bowl. Finally, I asked in English: "Why is your skin black?" Silence. The spoon went on turning around in the bowl. After a time, I added: "I wish I were all black, like you." The compliment was rewarded by a beautiful smile.

I recollect that when I was quite a child, in my bed, on the Rue de Passy, I wondered why I was not God, why He was up there and I in my room, whereas it might have been exactly the opposite, according to my lights. I dared not mention these things to my mother, but they tormented me. I was dissatisfied, as though it were unfair.

To go back to 1912, that year, unless I am mistaken, an event took place in Russia which affected me so deeply that I do not hesitate to note it. The Czarevitch hurt himself accidentally and bled. There was great anxiety, for he was hemophilic. A picture of him appeared in the papers and his face began to haunt me.

A religious ceremony for his recovery was celebrated at the Orthodox church on the Rue Daru. An English friend, Mrs. Gibson, took me to it. Why? I do not know. A child's life, as he or she recollects it, is full of question marks. Not everything is explained to a child, or the explanation, put off till later, is never given. I was glad to mix with the Russians, because in that way I was brought closer to the Czarevitch.

So there I stand with Mrs. Gibson, in a church where the golden icons and ornaments shine, where incense rises in heavy spiral curls to the vaulted ceiling, where the cantor's bass voice fills the air with its prodigious lowings answered by great, clear, and soaring cries from the male and female choir. Around us, the crowd is silent. A few people kneel on the paving. No one is seated.

I look and listen, perfectly motionless, frightened and delighted by the great tumult of voices rushing up as if to take heaven by storm. Never have I been in a place where the invisible is besought with such energy and almost summoned to act. It all resounded in me, in my head, my breast, my inwards. The incense goes to my head. In their own way, the priests' golden copes speak a new language to me. At the same time, my thoughts are fixed on the lovely face of the child, the object of prayers that sometimes sound like moans of distress, sometimes more and more pressing. I feel as though I may drop with fatigue, for the ceremony is very long, but nothing could induce me to leave, I am bewitched, stirred by renewed ardor, a strange enthralling world opens its monumental golden gates to me. Then comes the time when it all ends, when the priests disappear behind the iconostasis and the crowd silently makes its way toward the exit.

In the street, Mrs. Gibson puts her pince-nez in its case and says:

"Interesting, wasn't it?"

And I answer:

"Very."

And so it has ended, since everything must end, and that is what makes me despair. Once more streets, cabs, omnibuses, whereas I was—where? In heaven?

The ceremony on the Rue Daru settled in my mind forever and became much like a part of myself. The gold, the singing, the incense, all that trailed splendor after it. I could call it up at any time and find myself *elsewhere*, in a splendid, sonorous world where divinity swam in the invisible toward me, around me, in my heart as in an abyss, in my head as in a firmament. I closed my eyes, tried to imitate the cantor's voice: "Ba-oh! Ba-oh!" By paraphrasing the psalm slightly, I might say that I skipped like a calf before the Lord! I was drunk with God and did not know it.

I have said very little about my Irish godmother, Agnes Farley. She had married an American dentist who looked like Julius Caesar, and whom we thought mad. He occasionally turned prophet, was of the opinion that all the Latin races should be wiped out, called the Bible "a fool of a book," admired the Kaiser, etc., etc. All that was Farley, and no one paid much attention. He was small, slim, calm, and precise, given to violent fits of anger, fanatical anger, for there was a religious strain in him. One day, in the course of a discussion in which he tried a woman friend's patience to the breaking point, the latter, choking with rage, put a curse on him in a loud voice. Whereupon he caught her by the neck and while telling her he was acting for the good of her soul, tightened his grip, stifled and shook her until, not wishing to die on the spot, she took the curse back. As for us, for other reasons and by other means, he excelled at making us cry. To go to him, sit in his frightful black leather armchair, was more than any one of us could bear. Our parents' authority became necessary and the operation took place amidst tears and screams. For he belonged to the old school, the one that hurt the patient on principle. He announced the torture in a calm voice, prepared his drill with finical care. Beads of perspiration stood on our brows and for my part, I sometimes drooled with horror. "Open wider!" How well we knew that sentence. It was in itself alone a nightmare. Terrible moans followed almost immediately, long, useless shrieks. "I'm sorry, child," said Farley in a blank voice and the drill went *zzz zzz zzz*. The torment over, this mysterious man would wipe our face with his handkerchief. He was fond of children, felt for his victims a compassion more awful than his cruelty. In other times, he would have made a wonderful torturer. Maybe he did not know it. I have a charming letter he wrote me in 1912. It does not wipe out the memory of minutes of what might be called exquisite pain. Why did we have to go to him? On account of Agnes. Mamma said: "All dentists hurt. Farley is no worse than the others. So that's that." And then, once again, there was Agnes.

While Julius Caesar was tormenting his clients, she sat a few yards away in that little drawing room of hers that looked out on the Rue de la Paix, delighting her friends with her marvelous chit-chat. I remember her as a woman overladen with fat, but when she opened her lips, you forgot all about it. She battened on Zola, Maupassant, Huysmans, and Bloy, talked about everything so aptly that it acted like a charm. You were in love with a fat Scheherazade, eternally smoking small black cigars, her round face only visible through a cloud of bluish smoke. On her knees she held her beloved Judy, a yellow fox-terrier that smelt of cigars. That is how I recall Agnes. Around her neck she wore a long watch chain, the one I have given a good many of my heroines; the watch hid in the waistband of her skirt, and the whole of her bust disappeared under a frilly blouse. How far away all that seems! This was Agnes to us, with her jokes, her caustic remarks that never excluded an extreme kindliness; she captivated us one and all. She was the author of two books written with a lazy, gifted hand and today forgotten. In a general way, everything she said was false, but she stated facts in such a peremptory manner that it needed some courage to stand up for oneself. "Your French is incorrect," she said to Anne. *"Il faut dire: cette armoire sent bonne, puisque armoire est du féminin."* She believed only the most sensational news. Paris was to cave in some day or other, because of the subway. Then *le grand soir,* the great social upheaval, was near. It would begin by a general strike and, in expectation of this event, prudence recommended filling a bathtub with drinking water. The massacre of the bourgeois would follow very shortly after.

She was a Catholic and a great believer, but there was a shadow in her life, something of which I suspect the nature, without ever having been quite sure. Be it as it may, round Easter time began the tragedy of the annual confession. This is where my mother enters. Even though she was a Protestant, she wanted Agnes to do her Easter duty. I have often been told that the two women took a cab and went off in search of a priest who would consent to give the indispensable absolution. Innumerable little cigars were smoked. Then came a pause at a church and the poor sinner walked heavily to the door while my mother waited in the cab. After a long time, Agnes came out of the church, shaking her head. "Nothing doing. Let's try somewhere else." So they went from church to church, Mamma patient and determined, Agnes more and more uneasy. Finally, my mother saw her leave a last church, beaming. "I had a most intelligent priest to deal with," she said. "He gave me absolution."—"A little hard of hearing perhaps," murmured my mother. "Shut up, Mary, you're a Prot, you can't understand such things." And she lit a cigar.

I do not want to leave 16 Rue de la Paix without strolling around it a little longer. The drawing room, the big one, was dark and the gilt Louis XV furniture shone softly at twilight. Near the door was a bust of Napoleon as a Roman emperor. Often, as though by chance, Farley stood by the Caesarean head and sometimes there was someone to cry out: "Oh! Why . . . Oh! It's extraordinary! Mr. Farley, have you ever been told that you looked like Napoleon Bonaparte?" He smiled modestly and then returned to his victims. Entreaties and screams followed swiftly. One day I bit him and he slapped me. He had thrust a finger into my mouth, in search of some sensitive spot or other, and my jaws closed as hard as they could over one of his knuckles. I do not regret it, I avenged a whole lot of people.

I had remained incredibly childlike. Among the books entrusted to me by the Misses Chavanon were Hugo's dramatic works, of which I understood very little but which none the less went to my head. And I do not know why, but all this invariably produced a fury. The effect of *Le Roi s'amuse* was a little stronger than that of the other plays. How the king derived amusement, that I could not imagine. He sat a woman on his knees and said: "What a fine anatomy!" Obscure. Obscure to me. Doubled up over the book, I roared under my breath: "What a fine anatomy!" and turned the page. I expected murder, extreme savageness. At that moment I had to be careful not to roar too loud, because I was not alone in the Square Lamartine, but once at home, I could enjoy myself to my heart's content, particularly on days when Sidonie was present: she was really my best audience. Running to the kitchen, I took from the cupboard a four-pound loaf, one that was to be eaten next day, a little stale. I do not know if these broad thick loaves are still baked. Be that as it may, I wrapped half of my loaf in a table napkin and, knife in hand, rushed to the room where the seamstress worked. "My daughter!" I cried. "My daughter has been dishonored!"—"Whoever could have done that, Monsieur Julian?" asked Sidonie with a quiet little laugh, for she was used to these dramatic situations. "Who? The king! And she's going to die!"—"She is out of luck. First dishonored, then murdered . . . What has she done to you?"—"I'm her father, she's going to die. You're going to die, do you understand?"—"Don't come too close to me with that knife, Monsieur Julian!"—"Die! Die!" I cried, stabbing the bread over and over with the blade of my knife. Then the old maid removed her pince-nez and gave herself up to mirth. "What on earth have you been reading now?" she asked, throwing her head back to laugh more freely. I gave her a withering look. "She's dead!" I cried. And dropping the loaf to the ground, I raised my hands to the ceiling. "If I were you," said Sidonie, "I'd take the corpse back to the kitchen."

It always took me a little while to pull myself together. The stabbing had soothed me to a certain extent, but my emotion lasted a little longer, and agreeably. Something in me had been satisfied.

On the dining-room table was a suspicious-looking object that we all considered with a mixture of curiosity and agreeable fear. It was a small iron bell that Papa had found one day at an antique dealer's and which he thought interesting. And interesting it certainly was. The handle was a figure of Satan, no less, standing with crossed arms, horns on his brow and his tail wrapped around his feet. The little bell itself was a sort of tremendously Gothic cloister, and devils with wings like bats flew in and out of its columns. The whole thing was very black with lead-colored glints. When you shook Satan, the maid appeared. It was my mother's duty to ring the bell, and she did so with a queer expression of determination mingled with insuperable aversion. My father, however, admired with childlike ingenuousness what gradually filled us with horror: the finish of the scales that covered the fiend's body, the tiny twin columns that aped the style of churches, and lastly, the evil joy on the faces of the imps. "It really looks like a witches' sabbath," said Mary one day, sniffling sagaciously. My mother showed the diabolical bell to Agnes, who picked it up, examined it, laid it down on the table with a slight but most dramatic shiver. "My dear," she said, "it's a bell for black masses." She had to explain to Mamma what a black mass was: all its blasphemies, sacrileges, the enemy of souls clamored for, hideously adored by the damned.

I do not know what my mother said to my father that evening, but the next day she wrapped the object in paper and went to the Iéna bridge, whence she threw the bell into the Seine. Maybe it is there still. It was replaced by an honest bronze Swiss bell, the kind cows wear around their necks, fat, round, and heavy, with a most reassuring tinkle.

In the drawing room, on either side of the mantelpiece, were two low, black bookcases, and the last row of the one nearest the window contained the forbidden books. Who forbade them? No one. Forbidden by me. To draw them out, open them, look at them, one had to be alone, seated on the beige carpeting and cross-legged, a combination of circumstances difficult to achieve no doubt, as I do not remember having often turned the pages of these volumes. That I did so, however, is certain, not without actually wrestling with my conscience for reasons that escaped me. I did not know what I was wrestling with or if I really was wrestling. In any case, what I looked at was Dante's *Inferno,* illustrated by Doré. My heart thumped—that I remember distinctly—once more I saw the man plunging into the lake's black waters. In an indescribable manner I then felt the presence of evil. In the silence that always prevailed at such times, I knew myself to be surrounded by something more powerful than I. Any attempt to react was paralyzed, and also, there was something else that struck me later, on thinking it over: the advantage taken of circumstances: the flat was empty, no one would disturb me. I could look, look almost endlessly. My whole being centered in my eyes. How beautiful the lost soul was! But why, being so beautiful, was he in hell? And hell crept into me. One could not stare at that picture without suffering in an absurd manner. Yes, absurd, for after all, what did I want? That I could not have said.

Under the two volumes of the *Commedia* (I neglected the grim *Purgatorio* and evanescent *Paradiso*), there was something else, albums still bigger and heavier, very heavy. However, I managed to pull them out and turn the thick paper pages that made such a frightening noise in the stillness of the air and the things around me. *Gems of European Art* . . . This dull title meant nothing to me (the volumes dated back to the end of the last century), but I waited with a pleasure where horror had its part—my conscience worked on me—for the fascinating page that would show me "The Bearers of Evil Tidings." The Luxembourg painting, there it was at last under my eyes, it was mine, and mine alone, in the alarming solitude—the strange nature of which I vaguely guessed. Of course the magic of color, the skin golden as sand, were lacking, but with burning cheeks and open mouth I looked once more at the torturing picture. I suffered as much as a man can suffer, but the difference was that I knew nothing about the character of my pain, nor did I know what I wanted, nor why I felt so unhappy, I only knew that if I had been that savage pharaoh, I would have spared the messenger, even if he had brought me news twenty times worse. Then, talking to myself in my emotion and my insides tightening with inexplicable coveteousness, I closed the big album and replaced it on the shelf. And I forgot. I forgot with astonishing ease. Not a trace of obsession in my life. Only these very rare moments that prodigiously favored bold action. Then obsession took hold of my will power: I was thrown into the enemy's hands. With a dexterity fit to disconcert the most skillful people, he was careful not to prompt me to make dangerous gestures that might have enlightened me regarding myself, he merely contented himself with lodging in me, in my memory, as it were in my whole being, pictures that fascinated the child in order to bewitch the man, later on. . . .

In July 1912 our parents sent my sisters and myself to Saint-Valéry-sur-Somme for our summer holidays. Why did they not come with us? I do not know. Perhaps my father's business kept him in Paris and my mother did not wish to leave him.

At Saint-Valéry we lived in a small house beyond which there was nothing but the country. Our neighbor was the black-smith, Monsieur Tirard, whose daughter was epileptic. Once or twice she fell on the road, and I do not remember her screaming, but she was immediately surrounded by a small group of people who cropped up from somewhere or other and did what was necessary. I was not at all scared, but full of curios-ity mingled with the respectful admiration one might feel for a person who distinguishes herself, who steps out of the ranks.

Above all there was a magic spot, the immense, black smithy where the hammer's pure note rang out as it struck the iron on the anvil. Tirard wore a leather apron, and his tongs held a tip of the pale rose-colored metal on which the hammer's terrific weight came crashing down, but from all this din rose a sound like that of a child's voice; that was what surprised me most, that and the sprays of sparks studding the anvil. Horrifying to my mind was the metal's long-drawn-out sizzle of hatred when it was next plunged into a bucket of water, and the white smoke rising in the darkness, for no matter how light it was outside, the smithy in itself was night in a roseate blaze. I stood there motionless and intent. If a horse was brought in to be shod, I wandered a bit around the smithy, went toward the door, try-ing to pass unnoticed, and suddenly ran away. One should not look at a horse. Pure and Impure reared up before me like two great idols.

I often crossed the road, which happened to be narrow by the smithy, climbed to the top of a slope crowned with bushes, and there, amidst foliage that all but hid and isolated me from the world, I thought about the Czarevitch: there and nowhere else. That was the place. I remained motionless for minutes on end, dreaming about the child whose face I thought I saw. Through a sort of hallucination, I imagined myself far from Saint-Valéry, far from Monsieur Tirard's smithy, and, taking the hand of the little boy dressed as a soldier, I talked to him. Then I was seized with unutterable happiness, but a happiness mingled with great sadness. I did not know what I wanted, but I fancied that the bushes among which I hid carried me else-where. After some time, the dream ended. I went home with a heavy heart, but around me my sisters laughed, chattered, or sang and my sadness wore off quickly.

Sometimes we went walking as far as the mouth of the Somme and I was shown the distant shifting sands. I made people tell me about the frightful death of those who had been unwary enough to venture in that direction, and a shiver that was not at all unpleasant ran down my spine. I was warned: "If ever you are caught in those sands, remember to stretch your arms out at right angles, that would be your only chance of escape."

I looked at the multicolored houses on the opposite bank of the river: red, black, almond green, fishermen's houses. It was at Saint-Valéry that I saw the sea for the first time. It in-stantly filled me with horror. I imagined that all its waves were rushing at me and shivered in my bathing suit. The summer of 1912 remains in everyone's memory as one of the worst ever known. It was decided that I should learn to swim, because, as my sisters explained, if ever you are shipwrecked you'll be very glad to get yourself out of trouble. I immediately visualized the shipwreck and hated the sea more than ever. Nevertheless, I obeyed—I always obeyed. A young man seen around the beach, probably a swimming teacher, was commissioned to teach me the proper motions, and because I suffocated when sinking in the icy water, I was branded as a softy. However that may be, the young man who stood in the water, a cigarette in his mouth, seized me by the belt he had put around my waist and showed me what to do with my arms and legs. I remember that he wore a striped jersey and had bare thighs, which seemed to me distinctly impure, but I had no time to linger over such considerations. "If he lets go of me," I thought, "I'll drown." And as though he guessed what I had in mind, he did let go of me to light a cigarette which went out continually. I sank to the bottom at once and the youth fished me up. At this school, all I learned was to add another terror to all those of which I seemed to have made a collection. On leaving the water, I shook so violently that people thought me ill and my lessons were cut short.

Toward the middle of August, my parents joined us for a few days at Saint-Valéry. My room was given to my mother, and I had a bed in a small peasant house by the roadside, a little nearer the harbor where William the Conqueror set sail for England. My new room was very modest: a bed pushed into a corner, whitewashed walls. That is all I remember of it except that in my opinion its simplicity and whiteness lent it fascinating beauty. On waking, I had the feeling of having slept in the snow and finding myself in a region that was not of this world. All that made me feel happy, but before two days had gone by, we were given a piece of bad news. I can see my mother standing in the road, a blue paper in her hand and Anne saying: "Maybe it's only one of that silly Farley's sinister jokes. You know how mad he is." But the telegram said and went on saying: "Agnes is dead."

Our parents left us that same evening. I had no idea of what death could be and my mother's distressed face upset me. I had no place in her tragic eyes, she did not see me, she saw no one, she was silent. I remember that dressed as she was in a tailored suit, she seemed completely out of keeping with the landscape, the countryside. Her white lace frill was a marvel to me. And above that festive white frill, a wincing face: grief.

And how did Agnes die? She had already had two warnings, but that year, on August 12th, she was struck down by apoplexy. She had time enough to say to her husband: "Send for a priest!" I think she was forty-six. On the afternoon of the next day, she appeared at a friend's door, a friend who had asked her to tea. (This friend, Bibidie Leonard, had been Oscar Wilde's mistress and passed for a German spy, but that may have been one of the sensational stories Agnes was fond of telling.) A maid opened the door. Agnes stood on the threshold without going in. The maid returned to her mistress: "Mrs. Farley is waiting at the door, Madame." Miss Leonard went to see, but no one was there, and that evening she received a note from Farley telling her that Agnes had died the day before.

My sisters made me write a little letter of condolence to poor Farley, from whom I received a very fine answer written with a quill pen on blue paper (I have it in a drawer): "You are a very nice darling to have written me. . . . At Christmas you shall have a big picture book like the ones your godmother gave you. . . . May you love God and be an honor to His cause. . . ." Mad as he was, he did not lack heart, but he exasperated my father. I remember that one night, around 2 A.M., Papa got up, dressed, and crossed Paris to beg Farley's pardon after having had a very stormy discussion with him concerning the Kaiser. My father had said things that he bitterly regretted. "Wait until morning," advised my mother. No, his conscience tormented him. He left the house, found a cab. . . . I was struck by this story and did not find it at all funny, but mysterious and beautiful. In the middle of the night, to get up, go and ask to be forgiven . . . That sounded like the Bible.

We went home after the holidays and I returned to the lycée. I was now in the fifth form. I said nothing, made friends with no one. I was easily upset on hearing words whose meaning I could not grasp. Sometimes my schoolmates, six or seven strong, would drive me into a corner—I can see the dark red brick wall—and press against me as hard as they could. Their hot breath on my cheeks, my eyelids, my mouth, disgusted me, but I smiled, panting, since this apparently was a game and smile I must. I was winded. There was always some supervisor on duty to disperse them. I could not understand why such a game amused the boys. Others besides myself were submitted to the same ordeal, with the same impassiveness.

I do not know who decided, in 1912, that my education was not virile enough, that there were too many girls around me. My sisters' only answer was to turn to my mother and say: "He's your darling, it's your fault!" Mamma ended by agreeing on that score: a man should be made of me. As it happened, an organization called Les Eclaireurs—the Pathfinders—had just been formed in France, in imitation of the Boy Scout association founded in England by Lord Baden-Powell.

The full particulars escape me, but I do know that we still lived on the Rue de la Pompe, I can see myself, one fine day, dressed in khaki and can still smell the odor of that rough and *virile* fabric, as everything had to be virile at all costs. A red scarf around my neck, a shirt of the ugly color just mentioned, breeches that were short, but not too short, heavy boots, so much for the uniform, plus a hat with a stiff, wide brim. When it rained, the brim grew flabby and the glorious headgear drooped sadly, like the ears of a spaniel. Then you had to leave it at home and ask the maid to iron the brim. As nothing should be overlooked, I will also mention a heavy, very complicated penknife in the left-hand pocket, a hatchet over the right hip, and finally a very long iron-tipped stick that I shyly carried over my shoulder, like a halberd. All these trappings amused my mother. For there was in me a curious mixture of pride and gentleness that did not tally with this martial outfit. Nothing aggressive in my appearance. People told me that I looked like a woodland animal. However that may be, I joined my unit at some subway station or other, and that, Sunday after Sunday, deadly Sunday after deadly Sunday. We were the first French scouts, and my astonishment knew no bounds in finding myself among these pioneers, for I could form only the vaguest ideas about what I was doing in the midst of these boys. In the streets, people looked at us with curiosity, people smiled. Leading the van was a tall, resolute, handsome young man called Lannes. Bravely facing the cynical gaiety of the passers-by, he cried out harshly to us: "Now then, keep step, you Eclaireurs! Left! Right!" His strong, regular features have remained in my memory. An avalanche of black curls fell over his brow when he removed his hat. I think we were all in love with him, without knowing it. He often spoke to me, and a little roughly, but never unkindly, sometimes in French, sometimes in perfect English, for he was half English. I remember very little of what he said, except his assertion that all men were brothers and that any rivalry between nations belonged to an obsolete past. "It's a very good thing to come from the South," he said to me (I never concealed my extraction), "but it's just as much of a good thing to come from the North." I looked at him in silence and thought: "No!"—"Do you hear me, Green?"—"Yes, I hear you." That was all he could get out of me.

One evening, we were (I do not know how, I do not know why: if ever a pathfinder needed to be put on the path, it was I) in the Franchard Gorges, near Fontainebleu. The tent was unfurled, then pitched, and after a ceremonial in which fire and song played their part, we slipped under our blankets. At dawn I woke and, with a sort of wondering amazement, looked at a blade of grass heavy with dew. I have forgotten the rest. I went home, dog-tired. I was questioned. I answered all wrong. "Vague, vague, so vague!" murmured Papa.

On another occasion we were taken to the Saint-Cucufa

Woods. (I dared not say that name, which I considered improper, it went out of my head when Papa later inquired where we had been. "In the woods, Papa.") One memory comes back to me, more singular than others. We were walking down a magnificent avenue in the heart of the woods, shouldering the halberd-stick, and had been given permission to chat with each other. I happened to bring up the rear, not because I wanted to, but because a boy named Muselli had made me lag a little and talked to me under his breath. He had the prettiest face imaginable, with great dark eyes and an angelic expression that attracted me to him. I loved him, simply, without realizing it, not only because he was very handsome, but because he corresponded to the peculiar idea I had of purity. I was delighted by his gentle way of speaking to me, whereas all the other boys bawled or snickered, in virile fashion. At one moment, his hand touched mine and, turning, I looked at him with all the tenderness that filled my heart, for I loved love. Then it was that those exquisite lips shaped the coarsest words it has ever been given to me to hear, an artless invitation to pleasure of which I did not understand a syllable, but which remained forever in my memory. On seeing my amazement, Muselli dropped his hand and we quickened step to catch up with the group. What strikes me at present is that I had only the vaguest idea of what he suggested our doing together, but his strangely crude language affected me violently. "Impure," I thought, "he's impure!" And I did not know what impure meant.

It was around that period that my sister Eleanor came back from Africa with her husband. The latter had been taken ill, he had contracted one of those colonial diseases the cause of which is always a little mysterious. People talked of an insect bite. He and his wife rented a flat at the corner of the Rue de la Pompe and the Avenue Henri-Martin, in order to be close to us. Need I say that in those times, one chose the quarter, the street, and the house one preferred and that the whole business was dispatched in a few hours?

I remember my brother-in-law lying on a sofa in the drawing room with a view over the avenue's chestnut trees. He was then a good-looking young man with regular features and intensely blue eyes that reminded one of the sea. His accent, manners, and even the cut of his clothes were in my mind those of a man belonging to the British race. As a matter of fact, he did not care very much for the English and his family came from Cornwall. He was very polite and also very much of a scoffer, and I never saw him without feeling a little uneasy, being sure that at some time or other his gentle voice would imitate my way of pronouncing certain English words. Or else he would stare at me silently, with a cruel, amused expression. The fact that he was British put incalculable distances between himself and the rest of the world. He never said so, of course, but it was something that I vaguely guessed; I preferred not to be alone with him, exposed to the kind of silent merriment I aroused in the man. One day he signaled to me with his finger to come closer and, having looked at me most attentively, finally said very gravely: "You are probably the ugliest boy I have ever seen." Remaining mute and crushed under that pitiless ultramarine stare, without waiting for anything further, I left the drawing room.

It took me many a year to understand that he said this to keep me, he hoped, from a vanity that did not threaten me in the least then, for I had no opinion about my looks, but his unfeeling remark worked on me and made me even shyer than I was by nature. I looked so slim in my navy-blue jersey that my brother-in-law called me the maggot (for my pride should at all costs be destroyed, but I did not have that kind of pride, my pride was of another kind), and when I put on my round knitted cap, he said, with the smile of a courteous hangman, that I looked like a girl. Nothing could have hurt me more, but what could I answer? I blushed. Still more disturbing was my mother's affection for Kennie (as he was called). Since she was so fond of him, how could he be wrong? So I smiled at a man who made me quake inwardly, but something in me was destroyed when he looked at me, a little like a leaf shriveled by flame, and I lost heart.

How glad I was to run away from him to be with his son at the other end of the flat. I adored my nephew Patrick. He was two and I was twelve. He was called Gnomie because of his impish smile. I used to smother him with hugs and he would only laugh and cry out unintelligible things. It seems as though I spent hours with him in the dark little room that looked out on a courtyard. His maid took him to the Bois every day. That, in any case, was what she maintained. Eleanor had her doubts. And sure enough, one day, Patrick returned and, waving his arms, cried to his mother: "You must not say subway!"

At the lycée, in the big boys' yard where I sometimes ventured, I saw an inscription chalked on the pavement of a gallery: "Hurrah for the Three Years!" (A three-year military-service law had just been voted.) And all around it, the big boys, those lords that we middle boys admired from afar, hissed for all they were worth and cried: "Boo! Boo!" I did not understand a thing about it, but *what* did I understand? In my eyes, the whole world appeared as a riddle.

That year, an idea sprouted in my brother-in-law's mind, an idea my sisters did not much care for, but that appealed to my mother: we were to leave the Rue de la Pompe and all live together in the outskirts of Paris. A villa was found at Le Vésinet, commonplace but roomy, at the head of the Avenue de la Princesse. A large garden surrounded it, limited by the avenue just mentioned, the Boulevard Carnot, and another bit

111

of avenue bearing the name of Scribe. Magnificent trees, the remains of a great forest, shaded the lawns. One whole side of the house gave on a lake, a view that delighted me. Inconveniences were not lacking, of course. It took time to get to Paris, for instance. I will return to this later. My brother-in-law pointed out the healthiness of the air, and also, living in the country corresponded to some unknown dream or memory of his, and my mother asked nothing better than to see things through his eyes, although she did not much care for the country. I add that, being ill, he had a right to some consideration. That, at least, was what he himself thought. Moreover, he drew my parents' attention to the fact that by living together we would necessarily save money. My father allowed himself to be persuaded, probably from weariness and particularly because he saw that my mother was won over to this dubious plan.

Be it as it may, the beginning of 1913 saw us settled out there. I think it was in the spring. It had been decided that I would pursue my studies at the lycée, and small complications cropped up, for Mamma had to wake me very early each morning and prepare my breakfast. At a quarter to six she stood at the foot of my bed, holding a candle, calling me softly. I pretended not to hear, but through my eyelashes saw the candle flame shining like a star. "Get up, my little boy," she repeated gently. For the pleasure of hearing her speak to me so, I lingered a little longer, then suddenly, in the voice of conspiracy, I said: "Good morning, Mamma!" I felt that she loved me even more than she used to, but she saw me growing up and, for reasons that completely escaped me, dreaded some unknown dangers. With a serious, attentive expression, she watched me drink my tea on a corner of the dining-room table. The house was still asleep. All of a sudden my mother said: "If ever anyone speaks to you in the street, you must not answer." I shook my head, but the sentence seemed without meaning. It had a tremendous one, as we shall see. My mother also said, in the silence of half past six: "I don't want the boys at the lycée to teach you wicked things." Looking up at her, I asked what she meant. She looked at me, then, my expression telling her how deeply ignorant I was of what she feared, she said at last: "All right, my little boy. Remember that God sees you constantly." My breakfast over, I kissed my mother with a somewhat heavy heart and, leaving the house, rushed down the Avenue de la Princesse at top speed to the station. About an hour later I reached the Gare Saint-Lazare, where I suppose my guardian angel watched over me (he must have been slightly absent-minded on one occasion) and took the inner-circle railroad to the Avenue Henri-Martin. I made the journey alone, and that was what frightened my mother.

A short time afterwards, one of our maids gave me a little penknife with a crudely colored wooden handle. I had to return it and say (according to Mamma's orders) that I was much obliged, but could not accept presents. The poor girl's hurt face is still in my memory, but later I understood the reasons that prompted my mother.

At the lycée, I was still in the middle boys' playground, but each year brought me closer to that of the big boys. One minute before every hour, the concierge in the blue apron, with a soldier's long mustache and a big drum at his thigh, performed a rub-a-dub with admirable precision. That wild sound both pleased and disturbed me. I thought it brutal and splendid, but could not contrive to include it in the world of things I liked. It was gross heroism, battles, it was not music and it had a way of stopping suddenly that made me jump. The last rat-tat-tat left a void behind it that resembled a chasm.

I was a day scholar but did my homework at the lycée, watched (very little, I think) by a supervisor, which means that without sleeping at the school like the boarders in navy-blue uniforms, I ate my midday meal in the refectory and left the

113

study as early as five o'clock—by special permission—to catch the train and go home. The sadness I felt in the refectory at being far from home spoiled my appetite and I scarcely touched the food served us in aluminum bowls. The room was high and dark and the noise all around us upset me. By chance, I sat facing two brothers, Georges and Boni de X.; and I looked at the latter, mute with admiration, staring fixedly but unconsciously at him. Like me, he wore his hair in a stubble, but mine was brown and his golden. Something proud and energetic about his whole person fascinated me. In the midst of a babel of voices, laughter, metal dishes clanging on the white marble tables, I remained spellbound before him, as if I were witnessing a scene whose meaning escaped me, although it engaged my rapt attention. One day, at the end of a meal, he stepped over a bench and, passing near me, said: "You are awfully silent." I did not answer, but my heart was heavy. To see the boy gave me a strange joy mingled with the poison of some mysterious melancholy; yet I never gave him a thought except when I saw him.

The year 1913 must have been important to me, but I cannot manage to distinguish it clearly from the preceding one and the first months of the following year, at least as far as small events are concerned, those on which I want to turn my attention. I might be told that it does not matter much, and I would be only too ready to believe it, if I were not driven to go ahead.

My only good marks were in French and history. One day, Monsieur Mougeot gave as a subject for our French essay "Your Home." What does the term mean to you? That was his question. For me, "Your Home" was our Villa du Lac, with my mother under the trees, on a fine spring morning. Down at the bottom of the classroom, I felt like blubbering, because all that existed out there while I was here in this tiresome classroom, with boys to whom I had nothing to say and who thought me stupid on account of my incredible innocence. In

114

this frame of mind, I wrote an essay that obtained the best mark, whereas I usually came second to the boy who explained, sniffling, the secret of my birth.

When my mother was told of my little victory, she took my essay from me and, deeply moved (she ill concealed her feelings), made me sit down at her desk. "You must copy the essay for me and I'll send it to your brother Charles." I do not know why this irksome job seemed so hateful to me. Birds were singing in the garden and I had to copy "Your Home." "You'll see," André Gide once said to me, "the taste of laurels is bitter." I cannot say that I have eaten much laurel in my life, but that day I had a foretaste of that overrated foliage. I knew boredom such as I had never known before. Why? That is what I cannot quite make out, except that one holiday hour had been stolen from me, on account of good marks. And also, my brother Charles, whom I scarcely remembered having seen, lived so far away, in America. . . . On another occasion there was "The Clock," a paper I was also obliged to copy with feelings verging on despair. This taught me to be more modest and never to inform the inhabitants of the Villa du Lac that I had outdistanced everyone in Monsieur Mougeot's class.

Winter brought with it a sort of tragicomedy which I kept secret for years and years. My brother-in-law, always so smart, so furiously British, had a black overcoat the collar of which, will I ever forget it, was made of astrakhan. Thick and lustrous was that noble fur! To lay one's cheek on it gave a strange happiness, because not only were the tight little black curls soft to the touch, but they smelt good. What took place in the dear fellow's mind? Had he seen me stroking that fur collar? One day he told my mother that he no longer cared for that overcoat but, once shortened, it would fit me and, of course, nothing should be done about the collar. In winter, in very cold weather, I would be very glad to feel that nice fur rising above my ears. My mother, whose ideas about clothes were sometimes peculiar

115

where I was concerned (oh, not to be dressed like others, what a torture for a child!), my mother thought her son-in-law right, as usual, and I was taken to a tailor.

A few days later I went to the lycée, with the overcoat carefully folded over my arm, in order completely to conceal that impresario collar. It was cold, I did not mind. I preferred shivering to being ridiculous, for I was mortally ashamed of that fur, and from the Avenue Henri-Martin station to the lycée gates, I could be seen, the overcoat over my arm, as though I felt too warm. I particularly dreaded being spied by young B., who was so elegant, but suitably elegant, and who scorned me in my everlasting little navy-blue jersey, a poor boy's garment in the eyes of a little rich one. What would he have thought, what would he have said of that enormous and sumptuous dark mass in which my head all but disappeared when I was sure that nobody could see me? For there were happy moments when I blessed my brother-in-law, particularly from the Vésinet station to the Villa du Lac, when I had to walk up the whole of the Avenue de la Princesse on an icy evening. Then I would turn my chin this way and that, to feel all the little black curls caress my ears, but at the lycée I trembled. I put the overcoat on a clothes hanger in a dark corner of the study, turning the garment inside out to hide the sumptuous horror that no one should see, and I was very lucky, for no one at the lycée ever saw it.

One day—it must have been in the spring, for I was not wearing that dreadful overcoat—my mother told me to go with her to the village, as she called Le Vésinet. It was always a joy to me to go out with her. I wonder what we talked about, or rather, what I talked about, for, always deep in thought, she seldom listened to what I said and answered: "Ah?" absently, but she also had moments of sudden attentiveness and then spoke to me with striking seriousness. If only I remembered what she said! No, not a word comes back to me and I cannot induce myself to

116

make her talk. It seems to me that the more I think of it, the fewer the number of sentences I can recollect. What she wanted to say to me, she often conveyed otherwise than by words. Since my godmother's death, she had become more meditative and less given to expressing herself.

The day I am speaking of—it was a Thursday—she took me to the Vésinet Catholic church, a rather commonplace church, to my mind, that looked as though a child had designed it. So here we are, Mamma and I, standing at the end of the nave, exactly facing the high altar. My mother remains motionless for a long time and I wonder what she is thinking about, but I do not move and keep my hand in hers. Apparently, we are alone in the church. I look furtively around me, awed by the deep silence and more so by my mother's stillness. She does not say a word, her lips do not move, she simply looks. Such is the fact I can report with assurance, but from which I draw no conclusion.

Years after her death, I learnt that in Paris she went to see the nuns on the Rue Cortambert, among whom our American friend Roselys was there as a novice. One of these nuns has often assured me that my mother told her that she regretted not having been born a Catholic, and it is positive that she had at least one conversation about religion with the priest who was at that time the community's spiritual director, but she died a Protestant.

As I am on the subject, it seems the right time to say that from 1913 on, she appeared to have completely given up applying herself to my religious education, as she had done for all of my sisters. I learnt the first paragraphs of the Protestant catechism and the book was closed forever. Yet a daily reading of the Bible was never neglected. What strikes me most is that when I was almost thirteen, I never even heard the word "confirmation" mentioned. It was as though—am I mistaken? —my mother's heart was no longer set on handing down to me

117

the Protestant heritage that had been so dear to her. She could only talk of the Gospel.

The spring of 1913 has remained in my memory as one of the most rapturous periods of my life. I came home in broad daylight, seized with frenzied joy at the sight of the country in its young foliage. On Thursday afternoons I would roll on one of the garden lawns, a prey to a kind of silent delirium. Something seemed to grip my insides and, my face in the grass, I laughed to myself. I did not know what to do with so much happiness. I never asked myself questions, never wondered why I was so happy, in a way I felt as though my whole being were crushed under the weight of some unknown force. Turning over on my back, I gazed at the sky through millions of pale small leaves pierced by sunlight. I no longer seemed to be myself, I was part of all I saw. I was air, I was space.

The most absurd naïveté mingled with this sort of ecstasy. I do not know how a volume of plays by Labiche fell into my hands and, as I read everything, I devoured three comedies of which I probably understood very little. In one, however, was a young woman called Prunette; several men were in love with her, and I fell in love with her too. My head in my arms, stretched on the lawn, I endlessly repeated the name of Prunette with all the passionate violence I was capable of. I wanted to love someone or something, I would have loved an animal with the same foolish transports, and, not knowing what else to do, I laid my cheek tenderly on the little white volume of the Nelson series.

Need I say that no one knew anything about my state of mind? I was not secretive, but taciturn, and then to whom could I have confided such things? The youngest of my sisters, Lucy, was five years older than I. My mother thought me a very good, quiet child. My sister Mary alone watched me a little with a large black eye that suddenly became attentive whereas she was usually lost in endless dreams. I do not know why, she spied on me discreetly.

My room was at the top of the house. For the first time I had a room of my own. It was large and somewhat faintly lit by a small window through which I could see the lake between the trees of the garden and avenue. What delighted me in this view was its stillness and gentle melancholy. It seemed to me as beautiful as a station poster. For at the Vésinet station was a poster showing an autumnal landscape, a pool surrounded by golden trees. I am unable to fathom why the picture made me sad, although my sadness was an agreeable one. The same emotion laid hold of me when I looked from the window in my room, I sang to myself, airs of my own invention, mentally addressed to the pensive sheet of water that reflected the clouds.

To me this room was a small kingdom where I could entertain myself by making up stories. No one disturbed me. In the evening I went upstairs with a lamp, after having kissed everyone good night. "Don't read too late," my mother said absently. For she played backgammon with my father and her thoughts were elsewhere. And then, what was meant by "too late"? I put my lamp on the bedside table, undressed and, slipping into my sheets after having said my prayers, opened one of the volumes I was crazy about. They were three in number: *Les Misérables* (numerous obscurities in the text), *Notre-Dame de Paris* (same remark, but I read as a drunkard drinks brandy), and lastly an illustrated copy of *Les Mystères de Paris,* lent me by Sidonie. The last book overwhelmed me with pleasure. I remember that I used to swallow hard during the more unbearable dramatic moments and that the illustrations made me open enormous eyes. One showed a little girl looking in horror at a human foot sticking out of the ground. In a delightful terror, I gave a big sweeping glance around me, but everything seemed so peaceful in the country room: the big wardrobe where Mamma kept the household linen, the little table where I wrote, another table with a washbasin, the setting reassured me, I went on reading. The dreadful *Maître d'Ecole*, the *Chourineur*, the *Chouette*, the dens of thieves *under* the Champs-Elysées, Princess Sarah, Prince Rodolphe, Fleur-de-Marie, the tortures (I read these last passages over several times, for fear of missing a single word), scenes of vengeance . . . Suddenly there was a knock at the door and the book jumped out of my hands. "What are you doing?" asked Mary's voice. "Put your light out at once. It's half past ten!" I blew out the lamp, pulled the sheet up over my head on account of ghosts that might be wandering around my bed, but I had scarcely time to be frightened. Less than a minute after, I was asleep.

I drew a lot at that time, but all my drawings were of a kind that could be shown. The desire to produce the kind that were not had left me since young B. had allowed us to see what are termed the shameful parts of his body. It seemed as though this small event had closed the era of desires even as I left childhood to become adolescent. It should not be impossible to explain things that I understand so badly, but I can only say what I know to be true. At thirteen, I was far more innocent than at ten, or eight, when "The Bearers of Evil Tidings" made me faint with languor.

Of all the drawings I made in 1913, the only one I have kept is a sort of military picture in which the Kaiser is seen reviewing a regiment of soldiers in spiked helmets. This fits in very badly with Monsieur Mougeot's teaching, for he hated Germany, but I suppose that the painstaking, clumsy drawing was the result of conversations I had overheard in which people talked admiringly of this stupid emperor. Be it as it may, my mother, seeing my taste for the fine arts, decided to give me a teacher. A Monsieur Tisserand appeared one day in the Vésinet garden. He was a gray-bearded dwarf who held himself very straight and trod warily, his hand resting on the silver knob of a mahogany cane. His wide-brimmed hat and extremely dignified manners made my sisters explode with laughter. I do not know where my mother unearthed him, but he was poor and she wished to help him. What she did not know was that, owing to this, she was to have a whole family on her hands, as I will tell a little later.

Monsieur Tisserand made me draw pots of geraniums, brass candlesticks, chairs standing on tables (for perspective), balusters (for volume). He it was who gave a finishing touch to these scrawls, the indefinable something that made the thing correct and commonplace, and as he worked, he talked about literature, for he often arrived with a volume of Zola under his arm, "but," he said, "I strictly forbid you to read Zola." This had never entered my mind. Pure and Impure had never mentioned Zola to me. To show off my little stock of learning, I timidly gave the titles of a few novels by Hugo, among them *Notre-Dame de Paris*. "This will kill that," then quoted Monsieur Tisserand in a drone, for his bass voice would have done credit to a giant. I have forgotten to say that he was by profession a sculptor and that one day he suggested making a likeness of me: a terracotta medallion. So, the following Thursday, he appeared with white overalls and some potter's clay and, while exposing Zola's social demands, he made me sit for hours on end. The finished medallion cracked during the baking. My mother accepted it in spite of this. I still have it: a naïve, round-cheeked little profile. In order to reproduce the texture of my suit, the artist patted the clay with a nailbrush.

From time to time, my mother received calls for help from Madame Tisserand, my teacher's wife. Money and more and more money was needed or the whole family would face disaster, and money orders flowed from Le Vésinet to Paris. Monsieur Tisserand never took part in such things. He remained in the serene spheres of Art and Literature and the word "money" never sullied his lips. One Thursday, my teacher did not appear. To make up for his absence, his wife treated Mamma to a letter that was even more dramatic than usual. Grandma had died and how were they to bury her without money? "There's only one thing to do," said Mamma. "Send Julian to these poor people with clothing and all the help they need. I'm certain they have nothing." So off I went, provided with every necessity to lighten the Tisserand family's distress. It was not a very amusing way of spending my Thursday holiday, but Mamma said that I had to learn to be charitable and I did not kick. On reaching the Tisserands' house, I asked the concierge to tell me what floor they lived on. "They've all gone to the country," she said.—"All of them?"—"The grandmother is the only one at home. If you want to see her . . ." After hesitating, I went upstairs and was received by a nice old lady who made no fuss about accepting the bundle of clothes and the bank notes. I was so glad to be rid of the whole lot! On my return home, I gave an account of what had happened. My father held his sides and the girls burst into fits of derisive laughter. Mamma, who pretended to be angry, then laughed louder than we did and, on the following Thursday, Monsieur Tisserand came and gave me my lesson as usual.

Without knowing it, the little man had an enormous influence over me. I know very well that not everything can be laid at the devil's door. Nature—the devil's charwoman—and our own corruption take charge of the heavy work, but one cannot help seeing with horrified interest how our enemy takes advantage of circumstances and of the delicate mechanism of cause and effect. Monsieur Tisserand's lessons bore their poisonous fruits years later and hurled me into the most hazardous courses. He had no idea that he taught me to foster the carnal hallucinations of my twentieth year. In his opinion, the perfect imitation of a model was the acme of art, but he needed models, no matter if they were wood, metal, or flesh. What he did not know was that my imagination would furnish me with everything necessary, in due course. At the time, I was unaware of it myself. I learned well. I drew pots of geraniums and wastepaper baskets, applying myself to rounding out everything that was round, for that was my teacher's main rule: "It's got to round out, my friend. I *insist* on its rounding out." Was I gifted? I am not a good judge. Every writer is something of a draftsman, but I drew with a fury and passion that were well out of the ordinary. Yet I say once more that nothing I drew could have shocked anyone. I no longer thought of the forbidden albums. I entered into a period of apparent coldness, and to rouse my former hunger it would have been necessary first to conquer an ignorance that formed again, in spite of revelations made me about the "secret of my birth." With extreme care, I copied the engravings in my history book. I thus embellished my copybooks and reaped the compliments I thirsted for.

One day my sister Mary, who had gone to live in Rome with our English friend, Mrs. Gibson, sent me a colored postcard, the sight of which gave me an inner shock never to be forgotten. What weird inspiration made Mary choose a picture representing the head of one of the Sistine Chapel *ignudi,* the one *a destra del profeta Isaia*? And first of all, what were those big naked boys doing to the right and left of the prophet? I have always wondered. Apparently the young Titans' duty is to support scrolls, or to excuse their own laziness by noble attitudes that show off their superhuman beauty. The body's glory singing God's glory as the stars declare it? It is possible. Everything is possible, and I do not argue the point, but simply and sadly state that the effect of this carnal magnificence is not necessarily good. Of course, I had none of these ideas in mind when I received my sister Mary's card, but I ran for my sketchbook to copy that profile, serene and scornful under great tufts of unkempt hair. I applied myself with devouring zeal to transferring that face to a sheet of cream-colored paper, not knowing that I was, at the same time, establishing it in me forever. One after the other, my sisters leaned over my shoulder and Mamma also had a look. They all cried out in admiration. "For a child of thirteen, it's really not bad!" said my father, in turn, settling his pince-nez. "And look at the card," said Mamma, "that's it, exactly." My heart beat fast. I felt proud. But why did I also feel sad?

At the lycée, in the third form, you passed from the "middle boys' " playground to that of the "big boys."

To right and left of the covered court flowered clumps of lilacs behind which certain boys met, for reasons unknown to me. Attempts were sometimes made to lure me there, but I was on my guard. I preferred walking around the playground with the ugliest, silliest schoolmate I could find. Why? It is impossible to answer a question I have so often asked myself. I ran away from what attracted me most. I did what I did not want to do. As long as anyone had an unpleasing face and a brain a little below average, he was sure of being in my good graces, but inwardly I rebelled against myself and against the companion I had chosen with such care. However that may be, I was becoming less retiring and walked about chatting under the depressing galleries with their metal columns.

My father's office was 21 Rue du Louvre, opposite the General Post Office. He was special agent for Europe for cotton importations from the Southern States, and more particularly of cottonseed oil. The concern was called The Southern Cotton Oil Company, with head offices at New York. His own office, a vast, dark, and almost empty flat, was on the first floor of a black building. I remember it for having gone there several times with my mother. I was struck by the sadness of those big rooms. Nothing to be seen there but deal furniture, a few leather armchairs, and, on the walls, photographs of cotton fields, and what can be uglier than a cotton field? In the fields, Negroes. I had seen only two Negroes in all my life: Emily's cook and, like all other little Parisians, black Chocolat in his red dress coat, who made everybody laugh, he and his confederate Footit, an English clown. This reminds me of the day when I was at the Nouveau Cirque with Mamma, and the latter, leaning toward Chocolat as he passed by us—we were in the first row—asked the colored man where he was from. "From Georgia, Ma'am." —"So am I!" cried my mother, and they shook hands.

In the Rue du Louvre office, I looked around me, listened to my father and mother talking; because of the emptiness, their voices sounded different, and as soon as my father talked about business, he became incomprehensible. Bales of cotton, linseed, none of all that made much sense to me. To help him in his work, he had secretaries whom I remember perfectly: Mr. Turner, an Englishman with a pointed beard like King George the Fifth, and spectacled eyes both wise and prudent (what a tragic life the poor man led, but we knew nothing of it); Scherowski, a Russian who later died of hunger in his own country during the revolution; Ebrard, a gay, hard-working Frenchman who thought a great deal about the day when France would have her revenge on Germany and who was killed in the first months of the war. Finally, the latest-comer, my brother-in-law. For some unknown reason, it was agreed that he was not to stay in Paris, but would be given the Trieste agency. That, after having made us leave the Rue de la Pompe and settle at Le Vésinet! However, at the end of 1913, Eleanor and Kennie had left the Villa du Lac. Lucy, Retta, Anne, and myself remained with my parents.

My sister Anne had a beautiful room on the first floor with a view of the lake, darkened by heavy red damask curtains lined with silk of the same color. I admired the room on account of the curtains, of which I have made great use in my novels. Together with a certain number of pieces of Empire furniture, they came to us from Roselys, our American friend who had become a Catholic and left the world for the convent on the Rue Cortambert. It is time I went back to Roselys. We were all very fond of her, although she came from the North, but as Papa said: "Children, the war is over, so not a syllable about Sherman's atrocities and the word 'Yankee' must not be mentioned."

Without being pretty, Roselys was charmingly gay and amused us with her grimaces. A clown would not have amused us more. From time to time she dropped in with arms full of presents, gifts she distributed with remarks we found awfully witty. She adored my parents and considered us as her family. I have no doubt that her conversion shook my mother. Roselys lived on the Avenue Jules-Janin, at the point where the avenue bends sharply, in a small ground-floor flat that she shared with a companion, Mademoiselle Lainé, an old white sheep whose shoulders were always wrapped in a long cream-colored shawl.

It was in the tiny rooms on the Avenue Jules-Janin that the furniture just mentioned was assembled. Covered in pale green silk, it seemed both stiff and magnificent, and when I was allowed I used to play at sitting in all the seats, one after the other, to watch the drawing-room *change*. At the far end of the flat, in a bedroom, hung the red damask curtains. I admired the whole setting, the mahogany that shone like tortoiseshell, the pictures in their gilt frames. Alas, there must always be a shadow! My unthinkable inability to grasp the rudiments of mathematics gave Roselys the dubious idea of my having private lessons with Mademoiselle Lainé. That was when we still lived on the Rue de la Pompe. Once or twice a week, the peaceful, smiling setting became a setting for purgatory to me. The sheep wrapped in her big shawl, with fringes that swept the carpet, tried to make me understand the mystery of figures. She was patient. I would have preferred her fretting and fuming. That slow, quiet voice that seemed to come out of wool, repeating

126

twenty times over things that remained just as obscure, finally maddened me and I blushed as fright, shame, and despair overwhelmed me, each in turn. I clasped my hands between my legs, cracking my knuckles in a violent effort to understand the multiplication table. Today I can say that I was Pythagoras' martyr. My stupidity was unconquerable. "Now, child, you have two apples. You multiply them by two. . . ." Two apples. I could see them. That did not improve matters, quite the contrary. Why two apples? I would willingly have eaten them, had they been there.

The sheep died long ago. Roselys is in a convent, far away. The furniture is in Anne's room and mine, where I am writing this.

And so, at the lycée, there was a new breed called the big boys. The big boys wore trousers and had political opinions. Their talk was not ours, we who wore breeches. They did not run, they looked at us with contemptuous amusement, for in the third form you were not yet a big boy, but an indefinable something intermediate between an adolescent and a man. Here my difficulties began, for while I was so gentle with boys of my age, I showed an equal degree of insolence toward pupils who dressed like grownups. I have no idea why, but I looked them up and down contemptuously. If they spoke to me, I answered with an icy haughtiness quite unlike myself. They were certainly far stronger than I was, but thinking myself invulnerable, I never dreamt that anything unfortunate could happen to me, that anyone would strike me, for instance. I have said elsewhere that I could not even imagine myself capable of committing a serious offense and that, consequently, what I did could only be right, because it was I. Only the others were wrong. The big boys above all were wrong, and particularly so. No doubt because I did not care for the way they dressed. I do not know why they did not get together to beat me black and blue, which would probably have done me good, but they were patient and I was convinced that I was untouchable.

Untouchable—the word makes me dream. One autumn evening, in 1913, I waited on the platform of the little Avenue Henri-Martin station for the train that was to take me to the Saint-Lazare station, when a man of about forty came up to me. He had a serious face and wore a raincoat. My satchel under my arm, I stood perfectly motionless. We were alone on the platform. The man asked me politely if I spoke English and I answered yes. "Oh!" he said. A pause, then he asked: "Do you travel first or second?"—"Second." Another pause. The train was due only in five or six minutes. All at once, with a kind of sudden violence, the stranger pulled his wallet from his pocket, opened it, and showed me three or four photographs of naked men and women. He held them as one holds playing cards, fanwise, and placed them on a level with my eyes. I gave them a surprised glance and turned my head away directly. What was the meaning of this? Certainly something impure. Another pause, shorter than the last, then the man replaced the photographs in his wallet and the wallet in his pocket. "I see," he said calmly, "that you're probably too young for this sort of thing." I did not answer and supposed that, as the train came in, the stranger and I would part, but to my great astonishment he got into a second-class compartment with me. I can see myself sitting in a corner and he most precisely facing me. Was I frightened? Not in the least. The man did not say a word and I pretended not to see him, but I could not help noticing that he sat with his legs wide apart and that, half closing his eyes, he pretended to be asleep. I wondered what he could be doing. Without being uneasy, I thought the intervals between stations a little longer than usual and, at each stop, wished that someone would get into our compartment, but no one did. We were alone until we reached Saint-Lazare. Not a word was exchanged, and at the terminal the man vanished into the crowd as if by magic. I turned my head and he was gone. How many years later did I understand the meaning of this encounter? Six or eight, no doubt, when I was at the University and read the works of Havelock Ellis for the first time. Yet I still have an impression of something sinister: the compartment faintly lit by gas, the rather shabbily dressed man and the hypocritical glances he cast at me through half-closed eyelids.

No one knew about this. I did not mention it and then, not understanding what it was about, I forgot an incident that completely faded from my consciousness to stick in some unknown part of my brain and come to light suddenly around 1921. Since then, I have often thought of the man in the raincoat and, at a distance, I feel very sorry for him.

At the lycée, some of the boys, irritated by my innocence, circled around me laughing and saying things I could not understand. Their expression at such times, as well as their tone of voice, made me draw away. I was the object of an attention that made me ill at ease and there were whispers about me.

Since I had to take a train, I was allowed to leave the study long before the usual hour, as I have already said, and for quite a while was the only one to enjoy this privilege. Then it happened one evening that another pupil left early, like myself. He was a Swiss whom I will call Koenig, a tall, fat boy with thick cheeks of a purplish pink, like underdone meat. He told me that he would take me to the station, and why should I have refused? He spoke so pleasantly! At the station he suggested, without losing a second, our going up to the little gallery that straddled the railroad track. A large clock stood above the gallery and it was below this clock that, all of a sudden, he seized me in his arms. The platforms were empty, otherwise we could have been seen as clearly as actors on a stage. I thought Koenig wanted to play at wrestling with me and began laughing, but his face flushed crimson and his bulging, pale green eyes seemed about to pop out of his head. I turned this way and that to free myself, but he was far stronger than I and I could only shout to him to let me go. Taking fright at this, he ran off, with threats as mysterious to me as the rest. "You'll see!" What did he mean? What had I done to fat Koenig? You'll see? I saw nothing at all. Koenig ceased speaking to me and never looked at me except with an air of hostility.

On another occasion I was surprised to see B., the young Jew, come up to me, but so different from what he usually was! A dazzling white smile beautified his brown face, and he began talking to me in such a gentle voice that any coolness I might have felt for him changed into affection. I cannot express this otherwise. An outburst of feeling drew me to people who talked to me with that voice and smile. We were in the playground after class and all the day pupils were leaving, excepting young B. I think he spoke of reconciliation and took my hand. I asked nothing better than to be reconciled with B., but brusquely he ceased smiling and began murmuring incomprehensible things that threw my mind into a whirl. He wanted to drag me I do not know where, behind the clumps of lilacs or some other spot. Seized with uneasiness, I said I did not understand. "You're just pretending!" He flung the words at me under his breath with an expression of fury that I thought restored the diabolical beauty of his face. Running to the exit, he left me. What astonishes me today is the timidity concealed under those airs of violence, but he was greatly mistaken if he believed I was pretending, for I had literally no idea of what he wanted to do. A moment later, I had forgotten all about it.

I was getting on toward fourteen. At that time I was friends with two pupils for differing reasons. I walked around the large playground with one or the other after lunch. The first was a big, reasonable boy, always in a good temper, rather ugly and not very gifted. He was a Protestant and never said anything

130

coarse. On that account, I liked being with him. We used to have idiotic, peaceful conversations and I sometimes held forth on religion, such as I saw it. For I was already beginning to have that passion for converting that grew so strong years later, but I wonder what I wanted to convert him to, convert an honest boy who went to church every Sunday and read his Bible with the same seriousness as mine. I do not know why, but he was not very popular, scarcely anyone spoke to him. Perhaps he was as innocent as I was.

The second was very different. Small and even a trifle lank, his face was extremely mobile (while the other boy was very deliberate and slow, both in movements and expression). His magnificent black eyes sparkled with intelligence. He had the reputation of being able to understand everything, and no one ever surpassed him on scientific subjects, but he envied me the laurels I won in French and that proved useful in fostering, airing, and caressing my budding vanity. Philippe's engaging manners captivated me. He made a little fun of me without ever hurting my feelings. What he called my virginity or my purity roused his mirth, although he never told me its cause. His hands in his pockets, he literally writhed with laughter when I answered some of his most insidious questions. He was said to be very vicious and incredibly well informed about everything forbidden. This gave him a flattering reputation which, together with that of being intelligent, sheltered him from sarcastic remarks and blows. He was great friends with the boy who had revealed to me, with mysterious sniffles, the secret of my birth. The latter, a plump little party with lovely, dreamy eyes, was surrounded by a sort of small court whose underhand practices escaped me, although I suspected something and kept clear of it. As to Philippe, who sought my company, he never said anything wrong in my presence, and if he spoke of virginity and purity, it was only to take up the expressions I myself used very often without having the least idea of what they meant. "So you're still a virgin?" he asked. I answered yes and he roared with laughter.

One day, I no longer remember why, he talked to me about the Danube. The word filled him with wonder, for, as he explained, it seemed as though, on pronouncing it, he saw the wind blowing the linen hanging on a clothesline and that he saw the sheets swell and balloon out into the sky. I thought this mental picture beautiful and it seemed to open a world to me.

In the autumn, the plane trees' golden leaves strewed the ground and I used to walk on this marvelous carpet, shuffling my feet to hear the rustle. It sounded to me like the roar of a torrent. I dreamt endlessly about everything, about water scenes, about lakes buried in woods. Together with the Eclaireurs Français (not to be confused with the Eclaireurs de France, the latter being socialists, I was told), I explored, much against my will, the outskirts of Marly or slept under a tent by the ponds of Saint-Cucufa. And once there was a memorable journey that took us to Brussels to meet our Belgian comrades. We were shown the town, went into a tower where criminals used to be put on the rack. Torture— the dreadful word blazed in my mind. I wanted to know about everything, but all we were shown was rusty iron rings and, I think, some large tongs. I carried away in my memory all this sinister junk. On the Place de l'Hôtel-de-Ville, a meeting of the French and Belgian scouts took place. The Belgian boys were charming to us and some tried to enter into conversation with me, but nothing doing: I remained mute. For they made me feel shy and I hesitate to say why: they all wore white cotton gloves. And what sort of figure did we cut, we with our bare hands? Something else made me stare: almost all of them were blond, and I thought that nothing was more beautiful than to be blond. The Belgian boys seemed to have sunshine in their hair. I came home early next morning, having traveled all night in a third-class compartment. My mother, for some unknown reason, put me to sleep in her bed, which had just been made up. I still remember the freshness of the sheets, the voluptuous sliding into sleep. . . . On waking, I looked around me in amazement. Where was I? At Brussels? No, here, at Le Vésinet, in Mamma's bed. I called out. She came in and smiled: "My little boy, it's four in the afternoon!" I hugged her and jumped out of bed.

I look today with astonishment at the boy I was then. I thought him so pure, and no doubt he was, but so close to becoming the prey of everything he dreaded. . . . His photographs show him to be both determined and frail, proud and alone, with an unfathomable ignorance that exposes him to every danger. Has he not built up, with his mother's unconscious help, interdicts that rise up to the sky and separate him from the world?

Together with that of the year before, the spring of 1914 was one of the happiest in my life. In the Villa du Lac garden, an immoderate joy I knew so well made me roll and gambol laughing on the grass once more. Unknowingly, I was in love, but in love with whom? With whom could I share the devouring passion that turned me into a kind of semilunatic? A panic desire seized me, a desire that I did not know what to do with, that was both a torture and a delight.

No one seemed to have the least idea of what was taking place in me, and how should they have known? I said nothing, was reserved with everyone but my mother, in whose arms I took refuge, and who found such violent, sudden outbursts of tenderness quite natural. Sometimes, sitting on the dining-room sofa, she would draw me close, put her arm around my shoulder, and hug me without saying a word. I know only too well what she was thinking about. She wanted to protect me, she remembered a tragedy which had occurred five or six years before my birth and that she revealed to me only a few weeks before her death. When we were alone, she used to say to me under her breath: "Always remember that God loves you."

My sisters would make fun of us a little: "Look at them!" they said. "Mamma and her beloved!"

Time went by. One day when we were all at table we heard the little garden gate open and shut, and soon after, Farley appeared, a long cardboard box under his arm. Instead of coming toward the house, as we thought he would, he went down a small path, straight to the vegetable garden. There he put down his box with great care and entered a shed where we kept our bicycles and gardening tools. Behind the window curtains we watched these mysterious comings and goings with increasing curiosity, then Farley suddenly reappeared with a spade and, in a corner of the vegetable garden, began digging a big hole; there, bowed over with sorrow, he buried his box, filled in the little grave—for that was what it was—put the spade away, and left. We never saw him again. "He has buried his dog, Judy," said my mother. "Poor Willie!"

A few weeks later she decided to pay him a visit and took me to Paris with her. We two climbed the stairs of 16 Rue de la Paix. This is one of the most precise memories remaining to me of this period. It was so dark that we had some trouble in finding the door. My mother rang. A long silence was the only answer. She rang again with no more success, then knocked, but no one was there.

Weeks elapsed and a rumor went around that my godfather had retired to a monastery. At any rate, he disappeared completely. I was told what a monastery was.

One Sunday in July 1914, we were all sitting under the trees with a guest who had lunched with us, when the conversation rather quickly became incomprehensible to me, for it turned on politics. The word "war" often recurred, but in my father's opinion there was not going to be a war, because the German socialists would never allow the Kaiser to plunge into such a dangerous venture.

Nothing could be prettier than the light shadow of the foliage around us. Everything was peaceful. In those days, there were few carriages on the road and all we heard was the wind stirring in the trees. My mother seemed a little worried, but my father reassured her. She believed, as we all did, that Papa could never be mistaken, and yet, a week later . . .

When the news reached us, one of my sisters burst into sobs and it upset my mother so much that she made the following entry in the little memorandum book where she noted the daily expenses; it is before me now: "England declares war on France."

As for me, I went up to my room in a state of wild exaltation. War! Revenge for 1870! That was Monsieur Mougeot's dream. My hatred of Germany having passed all bounds, I threw myself on my German grammar and tore it to pieces. One thing sure, that was the end of those fiendish declensions and verbs flung, no, kicked to the very end of sentences.

Next day I bought little paper flags and stuck them in a map to mark the progress of French troops in southern Alsace, and my mother watched me do it. One day we saw an infantry regiment in red trousers march down the Boulevard Carnot and, a week later, in the opposite direction, refugees. My mother ran to them, giving everything she had on her, her money, her jacket, and even her hat, which they certainly had no use for, but she was beside herself with emotion.

Another few days went by, then one afternoon I went up to my room and saw Mamma standing in front of the big wardrobe where the household linen was kept. The wardrobe doors were wide open; the wicker trunk for the holidays stood a few steps away and my mother was throwing piles of towels into it. I asked

135

what was happening. She did not hear me. I repeated my question. She looked impatient. "The Germans are coming," she said. "Leave me alone."

For that very morning my father had had a telephone call from our friend General Filloneau, who advised him to leave Le Vésinet. "You're between two forts," explained the general, "you had better go somewhere else." I do not know where he wanted us to find shelter, but my father simply decided to take us to Paris, "for," he asserted, "the Germans will never take Paris."

So we landed in Paris the next morning. The city seemed empty, and there were neither porters nor taxis, the latter being busy elsewhere, as we all know. We were lent a handcart on which we piled our luggage, and my father himself trundled it, followed by all of us, to Passy, where he had reserved rooms in a boardinghouse, the Pension Mouton, which was to make a lasting impression on the family.

This pension was at 23 Rue de la Tour. I described it in one of my novels (*The Strange River*) without altering anything in its aspect. You opened the front door; to the right was a small drawing room where the landlady, a little woman whose face seemed worn away by life, spoke in a gentle, timid voice. She rented us the rooms we needed. My parents settled down on the ground floor and I in a room communicating with the drawing room and from which one saw the long garden on a lower level. For there was quite a large difference in levels in that part of the street; you walked down a whole flight to reach the dining room, a dark place most imperfectly lighted by the garden just mentioned, if you could call it a garden, a long strip of earth at the end of which two or three trees bent sadly over a chicken-coop. "Large, shady garden," said a sign on the pension's front door. This flattering description made Mamma smile, but we were glad to be quartered somewhere. Lucy slept at the pension. Anne and Retta, for reasons I have forgotten, lived a few steps away, almost facing number 43, in a flat—then vacant, and for very good reasons—belonging to young André Filloneau, son of the general who gave such good advice. In André's house, two floors below his apartment, lived his grandmother, known as Tante Kate. In her youth she had been the "grosse Kate Yapp" well known to specialists of Mallarmé. I remember her as an old lady, corpulent but alert, with a deep laugh exactly like a man's. She once showed me all the knickknacks that cluttered up her flat. In her room was the portrait of a girl painted by Regnault, who, she told me, had died during the Franco-Prussian War. "And who is this lady?" I asked thoughtlessly. She shook with huge laughter and replied: "Your humble servant!"

I scarcely remember anything about our first stay at the Pension Mouton (for there was another, far longer one). I only remember that Monsieur Tisserand gave me drawing lessons in my room. Once, before my professor's arrival, I had a visitor, my friend Philippe, with whom I played games that were most certainly innocent. Hearing Monsieur Tisserand approach, I hid Philippe behind a curtain, but almost immediately our fits of laughter betrayed us and my friend came out of his hiding place. "You must make a sketch of him," said Monsieur Tisserand. I still have that sketch. On another occasion I drew a spiked helmet picked up by Philippe's brother on a battlefield and sent to his parents. I showed the helmet to my mother. *Mit Gott für Kaiser und Vaterland*. This motto, inscribed on it, which I translated at once, gave my mother pause. "How can they have such fine feelings and behave so badly?" For the legend of the Germans' supposed practice of cutting off people's hands had begun its career.

Philippe's parents lived quite close to the pension, on the top floor of an apartment house where I went to see them one day. His mother, who was good and simple, looked anxious, not only because of the German armies' advance, but because news of her son did not reach her as quickly as she wished. He was killed a few months later.

I leaned out of the window with Philippe, I looked at Paris, at an endless prospect of roofs, domes, and towers. My heart went out to the city in a vague, powerful outburst of love, for the city was my city. I felt I loved it as I would love a human being and laughed with happiness. Philippe laughed with me. The seriousness of the situation never so much as touched us, even lightly. First of all, because my father had said that the French would stop the Germans, and that settled the matter in my mind. I do not know where he derived his optimism, but when told that many Parisians had fled their city, he simply remarked: "They're frightened and they're wrong. You'll see." And, I cannot tell how, he communicated his assurance to us all.

Today, I wonder what Philippe and I talked about. I am only certain of one thing: he never said anything at that time that could have disturbed or enlightened me. We played chess. My father had shown me the rules of the game and Philippe taught me the finesses, for he beat me at it, as one beats a child of five. With a sly, mocking air, he took my pieces away from me one after the other, saying: *"Toc!"* in a quiet voice.

One morning, it happened to be my birthday, I crossed the street to pass the time of day with my sisters and they greeted me, waving a newspaper. No questions of my birthday! It was the sixth of September, the Battle of the Marne had been won. Papa was right. Our relief was immense. Mamma laughed and cried, no longer knowing whether she was happy or unhappy. "I declare . . ." she began and tears streamed from her lovely gray eyes. Papa murmured softly: "I was certain of it." We returned to Le Vésinet a few days later.

Drawing lessons were resumed at the Villa du Lac. Every Thursday Monsieur Tisserand came to watch my progress in high relief. "It's got to round out, my friend, it's got to round out!" Then charcoal, pencils, erasers, Wattman paper, everything came into action. Shadows here, lights there, and rounded lines began to seem round, especially when the master's artistic touch added the essential and indefinable something. The illusion of relief filled me with admiration. It was in my opinion the aim and summit of art.

Meanwhile, trenches were being dug and the world settled down into war. My mother, who was mad with anxiety about my sister Eleanor and Kennie, heard one day that they had left Trieste to take refuge in Venice. They soon returned to us, with Patrick clasping to his heart a sawdust doll with *Onkel Zeppelin* inscribed on its stomach, and to part them was impossible. Behind them, carrying their bags, a magnificent peasant from the Friuli, a large Juno, strong as a man and called Teresina. She had faultless features, big, light eyes, enormous hands, a ringing voice, and the woman, who was tenderness itself, swept into rooms like a storm. Very pious, she made Patrick say his prayers in Latin, or what she took for such, and one night I heard them recite: *Benne-deeta too een booneer-boosse.* . . . It was only after my conversion that I understood: *Benedicta tu in mulieribus.*

The best room, which faced south, was given to Kennie and Eleanor (Patrick called them in one breath: Kenninor). It should be said that my brother-in-law was almost an invalid and quite unfit for service. Life went on, much as before the war. Once more, I felt myself grow pale under my brother-in-law's ferocious blue eye, for he spared me none of his quiet sarcasms. He had the idea, excellent no doubt, of helping me improve my English on Thursdays. I wrote down the *Times* communiqués, dictated by Kennie in a dreadfully patient voice. This operation over, he would take the paper from my hands, examine it and, with a diabolical smile, show it to one of my sisters, who burst out laughing. I changed color and corrected my mistakes as best I could, but preferred my mother's method.

When school reopened that year I made the acquaintance, in

the lycée playground, of four boys who formed a little gang, and three of whom at least decided to turn their attention to me. The fourth seemed less interested in this sort of conspiracy, but the other three spoke to me with ironical deference, and my art-less remarks made them exchange knowing looks ending in mysterious fits of laughter. I can almost see all four of them un-der my eyes, in the room where I sit writing. The first, very glib of tongue, was a Protestant. Sensitive and fated to pass through great suffering, he ran away at the least threat, hands crossed over the top of his breast, crying out a little too shrilly. What seemed strange to me was that he wore a pince-nez. Far from me any idea of smiling in recollecting behavior he could not help, for he was more of a girl than a boy. I looked at him with-out understanding. He would say to us: "See my pretty hands. I am taking great care of them for my confirmation. I will have to give the minister my hand." I did not know what a confirma-tion was, I looked at my schoolmate's hands and noted they were very white and faintly chubby. "Oh, you're so aus-teere!" he would say to me with his curiously affected pronunciation. I no longer know what prompted this remark, but it was one that recurred often and, singing very pretty tunes in a silvery voice, he would disappear from time to time behind the clumps of lilacs where I never ventured. His com-panions followed more slowly, in order to avoid rousing the supervisors on watch, who, it seems to me, did very little watch-ing, the gift of ubiquity not having devolved on them.

The second of these boys, also a Protestant, was a colorless person who snickered when others snickered and who, when others kept silence, did not speak. He was slim, rather ugly, very pale.

Mentally, I called the third of these boys the brute. There is always a brute per class. The brute in question filled me with horror. He was a strapping, square-shouldered fellow, some-thing of a redhead, with a cruel eye. He smiled occasionally, displaying the teeth of a young ogre, and, although he spoke little (the pince-nez was a great talker and talked for four), was much in demand. This intrigued me a little; I say a little, for as a matter of fact nothing intrigued me much. The brute came from Noyon, a city taken by the Germans. That was why the brute happened to be at the lycée. He was a refugee, a rather elegant refugee moreover, dressed in thick tweed. I worried about the city of Noyon's fate. Would it ever be retaken? For I supposed that no sooner would Noyon be recaptured than the brute would go home, but there was not much to be hoped for in that direction.

Finally comes the fourth and last member of the little gang. At a distance, he seems more interesting than the others. Tall and thin, with a small, tragic face that laughed unceasingly, he impressed me for several reasons. First, because he studied Latin and Greek. I did not know a word of these tongues, having most unfortunately been put in the sciences section where I floundered horribly, but I had an instinctive respect for the classics of which I was ignorant. Yet there was something else: the boy was a Catholic and made no secret of it. He said things that struck me, in his faltering voice. He gave me the feeling of being very learned, very different from the others and, in his way, very religious. Where is he now? I remember that his eyes were most precisely ringed with a mauve that shaded at times into violet. "The guy's done for," our friend with the pince-nez once said to us. Done for? Why? I did not understand, but asked no questions and looked at the "done-for guy" who smiled at me engagingly. He scarcely ever spoke to me and was most reserved where I was concerned. If my answers sometimes amused him, he laughed less loudly at them than the others. I would have liked to know him. I have forgotten his very name.

I should now probably talk about the lady who sold delicacies and whose tiny shop was queerly placed in the wall dividing the pupils of the third and second forms from the classical and top forms. The shop was more like a sentry box, and the lady sat there, her right profile on the side of the second and third forms, her left profile presented to the attention of the rhetoricians and philosophers. Stout and pink-faced, she seldom spoke, but smiled with a supremely hypocritical expression, because she knew what was going on around her and that her business profited by it. Displayed on a board in front of this puzzling character were sweets and little cakes tantalizing to our gluttony. I alone did not give in to it. For one had to pass behind the lilac clumps to reach the sentry box and its good things. The little gang often went there. I saw the four boys crowding each other, taking ages to choose their sticky candy and rum-flavored cakes. I could also hear the pince-nez's yelps.

"Stop being so aus-teere!" he said one day for the hundredth time. "What are you afraid of? Come with us and get yourself something; two sous, for instance, will buy you a nut chocolate." I do not know why, but I went. For the first time I had a close view of the silent lady's profile and noticed that she watched us under her lashes, from the corner of her eye. "Now take your time," advised the pince-nez. "One shouldn't choose in a hurry, isn't that so, Ma-dame?" The lady did not reply, but her smile remained glued to her side face. I hesitated, I was eager for sweets and there were so many of them. . . . Leaning forward, I felt several hands traveling over my body. With a violent effort, I struggled free and went back to the playground. My heart beat fast.

For several weeks, the little gang left me alone.

I knew nothing about the strange disorder that the sexual instinct introduces into daily life. Things happened at home, the meaning of which escaped me.

The kitchen was vast and, although in the basement, well lighted by two large barred windows that faced each other. It was sometimes the stage of violent and mysterious scenes of which I heard echoes, while they remained incomprehensible, for I understood what it was all about only much later.

The housemaid, whose name was Gabrielle, was a very pretty, sprightly, vivacious girl—rose-colored. I stress the fact that to see her was to be reminded of a rose. Now, every morning, and that is why I remember her so clearly, the girl drank a bowlful of blood. The bowl she carried to her lips with such evident pleasure was thick and white and the blood of a sinister black, ringed with red. I was told that she had delicate lungs and needed this treatment. Horrified but fascinated too, I watched her drink. Her hand flat on her hip, she threw back her head to enjoy the treat.

More mysterious still was Berthe, the cook. With her prominent eyes, drooping airs and perpetual smile flavored with malice and a certain slyness, she reminded one of the angel on the Rheims cathedral, but a dubious angel who had gone to the bad. Very intelligent and shamelessly thievish, she had the gift of charming whomever she was bent on pleasing. If I am not mistaken, she came from Picardy, and I can still hear her wheedling peasant voice.

Between Gabrielle and the kind of animated antique statue called Teresina, she led a pleasant life broken by terrifying storms, for her tastes led her at times from one to the other, and her caprices caused ferocious jealousy. I no longer know where the three women slept; I have forgotten the disposition of a whole part of the villa. At any rate, I knew nothing of their love affairs and it would have required a great deal of time to enlighten me as to what it all was about.

Left to myself, I was given to fits of wild gaiety. I danced about my room singing tunes of my own invention. I imagined myself as another being and in another century. The words I uttered had no meaning whatever. Throwing myself breathless on the bed, I laughed for no reason, so happy to be alive that both my gesticulation and cries freed me, as though a load had been taken off my shoulders. By rolling this way and that, I felt a curious relief caused by weariness. I then sank into dreams of grandeur, resumed endlessly, like fragments of a long story of which I never lost the guiding thread. I was an all-powerful character, giving orders to slaves. My grandfather had had slaves. I had some too. One knelt before me. I was good, with unexpected fits of homicidal fury I killed and had people killed. Such moments of semimadness were not rare when I was alone, but no one knew of them, they were my secret.

Of all my sisters, Lucy, whom not a soul understood properly, was the one who tried to draw closest to me. She was unsociable and very silent, but wanted me for an ally against the others, the grownups; although nearly nineteen, she had remained very much of a child, a little grumpy, a little secretive, concealing her affection. Arms crossed like a man, she looked at me sometimes with a smile in which she wanted to show tenderness, but one nevertheless resembling that of a wild animal. Much later, much too late, I realized all the goodness hidden in the heart of a strange girl doomed to every failure and to every disappointment. She too had her own private world of which she said nothing. She even expressed herself in a way peculiarly her own, in a tongue bristling with queer words, a mixture of French and English. I believe that she knew herself to be almost incomprehensible and suffered from it. A word she had invented became current among us, and even now I occasionally use it when talking to my sisters: BUNZEEM. A bunzeem could mean anything untidy or that hampered you, or that complicated life, but what was strange was that this very convenient word indicated the most insignificant details as well as events of major importance. A lock of hair standing out on your brow was certainly a bunzeem that should at all costs be smoothed. The fiercest discussion between friends: bunzeem. A general strike: bunzeem. A bomb thrown into a grand duke's carriage: a considerable bunzeem, but a bunzeem just the same.

I can see Lucy frowning, her great, beautiful, tragic sea-green eyes, shrugging her shoulders furiously. "Now what's the matter, Lucy?" She walked away brusquely, murmuring: "Bunzeems!" and without anyone knowing why, she would burst out sobbing and run to her room where some mysterious sorrow consumed her. Yet, at times, she did not run away, she did something far sadder: putting her fists in her eyes, like a little girl, she cried noiselessly. May the dead keep their poor secrets and forgive the living!

I have mentioned a "continuous story." This is perhaps the time to say a few words about it. It was born, I do not know how, at the very back of my brain and kept me busy in my solitude. I found the last episode when I laid my head on the bolster, and I think it developed according to unknown laws during my sleep. To dreams of grandeur and omnipotence were added stories about murders. Thus I was the last-born of an enormous family scattered over the face of the earth. In order to cause the disappearance of everyone related to me closely or distantly, I undertook long and difficult journeys. My mother was the only one spared from this scrupulous slaughter. I was never caught in the act, for I possessed an inestimable advantage, the gift of invisibility. I realize that my gentle nature corresponded very little with the studied ferocity of this mental game, but I cannot conceal from myself that, under my apparent gentleness, there breathed and stirred extreme violence. With time, all this passed into my novels.

Since everything should be said (otherwise why write a book of this kind?) I never saw a mirror without my heart leaping with joy, and if I was alone I looked at myself lengthily and with passionate interest. My brother-in-law's sarcastic remarks no longer affected me at such moments, I forgot them, fascinated by the image I discovered, so it seemed to me, on each occasion for the first time. That was what made the whole thing so

145

queer. I stood before someone to whom I spoke noiselessly, intently observing the movement of lips forming words that I am sorry to be unable to recollect. Was it I speaking? I tried to imagine it was not, that it was someone else. I adored the face that smiled at me, and if it was at night I moved the lighted candle this way and that around my head, to see my eyes shine or to make unexpected shadows play over my brow and cheeks. Sometimes I assumed a terrible expression, frowning, lips parted, or else, standing perfectly motionless without batting an eyelash, I waited for the moment when, by staring hard, I obtained a slow duplication of my face, and it seemed to me then that behind my head, somewhere at the end of the room, another person appeared. I put down the candlestick and turned with a cry, but the room was of course empty. The game impressed me as being so dangerous that I did not indulge in it often. Did I not run the risk of attracting the devil? Yet there were evenings when I felt myself invited to attend a sort of mystery, by something more powerful than I. Whoever suspected these singular pastimes? No one, I think, and my mother less than anybody else.

I now come to a very strange scene that took place on a Thursday and the memory of which has pursued me for many a year. It struck me so much that I really believe I remember it down to the smallest detail. It was a fine morning in the winter of 1914-15, a few weeks before my mother's death. She was ill that day, with one of the sick headaches she suffered from so often. I knew that no one should make a noise in the staircase, and I was in my room when someone came to say that she wanted to speak to me.

Her room was on the first floor and the sun came in through three windows, but Mamma's bed was in a corner where the light could not trouble her, even if the curtains were not drawn. I can very clearly see her brass bed with bars at its head and foot. My mother lay on her back, her graying hair spread like a wave over the whiteness of the pillow. In a voice I knew so well and that hurt me, for it was her distant voice, her suffering voice, she told me to close the door. I obeyed and stood, my hands on the bed's brass bar, already a little frightened by something indefinably tragic that showed in my mother's features. She let a few seconds go by, then asked whether Berthe talked to me sometimes alone. I said no. Did she make me little presents? No. (How weak her voice was, and from what a distance it reached me! Yet there was only the length of the bed between us.) Another few seconds went by. At last, she announced that she was going to tell me something. It was about her brother, my Uncle Willie. "He died long before you were born. I have never spoken to you about him, I couldn't, I loved him too much. He was handsomer than you."

At that moment she drew the sheet well over her face and gave a long moan of grief that made me start. "Mamma," I said, "you mustn't speak to me about him if it makes you feel too badly." She pulled down the sheet suddenly, as though my cowardice shamed her. "Yes," she said in a changed voice. "You must know. A woman fell in love with him. Do you understand? No one knew that they saw each other. On account of her, on account of that woman, do you hear, he fell ill. He could not be cured. He died very young."

I kept a horrified silence. What did this story mean, and why did my mother talk to me in such a fashion? Tears glistened on her cheeks. She suddenly raised her head and cried out. A few hairs, caught in the bars of the bed, had been torn away. She looked at me for an instant and said: "I want you to promise never to talk to any of the servants alone." I promised. She tried to smile and told me to leave her. I went out, very much upset, but having understood nothing except that I should never again laugh and chatter as I sometimes did with Berthe, with Gabrielle, with Teresina.

147

I knew nothing whatever about my Uncle Willie, whose very existence had been revealed to me only that morning. Now, as I had a carefree nature and, moreover, had not grasped a word of the story, the mere joy of living made me forget on the instant. It was only very long afterward that it occurred to me to ask for explanations, when my mother had been dead for years. I learned that my Uncle Willie lived in Savannah and was, as my mother said, remarkably handsome and that a servant had fallen in love with him. No one could tell me anything about their liaison, except that the temptress was syphilitic. When the disease broke out in Uncle Willie, he was cared for according to the methods of the period (this happened in 1892 or '93). Was his family informed about it? I do not think so. The fact remains that in 1895 his health was so much impaired that it was decided (a strange decision) that a journey to Europe would do him good. No one must have realized. . . . The poor boy must have concealed the nature of his disease and lied.

At that time, my parents and their children lived in Le Havre. It was my mother who went to meet Willie at the boat, but he was so much changed that she could scarcely recognize him, and there is also this dreadful fact: he had become almost an idiot.

The shock was terrible, and my mother never completely recovered from it. She was about to bring Lucy into the world and the latter, I feel sure, underwent the consequences of the effect on my mother's nervous system. What became of my uncle? I do not know. I think he was sent back to America and died shortly afterward.

A tragedy for which she was unprepared was such a sorrow to my mother that I can only imagine it with the deepest sadness. She had not been told that her brother was ill, and she loved him violently, wholeheartedly. Never again did she mention his name, except on that morning in 1914 when she drew her sheet over her face to conceal her distress.

So now, everything is far clearer. I can better understand a

148

mother, terror-stricken by an unforgettable ordeal, watching over her boy, looking out with horror for the first signs of sensuality, a sensuality that God had cursed in the person of her brother. I understand, without a smile, the bread-knife. I understand what was gloomy in Lucy's nature, she who received at one blow a weight of melancholy bordering on despair.

When I say that my mother's words were quickly effaced by the joy of living, I am wrong, for one sentence stuck in my mind, I admit it to my shame: "Your Uncle Willie was handsomer than you." Handsomer than I! I asked myself seriously if that was possible, and I also asked it of my mirror. What a monument of pride I was getting to be—without in the least knowing it—under the cloak of great modesty. . . . Today, questioning myself about a past so strangely remote, I realize that there was not a trace of sensuality in this self-adoration, because *I loved myself pure*. My mother had passed on to me her horror of impurity, and the sort of fascination this horror exercised over her, the moment her last-born was involved.

Now, my mirror reassured me. I was as easy to reassure as a lover about the love of the one he loves. The things I describe and that seem just a trifle ridiculous, I think many a boy and girl have felt, but will not admit, or will not remember them. Adolescence is narcissistic. I was to such a powerful degree that seeing a face that looked at me with such serious attention, I imagined that had it been able to leave its frame and talk to me as one to another, I would have died of joy. And that is the truth.

I must say, however, that this foolish self-worship remained at the hazy, unformulated stage of certain passions peculiar to that age, and that I was completely unconscious of my gigantic stupidity. I add that in my brother-in-law's presence I felt ugly, but once alone, not at all so. I sang and gesticulated gravely before my mirror in honor of the inaccessible being who copied my attitudes and my voice. I never looked at myself naked, nakedness being impure, and finally believed, in a vague way, that my

149

entire person was one of those only to be seen dressed and never to be touched, under any circumstance. My mother was the only one who could kiss me, and I grumbled a little when my sisters gave me their customary marks of affection.

From there to imagining that I could never be wrong was only a step. I was ripe for many a fault, pride calling for downfalls, but there was also a more serious idea that did not come from me, a crazy idea established in me for a very long time and that, with years, took on extraordinary weight: "Wrong ceases to be wrong as soon as you do it, *because it is you.*" Because it is I! How many times have I repeated this sentence that separated me from God! I did not yet do what is called wrong, but was apparently lacking in a certain kind of moral sense. And then, there were too many things I did not know. My religious education had been interrupted for more than two years.

I have no idea of what went on in my poor mother's mind. Her interior distress must have been very great, but how can one know what troubled her? No doubt she still talked to me of religion and with as much gravity as in the past, but in a rather more general manner. She told me that I must love God. I loved Him, since she loved Him. That I should not do wrong. I did nothing wrong then, I had not even the least idea of what an evil thought could be. And pressing me to her, she told me to thank the Lord for everything I had received. I said my prayers faithfully.

My efforts to recollect clearly the last weeks of 1914 are very strenuous, as though I might come across a secret, but they bring me next to nothing before the very last week of all, which was terrible.

I remember, however, that we sometimes called on American friends who lived in a charming villa bordered by large, old-fashioned gardens, Mr. and Mrs. C. and their two children Natalie and George. Natalie was about my age and strikingly beautiful.

My eyes were constantly attracted toward a face that pursued me for years as being one of the most perfect to be seen. An extremely sweet expression, a soft, fleshy mouth, skin white as a flower, there was something marvelous in all that for me and I stared at her without the least embarrassment, being unconscious that my admiration might be indiscreet. She smiled goodnaturedly at me with a sort of heavy innocence.

Her brother, whose intelligence everyone noticed, and who may have been a year younger or older than I, had a quite different appearance, for he should have been very handsome, but having, as a child, been knocked over by a large dog and badly hurt, he remained a cripple. A surgical appliance enabled him to stand almost straight, and he walked as best he could. I never saw him without a pang and must say that his poor, twisted body frightened me a little. He had the active brain of a cripple and argued sharply with me. Being proud, I always wanted to be right and, without quite knowing what I was doing, tried to humiliate a boy who suddenly turned into an adversary because he refused to give in to my arguments, but what did we talk about? I do not remember.

I used to go to see him in his room. Seated at a table, his beautiful face shining with light and resting on his fist, he talked—ah, how could I have forgotten?—he talked almost entirely about airplanes. He drew them endlessly, he made tiny ones out of cardboard and paper. Because his wretched legs played him false, he lived above the clouds. Leaving the earth that had wounded him, he flew toward the sky day and night, for all his dreams were made up of those prodigious leaps into the blue.

I could not quite see what was admirable in his enthusiasm, proof being that on beginning this page, I did not think of it, believing I had forgotten all about it, and it is only at present that I understand the beauty of a life tending toward an impossible goal. I own, to my shame, that I talked disdainfully of what I considered a mania in little George. I was too young and too violently enamored of myself to guess that the cripple, by freeing himself in this way, surpassed me by far. He laughed with joy, and when I talked to him about books, to make him feel my superiority, he made kindly fun of me with a good-natured smile. Had he flung his inkstand in my face, I would have richly deserved it. He never complained. He died a few years later, bearing away with him the dreams of which I understood nothing.

I have mentioned him, not so much on account of his airplanes that had slipped my memory, as because I thought him a Protestant, like the rest of his family. Neither he nor I ever broached the subject of religion, one that did not interest him apparently (and yet, who knows?), and so far as I was concerned, my mother alone had the right to discuss it with me. Coming from anyone else, I would have found it intolerable. Religion belonged to my mother. The idea of saying even a few words on religion to my father or my sisters would have seemed impossible. I would not have dreamed of talking about it to George, but at the bottom of his heart he was probably far more religious than I, considering how bravely he accepted all the pain and humiliating disadvantages that robbed him of his youth.

However, my mother said something one day that made me quiver with horror. I remember that all of us, my father, my sisters, and I, were standing at the foot of the staircase when she said, looking gravely at us: "Edward, we never go to church and Christmas is coming. I think we should bring the children together, with little George and Natalie, to sing hymns."

Sing hymns with little George! Oh, that was something I could not do! The mere thought was dreadfully embarrassing. I do not know what my father answered; the only thing I keep in mind is my mother's idea. There was a void in her life and she suffered from it. As I think I have already said, the only Protestant church at Le Vésinet was a Calvinist chapel. We were all to go there soon, much against our will.

To my great relief, the plan for a pious gathering was forgotten.

If I am so worried by the fact that little George was interested in aviation and that I had forgotten about it, how could I not be worried by the suspicion of everything that escapes me? Will I ever know what took place in my mother's mind at the end of her life? More and more often, she quoted St. John's words about God's love. "God is love. . . . Beloved, let us love one another." It was as though the whole of religion was summed up by the single word "love," and who could believe that my mother was not right? It was a kind of spiritual testament that she bequeathed me. "Though your sins be as scarlet, they shall be as white as snow." She left me, as a sort of viaticum, these words from the Old and New Testaments.

I have said that she latterly became far more silent. The idea of the war was unbearable to her, and there was something else that she probably knew: my father was on the verge of becoming a Catholic. Was it discussed between them? And what did she think of it? I have already mentioned her conversations with a religious of whom she asked explanations concerning Catholicism, but nothing definite resulted and I will probably never know how she was spiritually disposed when she died.

Two days before that Christmas of 1914, my sister Retta was sitting on a sofa in the dining room, looking out of the window; she called my sister Anne and told her to turn her eyes toward the garden's large iron gate. Men were draping it in black. One of them, standing on a ladder, was fastening the heavy mourning hangings that another man held out at arm's length. "Do you see them?" asked Retta. All that Anne saw was the big garden, death-stricken by winter and empty. "Just look!" But Anne did not see. Retta saw.

The day after Christmas happened to be a Sunday. That day,

after lunch, I sat by my mother on the dining-room sofa and told her once again how much I loved her. I snuggled close to her and she had her arm around my shoulder. I felt so happy, by her. "I love you more and more," I said. And her answer was to squeeze my hand. That was our last exchange, a farewell. In that big room, beautiful to me because it was home, I leaned against my mother and laughed. She wore the large gray shawl whose odor I liked so much, and on the table I saw a silver fruit bowl and in it a few oranges remaining from lunch, of a dazzling color on a rather dark winter day. Those are the last precise memories of a happiness so deep that I wonder if many children have known anything approaching it.

A little less than an hour later, I heard a cry coming from the drawing room where my mother happened to be. Almost at once, a new presence, immense and terrible, was felt in the house. People hurried to and fro. Someone carried a basin of steaming water to the drawing room. I wanted to go there and saw my mother seated on a sofa between two of my sisters. Her bare feet were plunged in the basin and the expression of pain on her face made her almost unrecognizable to me. She motioned me away and I took refuge in my room. Through the window, I saw the lake, motionless between the black trees. Nothing had changed. Everything was as usual, but my heart pounded.

I do not know very clearly what happened afterward, except that I was made to sleep that night in a small library next to my mother's room and remember that around nine o'clock, just as I was sinking into sleep, I heard a dreadful sound that was like that of a giant's breathing.

At dawn, one of my sisters put her hand on my shoulder and told me to dress and go for the doctor. I obeyed without understanding, I did everything I was asked to do, I went for my bicycle and crossed the garden where, in the wan light, I could scarcely make out the lawns and the iron gate. A moment later, I stood at the doctor's house and rang the front doorbell. A window opened. He leaned out, recognized me, and said: "I'll come right away." The fact that he asked for no explanations seemed more ominous to me than anything else, but I was living in a nightmare, a nightmare where I recognized nothing because, in truth, I was entering another world.

Having returned with the doctor, I went to the little library to be as near as possible to my mother. I had no precise idea of what was taking place on the other side of the partition. On a bookshelf, two or three goldfish swam round and round in their bowl. The sun was rising in the great melancholy garden, beyond which shone the waters of the lake. Was not everything as usual? Was it not possible to cling to that idea? After a while I went downstairs close behind the doctor, who had just left my mother's room. As we walked together to the gate, he said, with a kind of gentle brutality: "It's all over, you know. There is no hope."

I opened the gate and he shook my hand. I had not understood what he said. Whom was he talking about? I went in. The table was set for breakfast, but the dining room was empty, although it was eight o'clock. What to do with oneself? That was the minute when I felt how painful it can be to have a body. I cannot express myself otherwise. For there are moments when one does not know how to use one's body, where to put it, what to do with it. To walk about, come, go, sit down, get up, nothing else is possible and the weight remains, the weight of that strange, inhabited mass. Inhabited by something that is more our own self than anything else and that foresees too great a sorrow.

I tiptoed up to the threshold of the room where, the day before at that hour, I went to say good morning to my mother. The door stood ajar. I moved back. My father's voice reached me, not his everyday one, but a strangely gentle voice that was like a child's. "This is Retta . . . This is Lucy . . ." One would have thought he was introducing them, as he used to, when he presented his children to guests, but his voice had been so different then, jolly, happy . . .

Fear gripped me. I took refuge in my sister Anne's room. No one was there. A few steps led me to the window with the red curtains, and it was there that God broke my heart. For the first time in my life, I learned what it was to suffer. I understood, I understood everything. Without moving, without tears, in the deepest silence, I received the shock of death.

I remember that the room was a little dark, beautified by those blood-colored draperies. Outside, everything was still, everything was dead. The sky, the trees, the stones looked cold. It was like a picture where nothing moves and I myself, like a figure in a picture, did not move. There was nothing to do but to stand there without in the least understanding what you had at first thought you had understood and that had no meaning. I emerged from this strange moment very different from what I still was at dawn. Someone was born in me, not in tears, for I was far beyond tears, but in despair.

Lord, where were You at that moment? I felt neither Your presence nor Your sweetness, I found myself in a dreadful solitude. It seemed as though a diabolical machine hewed the air around me to shut me into myself, for I suffocated with grief, but I did not cry.

When I was able to break this kind of spell woven by sorrow, I went down to the dining room, where I found my sister Retta sitting on a sofa. Lucy sat by her, doubled up and sobbing. I dropped down on Retta's left and she, so mysterious, so taciturn, suddenly cried out loudly and opened her arms: "Come to me, my poor little ones, my little children!" I clung close to her, but Lucy moved away. I saw in Retta a new and unknown person. She was very pale, her eyes seemed to me huge, and her long black hair hung on either side of her face. She had never shown me any real tenderness, but all of a sudden, on the shoulder of this lovely and secretive girl, I sought the place I had had the day before, on my mother's shoulder.

Eleanor came in like a shadow, then a great noise of voices

drew us all to the foot of the stairs and I saw my father in his gray dressing gown, his arms raised in an attitude I had never seen him take, for everything was new that morning. When he saw me, he hastened down, moaning: "She was so proud of you!" And taking me in his arms, he hugged me.

That day was one of the most singular I have ever lived through. It seemed as though the house were empty. I do not know where I remained, I do not know where my father was, where my sisters were. I only knew where my mother was and I avoided her room, though all I could think of was that room. I heard doors open and shut too softly, as if one feared to wake the dead. The dead. Mamma had become the dead, and the day before, she was with us, laughing. From the top floor where I ran for shelter, I listened to the house noises, I waited. There was nothing in me but silence and an inexpressible solitude that I will never forget. At one instant I had understood, but for hours since then I no longer understood. I did not know what a dead person was. I wanted to see my mother again, and this idea, once lodged in my head, no longer left me. Now, I knew where my mother was, but I wanted to see her alone.

On the top floor of the house, I leaned over the banisters and watched, my eyes fixed on my mother's door. In the silence, my head buzzed. I waited, the wooden handrail cut into my stomach. How present those minutes are to me, with all that loaded them with the future! I do not know how long I stayed there, but I next see myself turning the doorknob with the wariness of a thief, and I went in.

The sun shone gaily into the room and everything was orderly. On the larger of the two beds, my father's, I saw my mother lying, her eyes closed. All fear immediately left me. I had feared something and I simply saw the one I loved. For a very long time, I stood by her. If anything could have troubled me, it was not her stillness, but mine. Why was it that I did not move?

She and I were like figures in a painting—once more I had that strange impression—and nothing seemed real. I vainly attempted to tell myself that my mother appeared to be sleeping. A sleeper breathes. In the same way, I vainly whispered: "Mamma!" She did not hear, I knew it and I also knew that she had become another woman, not the one who used to speak to me. She no longer thought the same things, she no longer saw me, and the more I looked at her, the more different she seemed. She had become someone as majestic as a queen, separated from me by great spaces, absorbed in a meditation that remained secret. I whispered once again: "Mamma!" but in such a low voice that even if she had been awake, she would probably not have heard. I was afraid of disturbing her. That was it exactly: I was afraid of disturbing someone deep in thought. I believe that the idea that I stood in the presence of a dead person never entered my mind. I stood before an unknown person who had Mamma's features, still as stone, but who did not frighten me. Death had entered the house a few hours earlier, but was there no longer. After a moment, I pressed my lips to my mother's brow and went out.

Where were the prayers one says on such occasions, where was religion? I do not know. It seems to me I gave no thought to all that. I was not even sad, I was amazed.

I returned to my room and glanced out of the window. What a fine day, and how peaceful everything around me was! My mother was not dead. That is all I had understood.

A quarter of an hour later, I went down to see Mamma again. How many times have I returned in memory to that room! The stairs creak under my feet. Once more I hold the doorknob in my hand, and although I am very careful, it makes a grinding noise, like a tiny cry. I go in. She is there, she is still thinking. Her hair has not been smoothed, it streams over the pillow. She looks more severe than usual, but younger. Her wrinkles have disappeared completely, she is very beautiful, I did not know that she was so beautiful. By dint of looking at her, I have the impression that she is drifting away on an invisible river, and yet she does not move. Her hands are placed alongside her body, the hands that washed the children's linen and that stroked my head. Everything is so strange this morning that it cannot be true. To die—what does that mean? Mamma is not dead, I was right. She died days and days later. We saw only too well that she did not come back.

When she heard the news, my sister Mary returned at once from Italy. She was given the room I occupied on the top floor, and from that day on I slept in the brass bed where my mother had died. For me this was not a source of fear, but an extraordinary comfort. It is difficult to find words to express such things, but it seemed to me that when I lay there, she was less absent. I saw what she had seen, I became to a certain degree herself, and amidst a sadness that I give up attempting to describe, but that never made a tear roll down my face, she was with me once more. One morning I noticed a few hairs caught in one of the round screw-bolts that topped the bars of the bed. I immediately remembered the cry of pain my mother had given in raising her head when she talked to me about my Uncle Willie. My heart beat with emotion, and taking these hairs, I rolled them around a piece of paper on which I wrote the date, December 27th. And that is all I have left of her. Of the woman who hugged me to her, whose cheek I felt against mine, just that, a few gray hairs.

The days went by. My father slept in the same room as I, in the big wooden bed that had always been his. The door of this room was left open so that when he came to bed, an hour after me, he avoided waking me. One night, just as I was going to sleep and had turned my face to the wall, I heard someone enter and kneel at the foot of my bed. It was my sister Mary. My legs were doubled up, and near them I felt the weight of her head and arms. She remained thus for a long time, and I wondered what prayers she could be saying (mine were short). I had heard that she had become a Catholic, in Rome, but the word did not convey much to my mind, arousing nothing but the idea of incense and Latin chanting. After a long time, Mary got up and bent over me. She stayed in that attitude for a few seconds and went away.

At the lycée there were the scholars, the playground, the cries once more. All that seemed horrible to me. One day when I waited with a line of boys at the refectory door, overcome by sorrow—but I did not cry—I turned to one of my schoolmates and murmured: "Mamma is dead." If only I could remember that boy's name and face. He moved back slightly, as though I had struck him, then silently came close to me and I think his lips brushed my cheek, but that perhaps is only what I would have wished. All I remember clearly is the sort of impulsive movement of sympathy he had for me.

I have a memory of the beginning of 1915 that I particularly wish to fix. I am in a horse carriage with my brother-in-law. The carriage is not an ordinary cab. It is all black and varnished outside, and the inside (can a child forget such things?) is wonderfully padded and upholstered. We drive up the almost deserted Boulevard des Italiens. It is like a dream. Where are we going? Rue du Louvre, where my father has his office. Why are we going there? That, I have completely forgotten. My brother-in-law is talking to me. Goodness, how British he is! His black overcoat is admirably cut, his cream silk muffler, his suède gloves . . . I do not even dare look at him, feeling so ugly by his side, so badly dressed, so inferior. . . . He talks to me of something or other. Mamma is no longer here. Everything is lost and everything is a matter of indifference to me. All of a sudden my brother-in-law clears his throat and looks embarrassed. He falters. "I know you are grieving," he says gently.

"So did I when my mother died. And I was very fond of yours. . . . ." Can it be he, talking to me so? I do not move. He goes on and from time to time coughs a little as though to apologize for saying embarrassing things, he even has the kind of stammer I have heard in so many men of his blood, when a few steps have to be taken toward the forbidden region of sentiment. He is offering me his heartfelt sympathy. I would willingly kiss him, if there were not something frightful about the very idea. I do not move, I remain silent, but with a beating heart.

As I think I have mentioned, I traveled from Le Vésinet to Paris in a second-class compartment. This was almost always full of evil-smelling people, but I forgot all that rather quickly as I lost myself in a book. During that sad month of January 1915, I read the story of Chateaubriand's *Atala* in a two-sous edition. I do not know what a boy of fourteen would think of it today, but it enraptured me. Its vivid beauty of imagery carried me to another world, and when I read the last pages I wept so copiously, although silently, that tears rolled down on the book. I might be told that, not having shed a tear when a real grave opened to bury what I held as most precious on earth, I was showing a great deal of sorrow for a fictitious death, and this is difficult to account for. I can only say what is. I only discovered my mother's death gradually, because I did not entirely believe in it. I was months in understanding it. . . .

Nunc animi opus, Aeneas, nunc pectore firmo. . . .

It is here, it is now that I need firmness to continue this narrative, but you must be silent or tell everything, if you wish to make yourself understood.

At home, there was no one now to talk to me about religion. My sister Retta, who tried to take my mother's place, said to me sometimes: "I hope you read your Bible." That was all. She came to wake me in the morning, holding a candlestick, and its flame lit up her lovely, rather tragic face, the first one I saw as day began. Like Mamma, she made my tea and kept me company, without saying a word. There was something in her presence so grave and yet so good that I could not help looking at her tenderly, and she stared silently at me with her great black eyes. "I hope you're careful when you cross the streets," she said. Mamma had used that sentence. Retta wished to continue the voice that was still. I dared not kiss her and she never asked me to. At night, she waited till I was in bed, then tucked me in. As she pulled the sheet over my shoulder, she touched my head lightly with her hand, and that was all. "Sleep well."

What happened at the lycée was very different. I am sorry to write what follows, because for me it meant a world that ended, and ended shabbily, my mother no longer being with us. The four boys I have mentioned gave me very little respite, except the one who was lost, according to what I had been told, and who looked at me from a certain distance with his violet-ringed eyes. The glib-tongued one of the gang, the pince-nez, took me aside one day and asked me if I knew what pleasure was. I said no, that I did not even know what he meant by the word. He explained it to me in terms of affected modesty and great bursts of laughter. "I hope I'm not shocking you. You are so austeere!"

That was one of the most mysterious moments in my life. The boy did not shock me, but I did not understand what he meant. The idea that it was sinful to listen to such things did not even cross my mind. Whereas they should have spoken very loudly, Pure and Impure were mute. Why? I have no answer to give.

My schoolmate resumed his explanations with great patience. The other three boys kept out of the way, knowing very well what we were talking about. The one I mentally called the brute looked at me anxiously.

Why was there no one that night to talk to me, to put me on my guard? Did nothing warn me that I was committing an error? I think I can answer no. I did not know what sin was. Of course I had been told about sin, of what was pure and impure, but never in a precise fashion. My mother, I have grounds to suppose, imagined that I knew enough on that score to avoid doing anything forbidden; she thought that I must have known what all boys of my age knew, and the extraordinary fact is that I knew nothing at all. As to the gesture in question, I did not connect it with any known offense. "That's what men do," my schoolmate said the next day. "Now, you're a man."

The most singular part of the whole story is that having committed the act, weeks went by without my having any idea of repeating it. At present, I cannot account for this. Something there escapes me. I retained the confused memory of a minute of stupor and dizziness. I was far from suspecting that from now on, there existed in my life a before and an after, and that what I had behind me was what a seventeenth-century author called the Lost Country. The gesture was humanly impossible to isolate. Its repetition was only a matter of time. Any priest would have shown me in a few minutes the danger toward which I ran, but I lived surrounded by Christians who remained silent, because one should not speak of certain things to a young boy. Such were the ideas of the times. What would have happened if someone had warned me? Would my life have been different? I am inclined to think so. I could be told that I am reasoning about a very simple thing and that it would have happened sooner or later, but that it happened "later" and not "sooner" had its importance. I am convinced that so long as my mother was on this earth, her presence guarded me in a way that neither she nor I could suspect.

With a subtleness that surprises me a little today, for he was not fifteen, my comrade with the pince-nez changed his manner of talking to me, in an imperceptible way that slowly brought me to see the world somewhat as he saw it. The word "austere" vanished from the boy's vocabulary and I became the object of compliments all the more agreeable since so far I had never received any. Yet the poison was only given me drop by drop, for one had to show patience with a being inexperienced as I was. There was sly laughter, and I kept silent. The brute said very little to me. I thought I saw anger and even hatred in his eyes. For that reason, I found the Allies very slow in recapturing Noyon. Had I been less innocent, I would have guessed that the brute was making schemes he dared not express.

The day came finally, at the beginning of spring, when the three conspirators suggested taking me to the station. I accepted without hesitation. Only the one who had been called the "done-for guy" refused to get mixed up in the affair. Need I say that I suspected nothing? At the Henri-Martin station we waited for my train, and when it came in, the pince-nez quickly chose an empty compartment. Unbeknownst to me, my companions had taken tickets (it was not difficult to draw away my attention, and their platform tickets had miraculously changed into train tickets). Hardly were they settled in the train when they behaved most strangely; two of them stood on the seats and glanced continually through the small glass panes that gave on neighboring compartments, and every three or four seconds they jumped down and came to reassure me. That was what I could not understand. Reassure me? Why? I did not budge and, facing me, the brute stared at me with eyes that started from his head. The base and mysterious gluttony I read in his face changed him in my mind. It was not an adversary I had before me, but a slave. "Quick! Quick!" cried the boys, jumping down from the seat in a sort of panic. Then the brute stretched his hand toward me with a beseeching smile. I remained absolutely motionless, motionless with the stupid immobility of an idol, since that is what I had become for these lunatics.

To see the scene in all its sadness and in all its ugliness, one should imagine the compartment, badly lit by gas, the seats covered with navy-blue cloth, the smell of cold smoke that clung to the partitions, the grinding of wheels, the boys' terror, for they feared that neighboring travelers might glance through the small glass panes. I need not enter into details concerning what happened, the triteness of which had something about it that was both gloomy and mechanical.

All this lasted only three or four minutes, perhaps less. I have the impression that we parted at the following station. However that may be, the three boys seemed eager to disappear as soon as possible, and from that day on they ceased hanging around me in the lycée playground. The compliments ceased. Spring came and the clumps of lilac flowered. I forgot everything. A scene that now seems so striking to me, faded from my memory for many a long year. I had no feeling of having committed a sin and, most remarkable to say, I did not have the least evil thought for several months.

As the brute took no further interest in me, I ceased to worry over the fate of Noyon. In a certain way, I once more became what I was before my mother's death. Sensuality no longer counted at all in my life. It was around that period that I became friends with a boy as grave as he was stupid and whom I took pleasure in humiliating a little from time to time, for I judged him inferior to me on all levels. His nonentity flattered my pride, which rejoiced at small expense. At the same time (these inconsistencies are not easy to explain), I laid myself out to play the fool with this schoolmate of mine, to talk like him, to relate ponderously artless little stories, to laugh idiotically and, like him, to roll a lock of hair around my forefinger as a sign of indecision. Why? That remains a mystery. It never occurred to me that I was not perhaps as attractive or as gifted as I was beginning to fancy, and I believe that what drew me to the boy was his innocence, one far deeper than mine had ever been.

Once more the words "pure" and "impure" trembled on my lips. If I speak of things that may seem insignificant, it is because they assumed an extraordinary meaning before the end of the year.

May came, and I changed suddenly.

Great silence reigned at home. My brother-in-law and his wife had gone to Genoa, where they settled until 1940. Anne and Retta were Red Cross nurses at Saint-Germain-en-Laye. Was my sister Mary with us? That I am unable to remember. At any rate, there remained my sister Lucy, who scarcely spoke after my mother's death, and my father, who was to be seen only at dinner. He too withdrew into a silence that he sometimes attempted to dispel and in his gentle voice told us stories about the other war, that of his childhood. He occasionally played cards with Lucy or, head in hands, he pored over a book placed on the dining-room table. What book? Probably a work proving we were right to secede from the Union (there were whole rows of such volumes in our library). My mother's absence created a dreadful void. I felt it more and more and fled a grief that grew in me almost day by day as I became a man. I realized that to wait for my mother's return was a dream of childhood. She would never come back, that was all. And yet, she did come back, but that I could not foresee, nor in what manner her return would be accomplished.

I walked under the trees, in the radiance of spring. The sun shone through the leaves and birds sang, but there was no longer any joy on earth. I wondered how I could ever have rolled on the grass. Monsieur Tisserand came every Thursday to give me a lesson and the seamstress came the same day, because they had to be helped as they were in my mother's time, but everything seemed futile. If Mary was with us, of which I am not sure, she must have spent her days in Paris before going back to Italy. All our lives were devastated because we lacked the person who, I do not know how, used to gather us all around her. For my part, it seemed as though I saw her everywhere, in the armchair where she fell asleep, at the window from which she leaned, shading her eyes with her hand, because the sun hurt her, but that was only my melancholy delusion. I envied my little nephew who, at the age of four, had really seen her after her death; one day when he was going down the stairs too quickly, she appeared on one of the steps to say to him, smiling: "*Doucement,* darling!"

I no longer slept in the room where she had died. I returned to mine on the top floor. That was my realm, the sphere of my dreams and of the "continuous story." Even on the finest days, the light was faint, but from the little window I saw the lake, and all sorts of thoughts that I could not manage to express rose in my mind. With strange outbursts of feeling, I looked endlessly at the sheet of water between the trees because it helped me, I do not know how, to recover my childhood. I imagined that everything was once more the way it used to be before our misfortune. I read Ronsard's poems and repeated them under my breath until my head swam, but boredom was creeping into my life.

As to my religion, it was reduced to the prayer I said at night, to reading a chapter of the Bible every day, and also to a thing that I can reveal only with some hesitation: my sister Eleanor had made me a present of her plaster crucifix and I had hung it in my room, although a Protestant, but in sinful moments—whose tyranny I ended by loathing—I took down the crucifix. Now in this secret sentence passed on my behavior there was the germ of something I did not suspect, and that is why I speak of it here. It is certain that I loved Christ as a living, present person. I firmly believed that He was there and that when I did wrong, thrown back on the bed like a murdered corpse, I had been bewitched by the dark angel. How dismal everything seemed to me afterward! The room, the days that followed one after the other . . .

Yet I became conscious of an inner change. I felt more intelligent, stronger. The desire to write pursued me without cease, but to write what? A history of France, a great book that would surpass all other books. The thing was to excel, to be first, to outdistance everybody, to dazzle. My ingenuousness being as great as my pride, I immediately began with ancient Gaul. I did not work in my room. The room was haunted by evil. I went somewhere else, I went down to my mother's room. Thanks to three windows, it was flooded with sunshine. There, I felt secure from myself and wrote all the afternoon.

I have forgotten to say that it was the summer when I wore trousers for the first time, laying aside forever the semilong breeches that came down below the knee. Thus, in my own eyes, I became a man. My hair was no longer close-cropped, I wore it brushed flat against my skull, without a parting, in the style set by South Americans before the war. I was distant, taciturn, locked up within myself and made even gloomier by faults that had so little relation to pleasure, for I was cold by temperament: the sight of a human face never roused the slightest desire in me. The world was empty. I did not realize that my selfishness had emptied it. For me, my neighbor remained someone unimaginable. No doubt my neighbor's suffering upset and even terrified me when I witnessed it, but nevertheless, I faced him without a gesture, and yet . . . A memory returns to me. As all the hospitals in Paris were full at that time, parts of certain lycées were requisitioned. Thus the first floor of ours harbored wounded soldiers who had not found room elsewhere. The more lightly wounded walked about the grounds in their horizon-blue uniforms and we were ordered to salute them, which, by the way, visibly embarrassed them. Above our heads, when we were in class, people came and went. One day my blood turned to ice on hearing a terrible cry followed by a sort

168

of galloping. We were given no explanation, but that was what we had above us. For me, that cry represented war. I supposed that a wounded soldier, suffering beyond endurance, had jumped out of bed to make his escape. I was frightened. The world opened before me, I could no longer deny its existence, it was there, like a hell. That was in the autumn of 1915. At home, on Thursday, I continued my foolish history of France with the help of a textbook by Seignobos and Larousse's small dictionary.

I think it was in October 1915 that one of the most singular events in my life occurred.

It should be explained that next to my mother's room (I always called it so, although my father occupied it) was a bathroom giving on the Boulevard Carnot. It was a very sunny little room in a corner of which stood a chest of drawers with brass handles; on top of it was a rather peculiar piece of furniture, a kind of long box, open on one side, with red and green striped curtains. By drawing aside these curtains, you saw my father's white shirts, carefully piled one on top of the other, with large, well-starched cuffs. Need I say that in my eyes these shirts did not offer the slightest interest. My father lived in a world absolutely foreign to mine. I respected him greatly but had nothing to say to him. We sometimes talked about the weather, or else he summed up in a few words his opinion of the morning communiqué, or from time to time a memory of America came back to him, the America of his youth. I listened silently to a voice that age and sorrow were beginning to muffle slightly and then said a word or two to prove myself attentive, but between us existed, not constraint, but a lack of intimacy that made me ill at ease. That he loved me, I did not doubt for a moment and I was sensitive to a goodness that distinguished him so much from other men. The fact is, however, that we did not know how to talk to each other. Was that due to the forty-three years between us? I felt myself unlike him and he could not find his way to me. All my memories of him are those of a rather awkward affection and a certain shyness on his part as well as on mine. "Hello, boy!" he would say when we met and he smiled at me, but his big chestnut-colored eyes had lost their gaiety since my mother's death. I loved him, in my strange way, I wanted above all not to offend him in any manner, to correspond exactly to all he expected of me. Yet what a distance there was between this respectful, rather stiff fondness and the transports I used to have for my mother! To my mother, I said "I love you!" a dozen times a day. Could I have said "I love you" to my father? Our attitude to one another was more or less that of two strangers.

One Thursday afternoon, when at work at something or other in his room, perhaps at my history of France, it suddenly occurred to me to get up and go to the bathroom. I began thinking of my mother and it seemed as though, in some inexplicable way, she was present. How is it possible to describe impressions that words can only indicate so clumsily? No sooner does one attempt to speak of them than they seem to vanish in a sort of mist, beyond reach of speech. I waited for a moment before the piece of furniture where my father kept his shirts, then, through a sudden inspiration, I drew aside one of the red and green curtains. Under a shirt, half concealed, slipped there like something that was to be kept to oneself, a book attracted my eye.

It was an abridgment of the whole doctrine of Catholicism, for the use of recent converts, by Cardinal Gibbons, of Baltimore. I began reading it. Immediately? I do not know, I no longer remember, but what I can assert is that within ten or fifteen days I had devoured the entire book. From the first word to the last, I believed all that these pages contained, I believed it strongly and joyfully. It seemed as if, when I was dying of thirst, fresh cool water were given me from an inexhaustible spring, a delectable water dispensing joy. What I wanted to know, I knew at last, what I wanted to believe was lavished on me, I only regretted there was not more of it. That water, more intoxicating than wine, transformed me at one sweep, I became a Catholic by intent, without any hesitation whatever, in an immense leap toward God.

Having finished the book, I reread it, it seems to me, several times, then I had to tell my father of my new frame of mind. I probably did not waver long. I felt in me the soul of a neophyte ready to face a Roman prefect. Why should I have been afraid of my father? I went to him and, trampling shyness and pride, told him that I had found the book under his shirts and wanted to become a Catholic. He smiled and laid his hand on my shoulder. "I myself have been a Catholic since last August the fifteenth," he said. "I will introduce you to a religious in Paris who will take charge of your instruction."

My instruction! "But I know everything!" pride secretly exclaimed. "I have read Cardinal Gibbons!" Yet I dared not argue with my father. In my eyes, he could not be wrong. He said nothing more to me that day, but I felt he was moved, and since he was as reticent as I was, we no longer talked about religion.

I went up to my room. The angel of solitary moments faded away like a mist. I fell on my knees, my head on the bed. God was there, I did not know what prayers to offer up to Him, but I rather believe that I laughed. Lord, remember that minute when You bent over me. You know so well what I am. Then give me back that minute and make it my eternity.

That year in September, as our lease was up, it was decided that we should return to live in Paris. To leave the Villa du Lac, where we had such heart-rending memories, did not seem difficult, and yet I remember that during the last days I wandered sadly in the garden where shadow and sun knew nothing of war and of death and spoke to me only of happiness. Peace in the stillness, light on my hands, at my feet, could anything in the

171

world be more real than what was given me at that moment? It was not easy for me to imagine anything else, I could not form an idea of a world where I was not present. There precisely lay a slant in my nature through which the devil was going to shut me within myself again.

Through God's grace, I knew my Creator and I knew myself, but it remained for me to discover that other self who was my neighbor. Now, on the eve of a great struggle of which I have not yet seen the last, I refused the outside world whose reality was beginning to seem doubtful, and with the world, all the voices that talked to me, all the faces that turned to me, all the rumors of distant suffering, the whole of grief, the whole cross.

Certain moments come back to me in glimmers. The furniture movers had taken away everything, the house was empty, it was time to leave. Then, in a sort of panic, I went down the winding stone staircase to the depths of the silent kitchen. I do not know what I wanted, what I was looking for. In leaving, I felt I was being torn away from something. My mother had gone up and down those steps, there was a place where she had fallen.

In Paris, while waiting to find a flat, we found ourselves once more at the Pension Mouton. It was the most convenient place for us all. The lycée was only a few minutes distant and my father took the subway at the Place du Trocadéro. I remember the sound of our footsteps on the little red-carpeted staircase. Everything seemed to me shabby and dark in this old-fashioned house, now filled with people from all over, stranded by the hazards of war, who were waiting for something or other, for the hostilities to cease, no doubt.

The dining room held ten or twelve persons, among them a very old lady who had retained very good manners in spite of a slightly addled brain. "Refined," "cozy," and "homelike" were the terms she used to qualify the sinister pension where we had drifted, terms that made us guffaw, even in those sad times. Next to her sat a big devil of a fellow, a Norman gentleman driven from his native province by financial reverses, a wiry, cynical, but extremely courteous old man. Eagle-nosed and pink-cheeked, he sat sideways, crossing interminably long legs, a table napkin thrown over one knee, holding a glass of apple brandy. His views were pessimistic and he had a peculiar way of snickering noiselessly when the word "victory" crept into the conversation. The way he looked at his neighbor, that poor tremulous mass of black, struck me on account of the forceful contempt he could put into his eyes, those of a bird of prey. Farther on, at the end of the room, a couple of very pallid ladies, with puffy faces and cheeks white with powder, two sisters, exchanged improprieties in muffled tones. Each of them had a son. One was called Hubert, the other Gaston. Hubert looked like an ape. Gaston resembled a pretty choirboy with big blue eyes. It was the time if ever to talk of purity when he turned his limpid gaze toward you, but that was a delusion rather quickly dispelled as far as I was concerned. Still farther, at the very bottom of the room, sat a plump South American whose spinach-green sweater molded her curves; she talked English, French, Spanish, anything you liked, so long as the conversation was spicy. I can see the black fringe that swept her brow and the long green jade cigarette holder from which she never parted except to eat. I must add that at table, the conversation never strayed into loose talk, barring the whispers exchanged by the two pale ladies and the South American, their accomplice. The boys laughed slyly. My father, plunged in sadness, did not hear them. Anne and Retta, when they dined with us on Thursday night, chicken night, occasionally raised an eyebrow but said nothing. Both were nurses at the Hôtel Ritz hospital then and, dressed in white, seemed to me very beautiful.

One also saw another lady, very silent and very modest, young and pretty, always in mourning, whose husband was at the front. Her eyes were often red. I heard that she came from Brittany. She looked at me sometimes with a serious expression. I remember one evening that having talked to some nuns that day, in a fit of absent-mindedness, I called the lady from Brittany "sister" instead of Madame; she saw me blush and said gently: "We are all of us sisters and brothers." That is the only thing she ever said to me. Occasionally we had transient guests. A soldier on leave, a quiet, disabused little man with a pince-nez and small black mustache. His horizon-blue uniform could not manage to give him a martial air. One day, he said without looking at me—his profile alone spoke—: "You're young. As for me, I'll soon be eating beets by the roots." His prediction came true, two or three months later. We were then plunging into the chasm of 1916.

On another occasion, there arrived an Englishman in khaki. His jaw shone. He looked at us with an undefinable expression that was beyond contempt, more like the interested amusement one could take in a meal between monkeys.

Seen from a distance in time, this pension now appears to me in the light of a caldron where something murky and poisonous boiled unceasingly. On the ground floor, the door of the room where one of the chalk-faced ladies lived opened (and shut immediately). There, behind a portiere, how much laughter rippled in a fog of cigarette smoke! One night as I was going up to bed, one of the boys suddenly appeared on the threshold of the mysterious room and asked me to come in, but I hesitated and stood for a moment in the doorway. "Make him come in!" cried the lady of the green sweater in Spanish. But I asked to be excused and vanished. I do not know what happened in the ground-floor room, but I imagine that the atmosphere was stifling. "Things are going very badly out there, you know!" cried the voice of one of the white-faced sisters, as the door closed. Out there, at the front. Pessimistic rumors circulated from top to bottom of the pension. We were the only ones not to believe them, and that we did not believe them was due to my father.

At the beginning of October he introduced me to a religious with whom my mother, giving in to the entreaties of her Catholic friends, had formerly talked. I heard later that their conversation had been a long one and that the Father had finally told my mother that as she felt happy and peaceful in the Protestant faith, she should remain in it. On the other hand, she told one of the Rue Cortambert nuns that she would have liked to have been born a Catholic, but that being born a Protestant, Protestant she would die. Those are the only remarks I have been able to collect concerning her. They leave in the background a whole aspect of the religious crisis she under-went during the last years of her life, and to such a point that I cannot honestly even venture upon a conjecture. Her apparent refusal to finish my religious education remains an enigma to me. She loved me, I know it. She loved me with the fierce, silent love an animal could have for its young, and I am not insulting her memory by comparing her love to that of an animal. What was more, she wished me to be a Christian, she wished me to be saved. Then why this silence about things she had so much at heart, about the Protestant faith in which she wished to die?

It goes without saying that I asked myself none of these questions when I entered Father X.'s room for the first time. He lived in the heart of Passy. The house was gray and rather sad, but inside, everything shone with cleanliness. You walked up a staircase that smelt of wax and Father X. lived, I think, on the third floor. The room seemed to me very large with a splendid view that took in a whole part of the city, from the heights of Saint-Cloud to the Invalides, under an immense sky with clouds racing across it. That was what first struck me, then the man in black, and more particularly his voice, a muffled, somewhat raucous voice that tried its best to be gentle.

Too shy to observe him at my ease when I saw him for the first time, all I realized was his extreme politeness and, sitting quite close to him on a rush-bottomed chair, the way he crossed his arms on his breast, holding himself so straight that he did not so much as touch the back of his chair. Slim, with very light eyes, he seemed of a venerable age to me, although he could only have been a little more than forty. His hair was graying around his ears and scarcely covered the top of his skull. His delicately shaped, thin lips were always ready for a smile. I know nothing of his extraction, but his face had a natural distinction seen in certain men of peasant stock. He told me that he was a Breton, and that is all he ever said to me about himself and his life.

My hands under my chair, out of sheer nervousness I tore away bits of rush from the seat, and that is my only memory of our first conversation. Many others followed. I bought Audollent and Duplessis's catechism and we went through the whole book in the space of five or six months. Page by page, we read it together on Thursday afternoons. I have an indistinct recollection of these lessons, but one that is still filled with emotion. This was the first time I had been spoken to in this manner of the mysteries at the base of faith, and I experienced a kind of interior rapture, something of which must have shown in my expression, for the Father watched me, and at times there were long silences.

I can say today that if ever a man loved me with a wholly supernatural love, it was that man. How was he with others? That I do not know, but for me he had the tenderness of a soul for a soul, and the hours I spent with him were not of this world. When he spoke to me of the infinite, it seemed as though we were not within those walls, but in indescribable regions where boundless happiness reigned. Afterward, I found it dreadful to go down into the street, to walk once more through the ill-lit city, but there were days when, on leaving the religious' room, I ran to the pension, threw myself on my knees, pressed my face to the bed to give myself up to an extraordinary joy from which I almost wished to be freed, for it crushed me like an overheavy burden.

Our talks were invariably preceded by prayers that we said together, kneeling on the floor: a Pater and an Ave. At such times, I almost always glanced furtively at him, because of the astonishing expression that spread over his face. For it seemed as though he saw something. His eyes filled with light, his brow and his cheeks turned pink as though colored by the setting sun.

Of his teaching, I remember about all I know of religion. His comments always turned on God's love for souls and in particular for mine, for it was of mine that he talked to me more and more frequently. Can one's innocence be recovered? I am inclined to believe so where I was concerned at that age. Sin appeared not to have any hold on me. That was what misled Father X., who formed a completely false idea of me, for although I felt I had a brand-new soul, I could not alter the fact that I had sinned, but as I did not examine myself on this point, it never occurred to me to mention it, and the misunderstanding could only grow from one Thursday to the other, all the more since I never had remorse for my errors and had not the least idea that these were serious sins.

The Father disapproved of my excessive sensibility, my immoderate love of literature and music, a love that he considered dangerous. "Loti!" he cried sadly. "You read Loti, my child? Now what can it matter to you that a writer called Julien Viaud exists?" (Julien Viaud's pen name was Loti.) He also worried about Hugo, who had enraptured me for a long time. "Wait," he once said to me. "I too read Hugo," and getting up, he took from a cupboard an anthology of the poet, published by Delagrave. He quickly found these lines and read them slowly to fix them forever in my memory:

> *"Soyez comme l'oiseau, posé pour un instant*
> *Sur des rameaux trop frêles,*
> *Qui sent ployer la branche et qui chante pourtant,*
> *Sachant qu'il a des ailes!"*

His hand on mine, he looked at me smiling. Once more, he spoke to me of my soul, of the soul's beauty. I was too shy to answer and, deeply moved, with my free hand tore a few bits of rush from under my chair. One day he discovered the trifling damage I had committed and exclaimed, laughing: "What! You're the one! So it's my Julian who is ruining my chair! I wondered what it all meant, those bits of rush after you had left. . . ."

Between us there grew an intimacy that I found delightful. Using the catechism as a means, he attempted to put practical ideas into my head. For instance, having realized that my knowledge of mathematics was nil to a startling and irreparable degree, he suggested my studying Latin, and persuaded my father to transfer me from the sciences-languages section of my class to that of Latin-languages, which was taking a great chance, but he went about it so skillfully that he taught me enough Latin for the transfer to be possible; the fact is that within a few weeks, having passed from one section into the other, I caught up with the Latinist pupils who had a three-year start on me. Everything about this tongue seemed easy and natural to me, and I fell in love with it at first sight. And then, it was the Church's mother tongue, and I felt that the Church was erecting itself around me, like an invisible fortress that sheltered me from the world. Latin circulated in me like a gush of fresh blood. I learned Book VI of the *Aeneid* with delight. As the summer holidays set in, I received letters in Latin from the Father to which I was to reply in the same tongue. *Cur non scriberem tibi lingua latina?*

However, no matter how long you took to read Audollent and Duplessis, you could not avoid finally reaching the terrible sixth and ninth commandments. I cannot help thinking that there was an idea back of the Father's slow progress, for if anyone ever watched me, it was he, and he lay in wait for me at the commandments regarding purity, but did not wish to come to them without very minute preparations. I passed through these difficulties with a peaceful soul and limpid eyes. "Just think," he said, "in lycées there are boys who do not even respect one another." I listened without quite understanding him. Boys who respected one another . . . I imagined well-bred boys exchanging low bows, and others, mere louts, doing nothing of the kind. The Father told me that in a Catholic school a boy had once gone up to another one and said to his face: "You're nothing but a dirty pig!" I listened attentively and did not turn a hair. What on earth had the dirty pig done? I did not know. And also, I was not much interested. Most literally, it left me cold.

I have no idea what the Father concluded from my silence and my expression. Perhaps he guessed that I had not understood much of what he said, and he was right. He should have spoken to me far more directly and immediately asked me precise questions. I would have answered with complete honesty. "Think," he said to me once, "that one should not tell a lie, *even to save the world*." It was unnecessary to tell me so. My mother had taught me that long before he did. On another occasion, enlarging on the dangers of excessive sensibility, he said this, and I cannot help thinking it was unwise of him: "A girl's downfall is caused by sentiment and a boy's perdition by sensuality." Perdition—the term was used instead of damnation. I listened without answering a word. I had never been quite sure of what was meant by sensuality but was convinced that I

179

had none. Paradise was the only thing that interested me, and on earth, music and literature, Ronsard's lines on the Gâtine Forest, for instance, and Chopin's Nocturnes, played to me sometimes by a friend of my cousin Sarah.

I must leave my religious for a moment and talk a little about this friend, since everything has a connection. I will call her Mademoiselle Jeanne. She came from a part of the country where French is spoken with a faintly singsong accent. At the Château de Groslay, near Paris, she had taught literature to young foreign girls who lived there as paying guests. I should have said earlier that my parents had sent my cousin to Groslay, that she had spent several years there, and that it was through this cousin that I met the young woman in question. For some reason unknown to me, she gave up teaching at the beginning of the war and settled in Paris in a flat on the Rue du Ranelagh.

The house faced a big garden at the end of which lived Father Janvier, a Dominican who had been well known in his day, I think, but in Mademoiselle Jeanne's drawing room, neither she nor I thought about Father Janvier. She talked to me of wonderful and daring things, of poetry, of novels, of journeys, and sometimes, in the evening, she sat at the piano and played me Chopin's Nocturnes. What exquisite hours! I suffered. Great distress overwhelmed me, tears came into my eyes, I regretted not having great sentimental sorrows in my life, such as those I divined in the sumptuous chords. It was really enough to take one's breath away. I cried, I was voiceless, I hoped the pianist would not see an anguished face, hidden for that reason in my hands, and at the same time hoped, without admitting it to myself, that she would surprise me in this interesting attitude. How romantic I felt! My heart was simply breaking. One evening she told me point-blank that she thought me handsome. The compliment went to my head. Naturally, I blushed. She proposed another Nocturne. All my father had said was: "Don't come home too late, boy." He knew Mademoiselle Jeanne and had no objection to the visits I paid her after dinner. So, another Nocturne, this one fit to make one scream oneself to death: the twelfth. I was standing. Emotion and fatigue forced me to sit down. The young woman stopped dramatically in the middle of a phrase and asked if I wanted something to drink in order to pull myself together, but no, I assured her, sweeping my hand over my brow, I was all right and would calm down. She looked at me anxiously and let me take my leave.

Poor lady! I did not understand a thing about her solicitude, her smiles. She was neither beautiful nor very young. Lively, with a big, scoffing nose, she did not care a straw for anything but art and love. With the great candor I had at the time (where was last summer's young man?) I talked to her about religion, I even talked about it with a fine flow of words, for I was beginning to have a taste for speeches. Words intoxicated me. She listened, raising one eyebrow, declared herself a Voltairean, then, sitting down at the piano, she made every use, good and bad, of this disloyal means of agreeably devastating me. Had she been a little bolder she would, I think, have seduced me, but she was probably hindered by divining in me a budding fanatic.

Spring came, I was at one and the same time all lyrical, all mystical, I could turn this way or that. When I left Father X.'s room, I was ready to face torture for my brand-new faith. Such a strange sensibility and its unexpected leaps worried the Father a little. Not without reason, he feared all he suspected to be vulnerable in my nature. And he did not know everything at that, for I did not tell him everything, I did not talk to him of what was most dangerous, not being aware myself that it was dangerous, not realizing, for instance, that I had fallen in love with one of my schoolmates to whom I had never spoken a single word.

181

What did I know about myself? Practically nothing. I only thought myself very handsome and very gifted. Those were the very convictions that I concealed under an unassuming aspect; another feature wantonly tangled everything up: I was drunk with religion. One day I confessed feeling sad to the Father. "Sad," he repeated and, rising, fetched a book from his cupboard. It was a Biblical concordance. "We'll see what Scripture has to say about sadness," he continued in his broken voice, and began turning the pages. *"Tristitia sicut tinea,"* he read finally. And he added: "You have the itch." I looked at him gravely. I was not very pleased to have my wonderful sadness compared to a filthy disease. Arms crossed, his eyes relentless, he repeated: "The itch." And once more he cautioned me against that wretched sensibility of mine. "The books you read, your love of music . . ." I thought it useless to talk to him about Mademoiselle Jeanne, not from deceit, but because I imagined that it would not interest him. How little I knew what a religious was like! No more than I talked to him about my schoolmate Frédéric, whom I adored and who did not even seem aware of my existence, for he had never once looked at me.

Be it as it may, the following Thursday Father X. questioned me a little about my sadness, which he no longer compared to the itch. Perhaps I was sad because I could not love God as much as I wanted? This supposition made me open my eyes wide, and for the first time in my life I had the feeling of being with a grownup who did not understand me. I was dumfounded, and to such a degree that I wondered if the Father was not right, for after all, how could a priest be mistaken? There was probably something I could not grasp. I certainly loved God and thought I loved Him with all my strength. Was there another way of loving Him more? I remained silent. I distinctly remember suddenly having difficulty in breathing and that I felt a tightness in my chest. I was frightened of what the Father was about to say, but he said nothing alarming, he only asked me if I could imagine myself in a monk's cell.

A cell? I had never in my life thought of one. My imagination showed me a charming little room with whitewashed walls and a window giving on an enchanting landscape of the sort described by Loti. Why not a cell? The Father seemed keen on it. A cell in a monastery . . . What more romantic than a monastery? I pictured myself dressed in rough homespun. What an effect that would produce! Julian has retired to a monastery. . . . I tried to think, to be serious. I would love God in a cell. "Yes," I answered. Then, to my great surprise, the Father got up and I did the same. Putting his arms around my neck, he lightly pressed my cheek to his. "I was sure of it," he said.

We sat down again and he began talking to me about the very great grace God had sent me in taking me out of the world. I suddenly had the impression of having unaccountably tied myself down, for I was far from expecting such talk and all the emotion I read in the eyes of such a serious and saintly man. According to him, my sensitiveness, my taste for study and for art testified to a Benedictine vocation. Oh, Father, did not your innocence equal mine? Did he not go so far as to point out the monastery where I could best work out my salvation? The Isle of Wight was selected, as I was an Anglo-Saxon. The place was described to me in a very attractive manner, but stress was laid on the happiness of a life wholly devoted to God, on the paradise that would follow this paradise. I felt I was losing my head. How was it that I had not known sooner that I had a religious vocation? The thing had seemed obvious to me for the last five minutes and I went mad with joy. The Father thought it advisable to wait before acquainting my family with what he called my decision, and I regretted not being able to communicate such an interesting piece of news to my relatives that very evening.

So God had chosen me. I ran home to throw myself at the

foot of the crucifix given me by Eleanor. I was drunk with love. I was also drunk with pride, but that I did not know. In all this ardor, all the impulses of a heart beating with supernatural passion, vanity found its advantage. Self-esteem was presented with a choice morsel. And yet I loved God. Therein lay the mystery. I loved God with a love that intoxicated me and made me forget my own existence at moments, but those moments were short. Everything brought me back to myself, even God.

Today, now that these things are so far away, I find it amazing that such an intelligent religious, one so eminently spiritual, should have been so greatly mistaken about me. He must have had good reasons to put the idea of a religious vocation into my head. Perhaps he thought that I would not be able to work out my salvation elsewhere than in a convent; perhaps, through an intuition that I hope with all my heart was a false one, he thought I would be lost if I remained in the world. Did he see, in a sensibility that inspired him with such keen fears, the germ of unconquerable passions? Did he foresee a great spiritual disaster, the pitfalls of love, of the flesh, of success? I am inclined to believe, as I write this, that he expected the worst and took it upon himself to suggest a vocation that would tear me away from hell. Why did I speak of innocence, a moment ago? He saw clearly and very clearly. The only thing concealed from him was the outcome of the struggle. Who is saved, who lost? That is God's secret.

These days, days that I used to keep in my memory like a treasure that no one could take away from me, how is it that in examining them very closely at present, I judge them less beautiful? Although I was more serious-minded than other boys of my age, I was also irresponsible and light. There was in me a kind of spiritual arrogance, and in a certain way the whole of the Gospel escaped me. I did not know what it was about, for pride blinded me and that, I think, is the case with us all.

I remember one day being at the window of the pension's little drawing room and, very gravely, reading a book. What book? The *Imitation*. I had no more desire of being seen than of hiding. I was alone and wished to remain so. But I was not alone very long. Soon the two boys I have mentioned entered, Hubert and Gaston, Hubert the little ape and Gaston the handsome choirboy. They asked me what I was reading and I told them with what I considered admirable simplicity. "What a prig!" cried Gaston, laughing. "You'd much better have a good time with us," said Hubert. I did not answer and continued reading while the boys went off to sit on the carpet, in a corner where they were half concealed by the piano, so that anyone coming in suddenly would not discover them for a few seconds.

I heard them whispering and noticed out of the corner of my eye that they faced each other cross-legged and that Gaston, his back turned, almost completely hid his companion from me. I did not know what they could be at and, moreover, was not interested, all I wanted was a silence that would allow me to soar to fresh heights! After a rather long interval during which I had forgotten the two schoolboys' presence, Hubert's voice was heard, sharp and provocative, but he used words I did not know: all the more reason for their burning into my memory.

Is it credible that I did not understand what the pair of them were doing in that dark nook of the drawing room? All I can say is that I peacefully finished reading a chapter and then got up and noiselessly left the room, I and my beautiful soul.

It may be that I judge myself severely, but I try to tell the truth as memory shows it to me today. I thought myself to be, not superior to others, but different. In my own eyes, I did not belong to any particular group. Above me, like a watchful angel, was my mother. Next came the Father who had undertaken my religious instruction and whom I reverenced. I gradually plunged into a sort of dream that took the place of life. Someone should have been there to shake me awake. I was like a sleepwalker lost in dreams, mystical delusions of grandeur.

One day, in the course of conversation, the Father chanced to pronounce the name of Jaurès, and I do not remember what he said about him except that this politician had formerly upheld a philosophical thesis demonstrating the reality of the outside world. "He must have been mad!" I cried. "As though it were possible that the outside world could not exist!"—"Mad, yes, yes," said the Father without dwelling on the subject. He was most certainly ignorant of what he had sown in my mind and what a harvest was to spring up later, for the idea that it was possible that the world did not exist settled in me, without my knowledge.

No doubt I was not absolutely such as I describe myself, I mean that there is always, way back inside us, someone whose existence we do not suspect, that we can never reach and that God loves. That someone, our real self, can get in touch with God and speak to Him. My mistake was to take myself for the one I saw every day in my mirror. I was not the proud and politely disdainful boy who kept the world at a distance, any more than I was the clothes that covered my body. In fact, I did not know who I was and passed blindly by my real self each day of my life. Perhaps, when death comes, the unknown self will rise up to reproach me with my blindness and judge me. He does not recognize himself in my wrongdoings. Have I ever allowed him to make himself known, to live in this world where God had sent him to speak to men in the great tongue of the invisible? Yet, in my sixteenth year, there were exceptional moments the meaning of which never appeared clearly to me, but I am quite certain that something happened.

At the pension I shared a room with my father. It was a rather large room whose windows opened on the long garden where a few hens cackled sadly under two small disheveled acacias. I remember that my father's bed was pushed into a kind of alcove, and mine being at the other end of the room, when we were both in bed it was impossible for us to see each other. In winter a good log fire burned from morning till night in the hearth (wood could still be found early in 1916), and it was in this room that I did my homework, in my sister Lucy's company. On washing days, the family linen dried on towel racks before the fire, and from wet flannel rose an odor that I could recognize on my deathbed.

This is where the dogs came on the stage. We owned three, not having had the heart to leave them behind us: two fox terriers, Loustalou and Annibal, and a rather large gray dog of the griffon type who answered when he felt like it to the name of Fox. These animals adored my father's room and, in bitterly cold weather, were allowed to lie on his bed, but there were rivalries among them that degenerated into fights. Wild fantastic chases took place among the furniture in an uproar of barks and yelps. Fangs gleamed ominously and many an ear bled. On an afternoon when we were absent and the linen was drying before the fire, one of these mad gallops threw the room into a disorder we should have anticipated. For on our return, we were greeted by smoke rising gently from flannel underwear and going up to the ceiling in spirals. The dogs, having made up their differences in the face of danger, had taken refuge on my father's bed and silently watched the slow combustion of towel racks, vests and underdrawers signed Jaeger.

This apparently insignificant scene has remained in my mind because it speaks volumes for those faraway days. We lived very modestly and, to all appearances, were just a little lacking in common sense. There was a touch of madness in all this. My father, who was the most reasonable one of the family, never scolded us, but merely shook his head, opened his arms slightly, then dropped them alongside of his body, heaving terrific sighs, to our great dismay.

He scarcely ever spoke to us after my mother's death. He smiled, asked us how we felt, and that was about all. I have never seen calmer despair or one more anxious not to disturb anybody. At night, in his gray dressing gown, he knelt by his bed and read his prayers from a little black book, then he removed his pince-nez, and from my corner my ear was keen enough to guess he was crying, but crying so softly that only a hearing such as mine could have perceived it. Around ten o'clock he put out the light and his slightly muffled voice traveled toward me, wishing me good night in an invariably kindly tone.

For my part, I had said my prayers and gone to bed. Sleep came quickly. One night, however, I could not drop off. Will I ever be able to forget it? I was lying on my back when, all of a sudden, a feeling of indescribable happiness swept over my whole being. It seemed as though the threats that weighed on the world no longer existed, that all sadness had suddenly ended, and that, in a deep and complete security, everything blossomed into joy. I have no idea how long this state lasted. I did not think of God, I thought of nothing, to speak truthfully, I did not think, I forgot who I was.

When I gradually came back to myself (is there anything more melancholy than to come back to oneself, once one has left that self behind?) I heard my father sighing sadly in his alcove. No doubt he was thinking of my mother. My heart grew heavy. Life on earth scared me. On all sides, man was in danger.

I said nothing about what had happened to me to Father X., which was probably a mistake on my part, but I considered it to be a secret, my secret, and then, how could that be connected with religion? Once more, I had not understood a thing. Much later I asked myself the following question: If it was God, how was it that I did not know it? If it was God, why did He not make me aware of it? Today, I still wonder. A delusion is always possible. In any case, relations between God and His creatures cannot be expressed in human language. Everything takes place in spheres unknown to us.

◇ ◇ ◇

No one at the lycée had any suspicion of the change that had taken place in my life, except Philippe, to whom I said a few words on the subject, and who stopped laughing to listen attentively. I do not know what impelled me to confide in him. Not without reason, I believed him to be more intelligent than us all, for I was not so stupid as to be unable to recognize the superiority of others over me. My pride was of a different kind. Yet the reputation people gave Philippe of being a thoroughly bad sort should have estranged him from me, but, as I have already said, with me he was on his best behavior.

I had trusted him with a secret: a passion as pure as it was violent for one of my schoolmates whom I have called Frédéric. The latter, to tell the truth, had very little to distinguish him from the other pupils except eyes of a wonderful blue that always seemed to look far away. Added to these, a pleasing face, a well-knit body, but an awkward gait that I unconsciously tried to copy. He walked a little like a duck, and I attempted without much success to walk as he did. For a year and a half I never said a word to him, I only looked at him when we passed each other, with a thumping heart, whereas the object of this emotion did not even see me. Finally (to be brief, but how can one say all?), having read *Madame Bovary,* for I read everything, I swallowed a handful of flour and tried to imagine it to be arsenic. This pretense at suicide will seem amusing to many a reader. Others will know by experience how much real despair can be concealed behind such strange gestures. What seems to me far more singular at a distance is that this insane love always kept close to my religious conversion, but I feel incapable of explaining these things and can only relate them. I would enter Father X.'s room, my heart wrung with sadness because of Frédéric, and the religious thought the melancholy in my face was due to not being able to serve and love God as I would have wished.

It could be said that I should have talked openly of the cause of my suffering, but I understood nothing whatever about my passion. If anyone had informed me that I was in love, I would certainly have answered that it was impossible, because the person in question was a boy. On the other hand, it was enough for the Father to talk about God for a far more mysterious love to blaze up again and tear me from this earth. At that moment, I keenly felt the nothingness of all that was not heaven and I wanted to die, but to die painlessly, die without bearing a cross. The cross was for others, and, in the first place, what was a cross? I wanted happiness such as I had known during that wonderful night, but the next morning, at the lycée, I once more passed by Frédéric and my heart turned heavy as stone.

No carnal desire tormented me. If my heart burned, my senses were fast asleep and I was exceptionally cold. The idea of laying a hand on Frédéric would have appeared to me perfectly monstrous, because I thought that nothing could be beautiful that was not pure, the word having, in my mind, recovered all the power that it had been in danger of losing.

As we are on the subject, it is time for me to talk of another boy whom I will call Roger, although that is not his real name. All of us, I think, were sensitive to his beauty; there was something radiant about it, and not one of us could compare with him. When I have said that he had very white skin, long, very black eyes, I will have said what is most important, for beauty is not to be described, but the fact remains that one never tired of looking at him. The nose, the mouth, the oval of his face all called to mind the idea of a perfection beyond which imagination could not go. In the "Burial of Count Orgaz," bending St. Stephen often recalled him to me, and that is about all I can say.

How could I, lost in dreams, have suspected that a boy with such pure features had a temperament that made him lewdness itself? Nothing of this appeared at first. His attitude to me was one of a rather ceremonious politeness. I remember that he always dressed in black. On the very first day when school reopened, he came up to me and said in a very firm voice: "I'm going to sit next to you." I was too much overawed by that angelic face to say no, and then, why should I have refused? So he sat down on my left and began his wiles. Had I been less innocent and less stupid, I would have understood quickly enough. He bent a charming profile over my copybook and whispered the most flattering words that had ever been addressed to me. They intoxicated my pride without acquainting me in the least with my neighbor's intentions. The latter, soon judging that my innocence exceeded all possible bounds, undertook to educate me by slipping under our desk books that he considered both voluptuous and enlightening. I took home and read, sighing wearily, *L'Orgie Latine* by Félicien Champsaur, or *Saint-Cendre* by Maindron, but these stories bored me to death. Then, showing his hand boldly, Roger lent me *Les Civilisés* by Claude Farrère. I read the book obediently and returned it to its owner. "What do you think of salacity at Saigon?" he asked, glancing at me sideways. "Not bad," I answered. I did not know the meaning of salacity. Timidly, he laid his right hand on my left knee. I remained motionless, feeling neither surprise nor emotion whatever. A few seconds later he removed his hand as gently as he had laid it on me.

The next day (for we must be done with this rather foolish story) the seat on my left was empty, and I glanced around for Roger without finding him. It was only toward the end of class that I caught sight of him at the very end of the room, seated on the last bench. From that day on, he began changing places each time we were assembled together and systematically went around the classroom, sitting sometimes here, sometimes there. I was too slow-witted to understand the reason for these capricious itineraries, and our professor, who was a very shortsighted old gentleman, did not see, or pretended not to see, anything. One day, however, he must have thought that things were

191

going a little too far, for he called Roger sharply to account and said: "I have an idea that rather fishy things are happening in your corner." (In French, *"pas très catholique"* means unorthodox, fishy.) —"Oh no, sir, you're mistaken, I assure you," replied Roger in his gentle voice as he turned a radiantly pure face toward the professor's desk. If the incident has a place in my memory, it is on account of the word *catholique,* the syllables of which possessed an indefinable virtue for me.

I said nothing about all this to Father X. For, in order to talk to him of such things, I would have had to understand them, and I was far from understanding. I had in fact become more or less as my mother had known me, having forgotten the little I had discovered. That is what appears to me the most singular aspect of that period in my life. Sexuality was once more absent, or hidden in such a way that I was completely ignorant of its presence. Evil no longer existed for me.

At the beginning of spring, Father X., judging my religious instruction sufficient, wrote to the archbishopric to obtain the necessary permission, and the ceremony of my abjuration was fixed for April 29, 1916; my first communion was to take place the next day, a Sunday. A question arose that I felt perfectly incapable of solving. As a Protestant, I had to abjure Calvin's heresy, or Luther's, as I liked. Timidly, I mentioned Henry VIII and tried to explain, not without stuttering horribly, that the Anglican Church was neither Calvinistic nor Lutheran, nor even, I had been told, Protestant. These reasons were waived as being too subtle and not foreseen by the archbishopric: "We'll say Luther, my child."

And so, on April 29th, I found myself in the crypt of the White Sisters' chapel, 20 Rue Cortambert, but I see that I am going too fast and have not talked of a quite different event that had taken place a month earlier.

My father had found a flat on the same Rue Cortambert, at

number 16, a few steps from the nuns and just in front of a Protestant church. This peaceful street then had the charm of a provincial one. It seemed as though the sun shone there more brightly than anywhere else, and on both sides of the street were a few one- or two-story houses standing in little gardens, as they did a century before. Our flat on the first floor ran the length of the façade and had six windows. The dining room and large and small drawing rooms formed a suite opening one into the other that took our fancy. The bedrooms looked out on the quietest of courtyards. My father told me to draw a plan of all the rooms, and when we moved in, in March 1916, we knew exactly where every piece of furniture should be placed.

It was there, within those walls, that I spent some of the happiest hours of my life, and I cannot think of it without a little sadness, for what remains of all that? Too many of us have gone, and my father was about the age I am now.

Be it as it may, we were delighted to see home coming to life under our very eyes, home as we had always loved it, that of the Rue de Passy and Le Vésinet, with its curious and charming chairs, a sofa of the kind no one had ever seen in France, its family portraits and the books we still have around us. How beautiful it all seemed to us! How we rubbed mahogany and marble to restore to these things what we artlessly took for splendor!

In a few days the last bits of straw had disappeared, order triumphed, our own particular order, to such an extent that it was as though we had been living there since our childhood, and my father glanced pensively around him, as if he were looking sadly for someone. He scarcely ever spoke, but he smiled and his presence was immensely reassuring. That was what he gave us, together with a mute and rather distant tenderness. From time to time we heard him hum tunes of his youth, and he occasionally talked to us about our family, but that did not interest me and I was wrong not to listen, although I seemed so attentive. After dinner, head in hands, he pored over some religious book, usually Sister Catherine Emmerich's *Sorrowful Passion*.

Years later, I learned how he had been converted. His office in the Rue du Louvre was quite close to Notre-Dame des Victoires, where he went sometimes, after Mamma's death, for a reason that he himself did not suspect. He only said that something about this church attracted him each time he passed the rather commonplace façade standing in a little square. One day he entered the church at the moment of communion. A great many people were going up to the communion rail and, Protestant though he was, he joined them, knelt, and communicated. The idea that this communion was anything but regular did not cross his mind. He knew practically nothing about the Catholic faith and very simply followed his inclination. Some time later he went to a priest and told him that he wished to be converted. That is how God took him by the hand and led him to the truth.

The crypt of the White Sisters' chapel was low and rather dark, particularly as one approached the altar which stood against the end wall. It was in front of this altar, my right hand on the Gospels, that in a ringing voice, such as could only belong to a timid person, I read the confession of Pius V, abjuring Luther and all heresy, stumbling, as might be expected, over the word "transubstantiation." After which, with a thumb dipped in holy water, Father X. made the sign of the cross on my brow as he pronounced the baptismal formula. The water did not run down my brow, in spite of the ritual's demands and, in Father X.'s mind, this conditional baptism added nothing to the one I had received in the Anglican Church. I would have preferred it to be otherwise and, as the Father's handwriting was very bad, I tried to read *unconditionally* where he had written on the certificate of baptism *conditionally*. For a new

194

baptism, having the power of a first baptism, would have delivered me from all my sins. An exhilarating idea indeed; I would have stood before God pure and unblemished. It never occurred to me that this exhilarating idea was in itself a sin of pride, for I wanted to be exactly like an angel.

Five or six nuns were present at the ceremony, with my sister Anne and a French friend of my cousin Sarah. Also present was a very pious old lady whose son had just been killed at the front. She paraded her mourning in long black veils, looking at me with a sadness and sweetness that pierced my heart.

The afternoon of the same day, I made a full and complete confession of all my sins to Father X. "I am afraid," he said as he listened to me, "that you are accusing yourself of too much . . . or too little." I was accusing myself as best I could, and sins against purity being clearly defined by the catechism, I accused myself as scrupulously as possible. To my great surprise, Father X. appeared dumfounded and later admitted to me that he had not expected anything of the sort, that he had believed me innocent of any such faults. "What a lot of fuss over such a small matter," I thought. He had to explain that I had greatly offended God, but the idea of offending God was so far from me at that moment that it required an effort to remember my former anguish and convince myself that the priest was right. I saw that he experienced a mysterious grief caused by my confession. I soon felt uneasy and my uneasiness rapidly developed into fright. Something of this must have been visible, for the Father pulled himself together and encouraged me unsparingly. No sooner had I received absolution than I went off with a light heart and that, I think, was the best thing I could do. I forgot all about my confession and thought only of the first communion that was to follow my baptism, at mass the next morning.

It was very fine, that afternoon. Absolution given, the Father came to our house where I received him with Anne, and in the smaller drawing room, sitting at the desk that had belonged to Mamma, he signed my act of abjuration. And while he was thus engaged, what was I doing? I was whispering to my sister. And what was I saying to her? Something fit to take one's breath away, but I was only fifteen and frivolous. So I was asking my sister if she thought I could go to the movies with my friend Jean S. I do not know whether she had time to answer, any more than I know (and will ever know) whether the Father heard me. At any rate, he got up and gave me his seat. I signed, then Anne. There were no comments. After an exchange of civilities, the Father left.

What do you do after being baptized a Catholic and absolved from your sins? Today, I would answer that you spend a little while in church. In April 1916, I did not know. I had received no inspiration on that point. However, it seemed to me better to postpone the movies to another day, and for that reason I went to my friend Jean S., who lived a few steps away, on the Rue Greuze. I gave him my reasons, told him everything, I always wanted to tell everything, as I still do now. He sniggered. Not that he was making fun of me. Simply because he did not know how to laugh and sniggered from embarrassment. He was a very good sort, a trifle stout, curly-headed, chubby-cheeked, and noisy. We had known each other since childhood, since the Rue de Passy (he then lived almost opposite us). It was impossible to have a serious talk with Jean, but I was fond of him. Stronger than I was, he teased and knocked me about a little, tripped me up and laughed continually. We ceased seeing one another, a little as you would cease spinning tops, without giving it a thought.

The day following that afternoon was, to use a stock phrase, the day of all days, and what lay uppermost in my thoughts? What I am going to say will appear most disappointing on the part of a neophyte, but facts are facts. It had been settled that I would hear mass in the choir with the nuns, a great honor.

Naturally, I would be seen by all the congregation assembled in the chapel, on the other side of the grille. Now I was very shabbily dressed, having only one navy-blue serge suit that seemed to me shiny in spots, worn and almost shapeless. Several weeks before, I had spoken about it to Anne, asking her if a new suit could not be bought for my first communion, but we were short of money at home or had barely enough. I persisted stubbornly and gently, and gently was refused. So that was the theme of my great meditations on the eve of the day of all days: a new suit. I dared to quote the parable of the wedding guest who had been sent away for not being properly dressed. Labor lost. The connection did not appear very clear to my family. And also—I should have said this earlier—my father was away, having been called to Copenhagen on business. He was the only one who could have given me the necessary funds. I suffered. No doubt, I tried hard to think about God and more particularly about the Eucharist. On that score, I think that I expected a sort of miracle, a most exceptional emotion, something like a rapture. What spoiled everything for me was my old suit. Will I ever forget it? It was composed of a vaguely military-looking tunic with big side pockets, of semibaggy breeches fitted below the knees into puttees, a pleasant reminder of the times we lived in. In short, I was dreadfully mortified when the Mother Superior (Mother Marie-Adolphine) and her coadjutrix, Mother Marie-Joachim, showed me into the choir, where, on the epistle side of the altar, a red velvet *prie-dieu* awaited me.

I went to my seat and stood, proud and despairing, from the beginning to the end of this mass. Not knowing what to do and thinking that everybody was watching me, I felt horribly ill at ease. It is extraordinary that the Father had said nothing to me about the way I should behave, but he probably had not thought of it. My pride bled from every pore on account of that wretched suit and also because I suspected that I should not stand, but kneel. I dared not, I was afraid of kneeling at moments when it was proper for me to stand. If one could die of shame, I would be underground for many a long year.

At the time for communion, a Sister came and motioned to the poor simpleton and, for a wonder, he understood that he should kneel on the first step of the altar. My heart beat terribly fast and my head swam a little. I thought I was going to faint but made an effort to remember what the Father had told me about the Eucharist that I was about to receive, and I communicated in a daze.

I recollect that, going back to my seat, I knelt and hid my burning face in my hands. I remained in this attitude until the end as though I had been turned to stone. It was even necessary for the Father to pass by to make me realize that mass was over and that I should leave. And what did I feel? Nothing. An impulse, a moment of happiness? No, nothing. My one idea was to hide, to hide anywhere I could. But there was no question of hiding. A nun signaled to me to follow her and led me to a dark parlor where I was awaited by the Mother Superior and her coadjutrix. The wooden grilles of the parlor screen had been opened in my honor and, on a table, a breakfast of croissants and hot chocolate was offered my greed to cheer the inner man. The nuns said a few charming words to me, looking so gay that I lost my tragic expression and, left to myself, piously wolfed down a breakfast of which not a crumb or drop remained.

What God was accomplishing in me that April 30, 1916, I did not even suspect, for He remains a hidden God whose light is for us almost complete darkness. From now on, I could no longer escape Him. The absent-minded, superficial little schoolboy had become His prey. Had I ever been anything else?

All I can say today is that I received communion in a state of imbecile agitation and, what seems to me sadder still, with the utmost coldness. That was the way with me. After a period of fervor that lasted several months, there came a period of coldness. There were seasons in my inner life. I could not understand why, and apparently there was no one to inform me about these peculiarities. Faith was certainly not involved, but it happened suddenly that a veil fell over a page of the Gospel. The words no longer reached me, no longer affected me. Spiritually, I turned stupid and this occurred, alas, on great feast days and on occasions such as April 30th, when I would have needed the greatest graces. What I did not know was that I stood on the eve of a series of religious crises, sometimes violent ones, that were to continue for many years, but then I didn't know that.

After April 30th, Father X. no doubt considered that the greater part of his task had been achieved and all that remained to him was to guide me gently to a cloister. Had he no intuition of souls? I do not know what reply to give this question. We will see later what should be thought of it. However that may be, he asked if I wished him to direct me, for a director was indispensable, and how could I refuse? I asked nothing better than to make my confession to Father X. Confession was no effort to me. I did nothing that seemed to me wrong. That was the important, the main thing, in the eyes of my director. Pure and Impure sprang to life again, but this time cased in steel like knights, one of which was angelic and the other fiendish, both of a gigantic size. Under their shadow, the Father and I hunted for the sins I might have committed. I found nothing. He, not without reason, saw pride and harried melancholy. "Now why are you sad, my child? Only those without hope are sad. . . . *Ceteri qui spem non habent.* . . ." I could not tell him that I was sad because Frédéric did not look at me. He would, I thought, have found that idiotic. Nothing of the sort could be discovered in the list of sins. "A longing for a cloistered life?" he murmured, directing his fine gaze toward the heights at Saint-Cloud. I did not know what on earth to say, I tore tufts of rush from under my chair. And thus an irreparable misunderstanding grew between this man and me.

I could not foresee that things would go wrong one day. I was far too unconcerned for that. The joy brought me by each hour was enough, and apart from the agony I endured because of Frédéric, I could count myself happy, often filled with an intoxicating happiness. When I was alone, I sang. I made up tunes, and these tunes were sometimes very useful to me. For if I had trouble in learning the words of a sentence, my musical memory was singularly faithful. To remember my Latin conjugations, for instance, I sang them to tunes of my own invention, and so with the rest of my lessons. The most solid part of what I learnt is linked in my mind with little melodies that still run through my head. This detail would be, I think, of small interest, except that it showed an optimistic nature and an unconquerable love of life.

I knew of course that the war was on, but I could not succeed in imagining a war. In the dark bedroom I shared with my father and where I did my homework, I hummed my little songs that seemed to me the prettiest in the whole world. At that age I had never heard an orchestra and, my sister Mary being absent, our piano remained mute, but I could go and get drunk on music, sadness, and misfortune at Mademoiselle Jeanne's. Chopin's lofty lamentations exactly described all I felt at the very name of the other Frédéric: "He is going to die. . . . Or rather, no, I'm the one who is going to die. . . . I am dead. I am being buried. Then my secret will be disclosed. He will know it and will weep, yes, he'll weep, but too late." I can smile at such things today. Yet, a few years ago, I met my friend Philippe again, he who was the confidant of my great passion. We exchanged memories, and the name of Frédéric happened to be mentioned. Philippe then said to me: "I'm no longer young, I know life and can assure you now that I have never seen a human being love another as much as you loved Frédéric."

I trembled whenever I saw him. "Talk to him," said Philippe, "he won't eat you." But my courage failed me. And then, what would I have said to him? Months went by, and I kept a silence on which fed a melancholy that had nothing to do with a longing for a cloistered life. In a novel, such melancholy would overrun everything, moving forward relentlessly, but, as I have said, there were hours of incomprehensible joy when my whole being bounded toward the light. I am not writing a novel; now, life does not care a fig for the novelist's logic. It writes its novels as it fancies, sometimes very badly, with flashes of genius that can only be envied.

"You who have received so much," said Father X. to me one day, laying his hand on mine, "look out for that sensibility of yours!" Now that the catechism was over, our conversations took a literary turn that enabled my director to cast an attentive eye on the innermost part of my heart, but I am not sure of what he discovered there. My enthusiasms did not seem to him of sterling quality, particularly for a future Benedictine. Loti's *Désenchantées* inspired him with some distrust, although he had not read the book. I reveled in these intoxicating pages. "Father, if you only knew how beautiful it is!" He raised his eyebrows. Next came Chateaubriand's *Martyrs*. That, the Father had read. He did not disapprove, no indeed, "but," he said, "there is the Velléda episode. My child, such things are dangerous." Dangerous? Why? The lovely priestess seemed to me perfectly harmless. I wanted to be Cymodocée. To die for the Christian faith before such a large audience and with such noble attitudes, yes indeed . . . I felt I had the soul of a stage martyr to a *T*. Under such circumstances, a word was enough to restore all my fervor and I would go home singing hymns, those of my childhood, Protestant hymns. "Onward, Christian Soldiers!" That was the thing, onward, onward! Where are your

201

racks, your lions, your leopards? Alas, next day, I saw a Frédéric go past me without even suspecting my existence and everything collapsed, I wanted to die, to kill myself.

Once back in my room, I softly hummed the lines of the sixth book of the *Aeneid*. What could a priest make of all this chaos? My Saturday confessions were colorless. They did not completely reassure my director. To speak in his old-fashioned way, they could not but provoke uneasiness in him. It was, if I may say so, the context that appeared strange to him. One fine summer day, I remember that he and I were walking down the Quai de Billy. What were we doing there? That, I do not know, but on reaching the magnificent cedar that has since disappeared and that then adorned a garden near the Place de l'Alma, I asked the Father: "Do you know whom I would like to be later on?"—"Now, what piece of folly is my Julian going to disclose?"—"I would like to be St. Francis of Assisi." (For he was the patron saint I had chosen at the time of my baptism.) *"Utinam!* my child. But hurry up. *Festina!"*—"But, Father, if I can't be St. Francis of Assisi, I would like to be Aladdin, yes, Aladdin, so that every one of my wishes would be immediately granted." The Father paused for a second and looked at me. I do not remember what he said, but he smiled sadly. I could not but provoke his uneasiness, poor Father.

There was indeed cause for it. The spring, then summer, put me in a state of effervescence. This is the only word that describes the extraordinary condition I had been in for a few weeks. One day I took down the crucifix above my bed and, my heart thudding like a ram battering at a door, I did the forbidden thing that, according to what I now knew, could cast me into hell if I died then and there. I did not die, but the act once committed, I was so terrified by what I had done that the blood buzzed in my ears.

I probably lost my head during the following minutes. At any rate, once I had calmed down, I did a strange thing: taking down the picture of the Blessed Virgin that my mother had been so fond of, I wrote on the wall, in tiny letters preceded by a cross, the date of this great sin. Then I put back the photograph as well as the plaster crucifix, but did not pray. "Impure, unworthy to pray," I said to myself.

An enormous difficulty then cropped up: confessing my error to my director. That, I could not do. To destroy the picture the man had formed of me, never. Cymodocée fell back before the lions and leopards of pride. Then it was that a gentle, reasonable voice I was often to hear asked me why it was necessary to make my confession to my director. Had I forgotten what he himself had said to me? "I will be your director only if you want me to be. If you find it embarrassing to confess to someone you know, you are quite free to go to another priest."

What a load was at once lifted from my shoulders! In my blindness, I did not see the danger of advice that made me no more no less than a hypocrite. Without losing a moment I ran to Saint-Honoré-d'Eylau and there, behind a rather faded olive-green curtain, confessed my sin, a sin that I bitterly regretted anyway, but, I fear, for human reasons where self-pride played its part. I had become impure once more. I was no longer an angel! How sad, trite, and miserable all this is!

The following Saturday I explained to Father X. that, having thought things over, it would be better in future—I made this as polite as I could—for a priest who did not know me to hear my confession, because it would be easier for me to talk to him. Father X. himself had furnished me with these fine reasons. He looked at me with his beautiful light eyes and unhesitatingly answered: "Very well, my child." Thus ended a spiritual direction that would no doubt have enabled me to avoid very great errors, but I did not know what I was doing. That was my only excuse and, ultimately, it is every man's excuse, as Christ said on the cross. I have often wondered what the Father thought of my decision and if he had a suspicion of the truth. A different kind of man would perhaps have struggled with me, but I suppose that he did not feel he had the right to do so, and wished to respect my freedom, as God himself respected it. "Mystery of human freedom . . ." he was to write me one day, under even more serious circumstances.

My error forgiven, the flattering picture I had of myself formed again almost immediately, for I had no feeling whatsoever of having cheated. In the afternoon I regularly attended Benediction with our neighbors the White Sisters. They had sent me a lovely spray of lilies the day after my first communion, and when the flowers began to wither I put one to dry between the pages of the *Commedia* (in *Paradiso,* I hope, but I am not very sure of that). I never looked at those terrible drawings by Doré that now left me cold, although at the age of six they set my brain on fire, but I thought nevertheless about hell: it only alarmed me for others for, having left the confessional with a well-washed soul, all clean, all saved, what could I fear? When I heard the Rue Cortambert nuns sing, something in me blossomed, but how can one describe such an emotion? I was with them, far away from the world. I became what they sang. This is meaningless and yet sums up everything. These peaceful melodies rose from the heart of past centuries. Wars and revolutions changed nothing. In spite of machine-gunning soldiers, cutting off heads, overthrowing governments, these chants, so simple and so beautiful, always rose to heaven. I was particularly fond of *Jesu dolcis memoria,* which made me forget the world, and even today I listen to it with the same feeling of happiness. All my fervor was restored to me by simply looking at the Blessed Sacrament.

How could this be reconciled with the rest? I do not know. For after all, the rest was there. My memory on this point is inflexible. In appearance, my life was most innocent, and perhaps not only in appearance. I had no evil desires, was obedient, got good marks. I had written my father a letter in which I gave him a fine description of what had happened on the 29th and 30th of April. The summer holidays were getting close, but going to the country was out of the question. We lacked money for that, but Paris was empty and so peaceful that it was like being in a provincial town. However, I was not to be alone. My friend Philippe was also to spend his holidays in Paris. Here, new difficulties began.

As Philippe's parents lived not very far from our house, I used to go to see him sometimes. At the far end of a very dark room, seated on the floor—that was his idea and I never argued —we played chess. In my mind, that black corner communicated straight with hell. I was sure of it. How could one otherwise explain the obsessions that beset us both? How is one to know how it all began? There is a shadow there that cannot be dispelled. I was seized with furious desires that I did not express and had no need to express. Did we ever talk of such things? I do not think so. Why did Philippe say: "Shall we wait until the game is over?" And I said: "Well, since you've already won . . ." What I secretly desired, he suddenly knew only too well. Looking at me with his black eyes, all of a sudden those of a man, he would begin whistling softly between his teeth, like an apache. That was the signal I waited for in a state of impatience mixed with horror. My heart beat too fast, my head swam. I felt as though the air grew thick, and the furniture uglier than usual. That was part of a terrifying joy that left me mute and trembling. I would get up finally and run away. In my room, I rushed to the mirror, looking for smutches on my eyelids, the incriminating shadow. I dared not raise my eyes to the plaster crucifix. If Christ had seen me . . . I could not bear the idea. I hoped that He had turned His head away. In my strange confusion, I loved Him. I threw myself flat on the bed to hide my face from Him, I tried to imagine that I was dead, then my heart beat less fast and I waited for the moment when I could go and kneel behind the olive-green curtain, at Saint-Honoré-d'Eylau.

Leaving the church delivered of my faults, I felt myself bounce like a rubber ball when it touches the ground. Everything seemed pleasant once more. Victor Hugo seated on his rock seemed charming. I sang. At such moments, I do not think that there was a happier boy on earth than I. The errors I committed with Philippe were rare and of such a rudimentary nature that they now appear to me as being at most relatively serious, but they created in me an enormous stir. One day when the happiness of knowing myself forgiven made me run and skip down the Rue Mesnil after a confession at Saint-Honoré-d'Eylau, I suddenly thought of Philippe and stopped dead: "Philippe is damned."

I remained perfectly motionless. "Philippe is damned on my account." There was only one thing to do. I ran to his house. He was busy at his homework. "Come with me."—"What's come over you?" I insisted so strongly that he obeyed.

In the street, I explained that having committed a serious fault with me, he risked eternal damnation if he did not go to confession. I can still hear his protests. "I went to confession at Easter. And also, it's none of your business."—"Philippe, if you die tonight, you'll go to hell forever." I had taken him by the arm. He began to laugh: "What's the matter with you? Has religion driven you crazy?" With a vehemence that I still remember, and dragging him to the Rue Cortambert, I described the torments of the damned to my friend. Need I say that Gustave Doré's illustrations provided my chief source of information? I went from horror to horror with a sort of fever that sent the blood to my face. Philippe struggled a little at first, then, finding it amusing, listened to me. Certain things I told him he found revolting and, at the end of his patience, said so, but I shut him up with unanswerable arguments. "So you're sure of living until tomorrow?" Reasoning all the while, I dragged him toward Saint-Honoré-d'Eylau and, I do not know how, ended by penetrating a very cold and very logical brain with an uneasiness that I took pleasure in slowly changing into terror. I do not remember what I said, except this sentence, spoken on the corner of the Rue Scheffer and the Rue Cortambert: "It's a quarter to seven. You have just time enough, but not a minute to spare." And seizing him by the arm I forced him to run to the church, where we arrived breathless. With inexpressible satisfaction, I watched him disappear behind the olive-green curtain. I waited near the holy-water font that stands by the door.

After some time, Philippe reappeared and joined me. I took him to his house. He confided that as the priest asked him why he had come to confession, he answered that a schoolmate had insisted on it. "You have no better friend," said the priest. My heart swelled with pride. Once more, I was an angel. Really, what a fine soul I had!

The idea I formed of Christ was both vivid and confused. He was first and above all a living person who saw me constantly, who never left me, and to whom I belonged. As He appeared in the Scriptures, so was He today, very present but concealed in the invisible. When I spoke aloud to Him, He listened, and the answer coming from the invisible was made of silence, and that silence was a language, God's language, not a silence like the ordinary silence that is only the discontinuance of noise, but really words perceived by the heart.

I found that same Christ in the Host. Yet there He was both visible and invisible. He showed Himself to me behind the veil of an appearance, and this appearance was only one because my eyes of flesh could not see beyond it. A very pure soul might perhaps have seen Him, the Christ of the Eucharist. Now, there reigned around Him a prodigious silence that, for me, ceased to be an intelligible silence. All I could do was to look at Christ and in front of Him, I had the feeling of not existing in the same manner as I existed, for instance, at home or in the street. There I could not speak to Him, for respect borders on fear.

For that reason, communion made me tremble inwardly. It was preceded and followed by palpitations, but never afforded me the happiness spoken of in books, or the feeling of divine intimacy so often given me when I read the Bible. The enormous and formidable silence came close and enveloped me, God's silence, I wondered if I were going to die, but said nothing about all this. To whom would I have spoken, and in what terms? The Father never questioned me on this point. He loved me deeply, dear Father X., but I had disappointed him; also he was interested in a soul far superior to mine and about which he sometimes dropped hints. He admired God in that soul. With me, he was absent-minded, then suddenly all attention, as though from a sense of duty, for with me he lapsed into the childishness of vanity and of literature, and when I talked to him of Victor Hugo he would say with a sort of brusqueness, his arms folded: "Glory, garish glory, that was what he wanted. Read Biré, my child." If only he could have known how to brush aside all that was frivolous in me to reach what was serious and of which I myself was unaware! In his eyes I was impure, the game was jeopardized on a certain spiritual level, one had to climb down to the commonplace, down to the commonplace "defilement" that filled him with disgust. I felt all this vaguely, because I myself had this disgust, but the devil had entered my house, or at least he had one foot inside the door.

From time to time the Father asked me if I still thought of the Isle of Wight. It occasionally disappeared from my horizon like an *ultima Thule* and sometimes came back unsullied, full of monks who sang, when I was at Benediction. I said to myself that once over there, everything would be all right, that dressed in black homespun I would be saintly and pure. The dream vanished suddenly, as though shattered by a great, sinister, mocking burst of laughter on the days when, sick at heart, I wrote a date in tiny letters behind Murillo's "Blessed Virgin." I would rather die than do such a thing again! Such was my state of mind when I ran to Saint-Honoré-d'Eylau. Hence my fits of happiness when I returned home, forgiven. It was finished —finished forever—for three weeks or a month. The lesson was of no benefit to me. From humiliation, something like humility should have sprung up. Nothing came of it but pride, and pride precipitated downfalls. For I could not manage to grasp that a bond links pride to impurity. I still imagined that I would become a saint.

In the course of the year 1915, I sometimes went to see Anne and Retta, who were nurses at the Ritz hospital, but my visits were not encouraged, largely, I imagine, on account of the dreadful things I might see there. It was certainly one of the spots in Paris where people suffered most, and I never go down the Rue Cambon without remembering it. More often, I saw my sisters in corridors. Both were very beautiful and talked gaily to me, but their life, I know, was a hard one and the constant proximity of human suffering made their youth a strange one. My sister Retta was to die in harness, in January 1918. Anne, who was more robust, managed to hang on until the end of the war. Both received the *médaille des épidémies,* a decoration not easily given.

I was sometimes allowed to see one or two of the wounded convalescents, but I left them in dread. They were young, they smiled at me without a word and, when they could, held out their hand to me. I attempted unsuccessfully to imagine that I might someday be in the same state. War remained for me something incomprehensible, because I still retained from my childhood the absurd idea that my elders were necessarily right; now, the war was their doing, one can even say that it was, and still is, the masterpiece of human stupidity.

I remember one day standing near one of the Ritz windows, waiting for my sisters. The weather was magnificent. The cloudless blue sky dazzled the eye and spoke only of happiness, when suddenly I heard the light droning of a plane over the city. This distant murmur meant the ever present war. A feeling of sadness came over me such as I had only known when my mother died. Man turned the world into a hell. He had to kill, to kill at all costs and by every means, like a maniac. That was the end of all politics, sooner or later. I think that this moment of sadness, overwhelming to a certain extent, was one of those that molded me and taught me most about the incurable ferocity of the human race. To be truthful, the impression faded from my mind, but it left something behind that I found later.

My sister Lucy had gone to spend a few months with our relatives in Virginia, and I never think of her without a pang, for I know only too well that she was as unhappy over there as she was at home, but that we could do very little to alter the fate that brooded over her. Under a proud and almost aggressive aspect, she hid an extremely tender heart whose secret was never clearly known. For my sister Retta, she had a kind of mute adoration that could be read in her great sea-green eyes. She made a little fun of Anne and myself and even of my father, but that was her way of saying that she loved us. On the other hand, she fought madly with my sister Mary, who made us all quake in our boots; Lucy was the only one who was not frightened of her. "I can see the devil peeping over your shoulder!" cried Mary, the visionary. But Lucy did not give a hang for the devil. The air rang with their dreadful exchanges and we listened, dumfounded but interested, for both of them had style.

So with Lucy in America, Mary in Rome, where she unknowingly worsened an incipient tuberculosis, and two of my sisters being at the Ritz, I was the only one at home with my father, who had returned from Denmark. I was not at all bored. Every room was well provided with French and English books, and I read anything I could lay my hands on. That was the year when

I began reading Baudelaire more attentively, and it seemed as though the world around me underwent a change. The earth's great sadness appeared to me, but beautified in such a manner that it became enchanting. Beauty reigned over these poems like a queen in mourning. I did not understand everything, I skipped the blasphemies, but all these very simple words intoxicated me with a melancholy joy, I was unhappy without knowing why and enjoyed this unhappiness. All the sensuous passions in question retained a mystery that made them harmless, but the perfection of the verse, and even its imperfection, possessed a magical power for me; what I found most peculiar about it all was that I always imagined reading the poems for the first time because, in some inexplicable manner, they changed between two readings. This was probably due to my faulty memory, which had trouble in retaining words, or to some unknown spell cast by the poet. I never for a moment had the impression of reading something impure. I must say, however, that our edition was that of Calmann-Lévy (with a fine steel engraved portrait) and that the most suggestive poems had been omitted. The idea of mentioning this to Father X. never even crossed my mind.

At the beginning of the long vacations, I fell ill. It was only a slight liver attack, but I had to keep to my bed. Philippe came to see me and, looking down from the heights of sickness as one would from the heights of a pulpit, I let forth on religion, my French Bible open at my side, or else, with an unconscious inconsistency, I talked to him of Frédéric, whom I was not to see again before October, but in spite of every effort I cannot remember what I said about the blue-eyed boy whose very name pained me.

My illness over, Papa decided to send me to my sister Eleanor in Genoa for the month of August. The day before I left, my cousin Sarah brought me a bag of salt crackers for the journey. She was a light, slim girl whom we scarcely ever saw because she lived at the Château de Groslay, where she was improving her French. She certainly had a kind heart but was irritating, I do not know why. Wearing a three-cornered hat, her skirts flaring from the waist like a ballet dancer's, she found it easy enough to turn the heads of the American Red Cross boys. "As for legs," she said, "no one can hold a candle to mine." A golden fringe hid her brow, and what with her light eyes and pert airs, she had all that was needed to be attractive and it is certain that men ran after her. She was the granddaughter of a Protestant bishop, a great believer, very much shocked by my conversion, but she was affectionate and also flattering. One day when she was making fudge—in the middle of a war when everything was rationed, so I do not know how she managed to procure what she called the ingredients—she talked to me about the happiness of youth. I can see her now, bending over the saucepan, stirring with a long wooden spoon in a voluptuous odor of chocolate. I listened gravely to what she had to say, then, with all the heaviness of my age, reminded her (everyone knew about it) that I would be in a monastery someday. "A pity," she remarked. However, the day before my departure she made me a present of those salt crackers with an "and now you must excuse me, I have a date."

Two days later I arrived in Genoa. It was my first sight of Italy, and my admiration was boundless. I think that what most struck me there was to see so many houses painted different colors, and the hills around Genoa, though so bare, seemed excitingly beautiful. For in a landscape so new to me, I felt another person, capable of great things, of great poems. I had the impression that a splendid future lay open to me, that the whole world smiled at me. This was the beginning of a strange rapture which was to continue during my entire youth.

Genoa, however, was an unsmiling city. My sister and brother-in-law lived in a house at the very top of a little street that overlooked the whole city and its outskirts. From the Piazza Corvetto, you climbed the interminable Via Assarotti, at the end of which was a flight of steps leading to a bridge. The bridge crossed, you walked up an alley, the Via della Crocetta. Dragging behind me a suitcase full of books, I rang at number 17. On the last floor, Eleanor waited for me.

The flat was vast, paved in marble, with whitewashed walls. Very early in the morning, as you would protect a treasure, green shutters jealously kept the rooms dark and cool. The one I was given delighted me, for I had only to peep through the slats of the blinds to see the whole city at my feet, and into this room I shut myself. For once there, it was difficult to move. To go down to the port and come back again meant a certain fatigue, even for a boy of my age, for I had no pocket money. No one had thought of giving me pocket money. My brother-in-law gave me what was necessary to take the tram, but not every day.

When I think of those weeks spent in Genoa, they seem among the strangest in my life, but I have too much to say about them to know how to begin. My sister was kindness itself, all laughter and smiles and letting me do as I liked. My brother-in-law appeared only in the evening. I was my own master. In my suitcase were a couple of shirts, some underwear, and a toothbrush. It was one of my father's suitcases, heavy, enormous, in thick leather covered with the labels of different countries from Russia to Turkey, Italy to Sweden. In addition to the articles I have mentioned, it contained all my schoolbooks, including a Latin dictionary, novels, volumes of poetry, seeing which, Eleanor laughed softly and said nothing. I wrote in Latin to Father X. telling him about my journey and my enthusiasms; this entitled me to a reply by return post with a complete list of my mistakes in grammar and useful advice regarding my dangerous sensibility. *Me juvat te delectare Italiam* . . . He little knew what a trap awaited me, poor Father! Right at the bottom of the letter, in French and as though under his breath, he asked if I went to communion. But to communicate, I should have gone to confession, and how could I make my confession in Italian? I considered the problem solved. Simply, Italy had gone to my head. I was no longer the same. To see those great hills, like giant shoulders under the blue sky, filled me with such extraordinary emotion that I raved inwardly. It should be said that I had scarcely seen anything in my life but Paris and the Seine-et-Oise Department. Be it as it may, I think that for several days I remained in a state approaching lunacy, but I was a seemingly very quiet madman and sang only when sure of not being heard. Yet it was no longer a matter of singing my Latin conjugations. I myself became the object of poetic enthusiasm, or else Frédéric with his ducklike gait suffered a violent change and turned into an Italian Renaissance prince. I wrote Philippe a letter of which I can only recall one sentence that he served up to me for years in fits of uncontrollable laughter: "Frédéric obsesses me." But I did not know what I wanted. I was at the same time unhappy and mad with joy, and delirious about my own self. I wrote narratives that took place in Genoa. The hero, no other than myself, threw himself from my sister's terrace into the Campo Santo, one stormy day.

In the evening I dined under my brother-in-law's steely eye watching me sideways to see whether I held my knife by the top of the handle, without my forefinger touching the blade, but on that point I had nothing to fear: I knew. Anyway, he was nice to me, since I was his guest, and I finally spoke English in a manner he judged acceptable. The silver shone in the candle-light and conversation was of the simplest. Neither my brother-in-law nor Eleanor had any inkling of what took place inside me.

My books no longer being sufficient, I began reading those I found in the house. That is how I chanced on a translation of Boccaccio. If the *Decameron* is a wicked book, it was the first I lighted on. The harm it did me is practically incalculable. The pleasures of the flesh presented as the most desirable thing in the world found a sudden echo in me that covered the voice of religion. The Isle of Wight vanished from my horizon to be replaced by a confused vision where boys and girls in fourteenth-century dress rolled about on the grass in orchards. Voluptuousness! Every time the word recurred in these tales—and it happened often—the blood rushed to my face.

To tell the truth, I had no idea of what was meant by voluptuousness, but something in me must have recognized the presence of danger, for, together with a joy that set my blood aflame, I became conscious of sin. Now, iniquity settled in me with a frenzy that was not that of pleasure, but of the idea of pleasure as the great Italian described it. How beautiful life seemed to me, and how could I have run away from it? There was something in danger that dazzled me.

None of all this showed outwardly, for these things still took place in my mind, but before long I went downtown in the tram to the Piazza Deferrari, where the theater stood. There, full of confused ideas, I was almost killed by a barouche driven at a fast trot. The coachman checked his horses less than a yard away from me and, without a word, threw me a terrible glance. I ran after my stiff straw hat that rolled like a small halo to the entrance of an alley where I caught it, glad to hide in the cool, dark street humming with voices, laughter, and songs. Right and left, houses, every window open, rose toward the relentlessly blue sky. Around me, the Genoese crowd with its songs, cries, and rather rough good nature, guttural calls from vegetable and fruit vendors in a dialect of which I did not understand a word, all that was enough to remove me from my element and I must have looked bewildered in my suit of small black and white checks that, after belonging to my brother-in-law, had been altered for me the year before. And that straw hat . . . The street was narrow and people jostled me a little, for I walked like a somnambulist. No question of the *Decameron* now! From alley to alley, I got lost and had to ask my way to the

Via Assarotti, not once but twenty times. People smiled at me, took me by the arm, I met with nothing but the most charming kindness, and an hour later, my knees shaking with fatigue (for I had decided to walk home), I threw myself on my bed. A great hum filled my head, like a sea shell. Life, the earth, happiness . . . How far away Paris seemed, with its women in mourning and its hospitals! The Rue Cortambert too, in its banal peace, and Philippe, and even Frédéric and the gloomy lycée. I wrote Father X. *Genua quae nominatur superba . . .* But my heart was not entirely in it and I did not answer the postscript of the religious' beautifully turned letter. That Friday and all the Fridays that followed until my departure, my sister and brother-in-law took me with them to Nervi, where one of their friends had asked us to stay. I have only a vague recollection of Mrs. Kreyer, but she seemed to me immensely old, although she could not have been much over fifty. She was fat and flabby, and her wrinkles wreathed themselves into a smile for one and all. In spite of having a German name, she was English. Her husband . . . I do not know where her husband was, but his wife had been allowed to keep the very fine villa belonging to him. As in Bluebeard's castle, only one room had been placed under seal by the Italian government. Regarding the house, as I will explain later, I have a few very precise memories, plus a quantity of very vague ones, but the vast garden that ran down to the sea made an unforgettable impression on me. Among the intoxicating scents of flowers, you walked under shady trees flecked with sunlight. Canopies of heavy foliage opened to show the sky and, at the bend of a path lined with oleanders, I had a glimpse of the Mediterranean, blue striped with black. I immediately thought of the Garden of Eden, but kept my opinion to myself, for my brother-in-law was with me and I knew that in his opinion one should never express any emotion. "How pretty!" I exclaimed in a calm voice. "Very." On reaching the end of the garden, we opened a small iron gate. There, magnifi-

216

cent bronze-colored rocks beetled over the sea, on which I could not help casting a hostile glare.

As though he guessed what I was thinking, my brother-in-law gave me a cruel smile. "We're going in bathing," he said. "But I don't know how to swim."—"That doesn't matter in the least. You'll do the same as I do. Undress." I had no bathing trunks, but that also did not matter in the least. I obeyed. My brother-in-law undressed too, but under his suit he wore black bathing trunks, whereas I was stark naked. Taking me by the hand, he led me to the edge of the rock and said: "Hold your nose and close your mouth. Keep hold of my hand. We're going to jump straight in." About three yards below us, the water was transparent and showed depths that made me swallow hard. "Anyway," I thought, "if I'm frightened he shan't know it, and if I get killed it will be his fault." I had the sensation of passing through a precious stone, for all around me was that inexpressibly beautiful, limpid color, and for an instant I believed myself in another world. The idea of possible danger left me suddenly, but I had no time to examine my feelings. My brother-in-law's powerful grasp already brought me to the surface and I threw myself on a rock. It was easy to climb to the top. "Dress yourself," said my brother-in-law. "I'm going to have a little swim." So off he went, and I dried myself in the sun. He probably wanted to know what stuff I was made of, whether I would draw back at the last moment. That showed he knew me very badly.

The house was large and cool. We had tea in a drawing room where elephantine chintz-covered sofas and armchairs took you straight to England.

A tall and rather mysterious girl kept us company. She was called Stella, painted water-colors that I found lovely, and talked to me with a mixture of coolness and kindness that I liked. Next morning, although a Protestant, she wished to go to mass with me at the little village church that was not far from our villa. Peasant women draped in shawls sang in fine, guttural voices, and after mass came Benediction, preceded, I think, by the Litany of the Blessed Virgin. I can still hear that litany. It was so brisk and, at the same time, so strange. . . . It sounded like a marching song, and the melody roused my slumbering mysticism. I was proud of being a Catholic. When we returned to the villa, Mrs. Kreyer, I think, ventured a slightly condescending remark about the Church of Rome. Thereupon Stella cried in a sharp, clear voice: "That may be so, but we others have broken up into I don't know how many churches, whereas Catholics stick together."

I now come to one of the most singular events in this narrative. Eleanor had taken me around the house—it tired Mrs. Kreyer to climb stairs—and shown me my room. Almost facing this room, on the other side of the passage, was a door to which my sister called attention with a laugh: seals had been affixed there, but had been broken into fragments. For someone had been bold enough to go in. Anyway . . . She opened the door and I saw a dark place with lots of books on shelves and tables. "This is where he used to work," she said, closing the door. I wondered why she had laughed.

That night, when I went to bed, I could not get to sleep; the business of the seals stirred me up to such an extent and my curiosity became so pressing that after a while I got up noiselessly and crossed the passage.

In front of the forbidden door, my heart began to pound. I went in, however, and turned on the electric light. What a lot of books! And on the wall behind the door, the painting of a faun and a woman clasped in each other's arms. It took my breath away. I had never seen an erotic picture. This made me understand in a second the kind of library I stood in. A book picked up haphazard contained, I remember (how could it ever be forgotten?), engravings by Albano that left nothing to the imagination concerning what a man and a woman can do together. Another showed me figures by Giulio Romano. Yet another, more pedantic, presented my astounded eyes with reproductions of paintings and statues, all of which celebrated physical love, with a care and attention to minute detail that staggered me. I began to tremble. If anyone came on me unexpectedly, it would be dreadful. I glanced through a book or two more—the subject did not vary—and replaced the volumes most regretfully. On going back to my room and slipping into bed, it seemed as though the blood were boiling in my veins. How could I get to sleep now?

It would be wrong to think that I smile at such things. In spite of being intoxicated by the idea of a pleasure that I did not yet know, the feeling that I was no longer *alone in my solitude* became more pronounced. Coming out of my infancy, it seemed to me that someone approached and suggested thoughts that turned into mental pictures, thanks to all I had learned in the forbidden room. For each time we returned to Nervi, I found a propitious moment for my investigations and crept into the library in the middle of the night. I never stayed there long. I was frightened. On looking back, what astonishes me is that I always lingered over the same works, fearing no doubt that the others would not prove as interesting.

On leaving the room, I trembled. Desire mingled with a terror I could not analyze. These engravings showed me nothing but lunatics in alarming attitudes. My elders, who were usually dressed and reasonable, I suddenly discovered naked and gesticulating like lunatics in an asylum. I myself wished to behave as they did, and this humiliated me, for having thought I was set apart from everyone else, I saw that I was like a demented humanity, but once more, I realized it all only in the vaguest fashion.

I usually went out alone in Genoa. One day a walk took me by chance to San Lorenzo, the cathedral of white stone layered with black, in the Moorish style. Marble lions mounted guard at the door. I entered. In the vast church, dim as a forest, I suddenly felt all that was mysterious and terrible in the Christian faith. I advanced along the vaulted nave as though God was waiting for me in the darkness of the apse. I did not see Him, but He never ceased watching me. After a time I stopped, seized with great misgivings. It occurred to me that God had seen me in Mr. Kreyer's library, and for the first time I was horrified at myself. Pray, I could not, but I made a big sign of the cross and left.

Is it not strange that I looked at no one in the little streets full of people where I used to walk? Yet there must have been some very beautiful faces in the crowd, but I did not see them, or perhaps was not sensitive to the Italian charm. To be truthful, I desired nobody. I did not even know what desiring someone meant, and when I met the expression in a book, I passed it by without questioning myself. I desired the voluptuousness spoken of by Boccaccio, but how was that to be found?

Once back in my room, I became the prey and something like the plaything of the devil. It was he who instructed me as to what he judged right for me to learn. Certain that no one would disturb me, on a table drawn close to the window, I spread a sheet of white paper and began drawing. Long hours were spent in this way, the only interruptions being meals. "Julian is hermetically sealed up in his room," Eleanor said, laughing. If she had only known what I was doing! But had she known, it is probable that she would have laughed, since everything made her laugh.

All these drawings have left my memory, save one. Was it inspired by what I had seen in Mr. Kreyer's library? I suppose so. With time, I may perhaps forget some of the finest paintings I have seen in European and American museums, but that wretched little drawing, never. It was really dreadful and, in its obscenity, not without a certain innocence.

How sad it is to think that, with a black pencil and paper, I was unwittingly searching for the immemorial dream of fallen humanity, the voluptuousness that would tear a man away from earth without letting him fall back on it. . . . . I searched for it as best I could, not knowing where to pin my desire. What I cannot describe is the kind of trance in which my patient work threw me. I think that if someone had struck me, I would not have felt the blow but outwardly remained calm enough, for everything took place in my head. It would be a mistake to believe that I gave myself up to excesses of a physical nature. Perhaps it would have been better so, in a certain way. The fact was that everything became mental.

At night I hid the sketch in a drawer and next morning, throwing myself on it, imagined that it had changed. I did not recognize it immediately. Had I perhaps forgotten it in my sleep? A kind of magic was at work. The sketch did not remain dead and motionless in its drawer, as illustrations do in books, it changed, I thought. Seized with fear, one day, I tore the paper into such small pieces that it would have taken weeks to put them together again. I trembled as though I had destroyed something living, and a whole part of my being regretted it. The shadows were so good, the volumes so faithfully reproduced. . . . . I had benefited by Monsieur Tisserand's lessons. He would have thought that everything "rounded out" to perfection. At the same time, I knew I was in danger. For that reason, I wrote Father X. a letter that I fancied to be in Latin, and my nature being so unconcerned and so frivolous, having prayed that night as usual, I gaily climbed on to a brand-new pedestal, believing myself clean and pure once more.

What I gather from this business is that an intellectual mechanism was making formidable progress. Hallucination was turning into a system. The truth was that any drawing became useless, because a fascinating (in the strongest sense of the term) representation was being born in my mind. What I imagined, I saw, as a visionary sees a vision.

From that day on, and for a considerable length of time, there were no more drawings. I studied quietly, I began a novel that

221

took place at Nervi. One day my sister took me to the top of a hill reached by a funicular. A rather mysterious young lady went with us, dressed in white, with a white sunshade and a white veil that wrapped around her large hat and concealed her face. She was called Mademoiselle Schiavone and was said to be very beautiful, but how could one tell? All three of us ate snow-white sherbets in a charming café. I saw Mademoiselle Schiavone raise the border of her veil to eat a small portion of her sherbet, thus showing a pretty little mouth that reminded one of a cherry. The sherbet finished and the veil drawn down—and why that veil? to protect a delicate complexion?—the young lady talked and laughed a little in a subdued voice. I imagined that I might have behaved with her in the way Boccaccio's boys did with their lady loves, but all those veils swaddled her in clouds. I asked Eleanor if Mademoiselle Schiavone was as pretty as Emily. "She's a different type," Eleanor replied, "but very pretty."

At the end of the month I left Genoa by train to return to Paris. We stopped at Modane, where, for some unknown reason that probably had to do with the war, we were delayed for several hours. I took advantage of it to climb into the mountains, and the higher I climbed, the prouder I felt. I sang. On reaching a meadow where it seemed as though I could see all the kingdoms of this world at my feet, I felt myself to be the lord of creation or a king and at any rate someone exceptional. Lying on my back, I was intoxicated by the blue above me that entered my head through my eyes. Was I demented? It occurred to me to brave Heaven.

To brave Heaven ill expresses what I wanted; if the words have any meaning, to brave the blue would be nearer the truth. I wanted to show myself to the clouds, the rocks, the whole of nature in this vast solitude filled with light. I became part of the air, the earth, the sun, I was free.

It was only on going down to Modane that I felt horrified at myself. It seemed to me that I had gone back to paganism. That

222

hour has remained in my memory, but how many others have slipped away from me, hours that would have allowed me to decipher the riddle of my life! I am pursuing a phantom.

I scarcely remember anything about the end of that summer in Paris except that I went to see several churches, in particular Saint-Séverin and Saint-Julien-le-Pauvre, of which I am still very fond. Without being aware of it, I staged a show for my own benefit: at Saint-Séverin, I was Gothic, romantic, and mystical. I prayed there with delight, especially when I found myself alone. The stone palm grove provided me with a rapture where art lent effective help to piety. On looking at the vaulting and the wonderful gaudy colors of the stained glass, I felt happy to be a believer and decided to be a saint. My soul became voluptuously disincarnate. I stress "voluptuously," for a sort of spiritual lechery was what it now reveled in. How all that comes back to me! All sensuality seemed far away and disgusting. Such things I left to others, to anyone who wanted them. I was of a different kind, I was. First of all, I had a religious vocation. Father X. had told me so.

Leaving Saint-Séverin, I went to Saint-Julien, which was only a few steps away. There, I blossomed. I felt myself at home in my patron saint's church, with the eye of a connoisseur, I admired the capital of a column with its sportive sirens. I said long prayers, I took care to genuflect properly, I unconsciously admired my fine attitudes in this perfect church. Had there been a mirror, I would probably have looked at myself in it. Perhaps I am being severe, perhaps I am being more severe than God was Himself at that moment. Who can say? If only I could be given back that foolish little soul of mine!

Having left the church, I wandered in the charming empty lot that bordered it at the time. I looked at Notre-Dame in the distance, thinking: "This is my city, it is mine, I belong here." And I went home as I had come, on foot, because I had no money, but what did that matter? In my room, I wrote poetry, a sonnet

223

on Saint-Julien-le-Pauvre (that was just it, he could not have had any money either, with a name like his: one more point where I resembled the saints; he had cut his father's and mother's throats, but that was a detail of which I was ignorant). That sonnet was printed later, no one will ever know where, and I almost burst with pride, but I am going too fast.

I walked about the old streets of Paris, imagining that I belonged to other times. Rue Cortambert, in the White Sisters' chapel, where the Sisters sang so well in their colorless voices, I was a medieval Catholic, and once back in my room, I sang *Jesu dulcis memoria* until my head swam. I went to communion every morning. All my sins had vanished behind the rather faded olive-green curtain at Saint-Honoré-d'Eylau. Of Christian life, all I knew was sweetness, an untroubled conscience, and the joy of a salvation that could reasonably be hoped for.

Such was the month of September of that year in which so many tears were shed.

I have already said that the war affected me little. Yet it was going to overtake us finally. Although we had no relatives at the front so far, my sister Retta, in spite of being so brave, had not been able to weather the hardships of a nurse's life very long. She fell ill in 1915. Then began a lingering martyrdom. Her lungs being impaired, she was taken to the South of France, in accordance with the ideas of the times, and temporary improvements in her health were succeeded by dreadful relapses. She was operated on, but nothing could be done for her. When she seemed in less pain, she was brought back to Paris. It was then I saw her, serious as ever and, I thought, more beautiful than before, with immense eyes in the face of a peaceful and attentive angel. She never complained. She smiled at me, made a little kindly fun of me, gave me pieces of advice, as to a child, for she had the idea that she should in a certain measure take my mother's place in my life. With terror, I gauged the distance that separated her from me, for in my eyes she was perfect, and in spite of convincing myself that I was pure, in her presence I felt that I was not. What struck me most in her face was the contrast between her black hair and pink cheeks, too pink, alas. She was the only person who awed me. On hearing that I had become a Catholic, she merely said that it was all right. Her own religion, as far as could be known, for she kept such things to herself, was confined to reading the Bible, but her very last moments revealed her deep faith. I think that of us all, she was the one in whom our Scottish blood showed most strongly. Her sweetness and goodness concealed an unyielding character. I think of her with a sort of wonder, for if I have ever on this earth known someone approaching the idea we form of saintliness, it was the smiling, tortured girl who was my sister.

On returning to the lycée in October, I once again found the big dreary playgrounds, pupils who seemed a little anxious, and a greater number of wounded soldiers. We descended into the third winter of the war, as into a darker and darker valley. Rumors of bad news circulated. I ended by leaving the kind of waking dream in which I had lived so far. One day, Roger, who had resumed his seat next mine, lent me *Le Feu,* by Barbusse, and the book gave me a shock that only threw me back into myself. History in my eyes was no more than one of the aspects of hell. Although I opposed the Gospel to it, at that moment Christ's voice was covered by the long-drawn-out barking of guns. Vainly the last leaves on the plane trees simulated gold in the still blue sky, vainly we were fifteen, sixteen, seventeen years old, humanity was cursed. The butchery went on at all hours of the day and night less than sixty miles from the classrooms where we studied. A whole France lay dying. I returned the book to Roger without a word. He occasionally quoted some of the coarsest remarks exchanged between soldiers in this book, he quoted them to me, just to see.

To see what? I am thinking about this strange boy, about the

225

pleasure he took in saying certain words that seemed shocking on such purely shaped lips. One would have had to be blind not to notice that he had become more handsome during the holidays. His face produced an effect of amazement such as might be caused by an apparition. When he looked down and his long black eyelashes cast a shadow over his white cheeks, he reminded one of a girl, but under a very slightly effeminate aspect he was a rough, imperious boy, in spite of the courtesy he affected when with me.

I admired him, considered myself less good-looking than he, but even when we sat side by side, I thought of him very rarely. A change was taking place in me, of which I did not suspect the meaning. The world's diabolical nature seemed to me obvious, and against it I could see no other refuge than the interior kingdom spoken of in the Gospel. All this, need I say, was not very clear in my mind, but I felt all the power of Christ's word, revealing that the kingdom of God is within us. There lay the protection against misfortune, against sadness, against impurity. To the best of my ability, I said all the morning and evening prayers, I found happiness in them since I was searching for happiness while I thought I was searching for God. The masses sung by the White Sisters delivered me of all fear, spoke to me of a world both present and far away, of the home of souls against which mankind's wickedness could not prevail. In the peaceful, indefinitely drawn-out melodies of Gregorian chant there was a sort of spell that gently carried me out of myself. Low masses were far from having the same effect on me. This shows the spiritual level I was then on. Beforehand, I granted myself a good place in the Catholic paradise, since everything was going so well. Heresy appalled me. I put aside my mother's Protestant Bible and took to Crampon's (the French Catholic version). The fanatic woke in me, rather timidly at first, for there were many Protestants in my family and I sounded my conscience regarding their salvation. Mingled with these cares was a completely unconscious arrogance. Modest in the eyes of the world, I was full of myself, I had introduced into my life that nuisance of a man, the fighting Catholic, bent on proselytism. Had I been a little bolder I would have undertaken to convert the lycée, but native shyness closed my mouth before certain somewhat scoffing glances, and I became garrulous only with Philippe, whom I was determined to turn into a saint (like myself), and the wretched Calvinist, whom I crushed with my learning and to whom I asserted that God was not in his church—"*dans ce que vous appelez vos temples*" ("in what you call your temples": French Protestants call their churches *temples*). He looked at me sadly, instead of giving me a good clout that would have put my theology in its place. To speak plainly, I am not very proud of the figure I cut then, which was that of a pious simpleton.

The winter of that year was one of the most severe of the war. At home, there was just enough coal to keep up a small fire in the dining room, a fire more ornamental than useful. We shivered in our overcoats. Chilblains swelled my fingers and broke, leaving for years the scars of little wounds. Other people managed to heat and feed themselves normally, but we lacked the funds for that. I do not remember having suffered much from such circumstances. Religion carried me through. Saints had had privations! I was cold and hungry: all that was necessary to be happy, according to St. Francis of Assisi. Yet it was not wise to fall ill. One day Anne came in with a big parcel under her arm. "I've found some coal," she said to Papa with a happy smile. The parcel was immediately emptied into the grate, where a few egg-shaped bits of compressed coal dust smoldered modestly. We waited. After a while, smoke rose in the hearth. "It's taking." Yes, it was taking, already we held our hands to the fire, but our joy was short-lived: Anne had been sold stones coated with coal dust. "My poor children," said my father simply.

Doubtless because of this difficult winter, the spring that followed threw everyone into a kind of subdued effervescence, for after all the war was still on. The champion of faith, the candidate for martyrdom, also had his little share of the general running wild at the lycée. Young shoots glistened in the sun and the milder air went to our heads: we were like young animals. One day my schoolmate Roger talked to me more freely than usual, and I suddenly found it interesting to listen to him. He advised me to go to a brothel. I did not know what a brothel was. He explained, gave me an address near the Bourse, said it would cost me twenty francs, "but," he added, "you won't regret it, and then, no one is a man unless he has been to a brothel. Of course, if you want to sleep with Mademoiselle C." (he named a celebrated singer) "it will be more expensive." I went home, absolutely flabbergasted by this discourse. Since one had to go there, I would think about it. Today, I am still wondering how this agreed with my religious ideas. Perhaps with the inconsistencies of my age and nature, I never gave it a thought. Anyway, I can give no explanation of the fact that I began saving to collect the necessary sum, most literally sou by sou.

Finally I had twenty francs, and the following Thursday I walked up the Boulevard des Italiens, my head on fire and a lump in my throat, for Roger's attractive words rang in my ears (I had told him that the thing was to take place that day) but I was scared. The delights of the flesh, Voluptuousness—at last I was about to discover these mysterious joys, but I was scared. I suffered. Each step brought me closer to the street famous for its bawdyhouses, and I felt that nothing could prevent me from going "down there," when all of a sudden, passing by an expensive-looking shop, I was attracted by some gloves. I had never seen finer ones. Not to be compared with the woolen gloves I wore: these were leather gloves, suède gloves. For twenty francs I could treat myself to a pair. New debate: would I dare to enter a shop glittering with lights? "But," I thought, "if you dare not go into a shop, how will you dare go into a brothel?" Was it at Les Trois Quartiers that I bought those gloves? And how long did my hesitation last? I cannot answer. All I know is that I went home that afternoon, my hands concealed in those gloves that seemed to me so beautiful that I never tired of looking at them, opening wide my fingers, stretching out my arms, striking all sorts of attitudes in my room, and sniffing the leather, intoxicated by its odor. Next day I put them on to go to the lycée and kept them in a pocket during class. Roger asked me at once if I had gone "down there," and I said no, that I had not felt like it. He did not answer but his profile assumed an extremely sly expression. I could not resist showing him my gloves. Was not that why I had put them in my pocket? He was so smartly dressed and I, so simply. . . . He would see, for once. "Look at what I bought myself yesterday." He took the gloves, examined them, and bending a little to avoid being seen, he raised them to his face, smelt them as one smells a flower, then returned them to me without a word.

Some time later, Roger passed me in a playground that was not ours and where we knew no one. I had a feeling that he was waiting for me. He wore a gray gabardine raincoat belted in at the waist and, on his hands, gloves quite as fine as mine. I do not know what he said to me, but he spoke very gently and with a kind of humility that surprised me. As though he were asking a favor, he suggested our taking a walk in a little avenue, after class.

I knew the avenue very well. It was charming. With its gardens and trees, it took you straight to the provinces, and at one point the city noises were scarcely heard. I add, since everything must be told, that it enjoyed a rather mysterious reputation, but I had very little idea of the whys and wherefores of all this. Boys used to linger there. That was all I knew. Roger looked at me, waiting for my answer. At that period I was not yet too sensitive to beauty and there was something disdainful about the boy that made me avoid him, but that day he was not the same, he laid himself out to please, his eyes spoke and he smiled at me with a tenderness I had never seen in a man. I distinctly remember my sensation of being bewitched by some unknown thing, a dark power all the more fascinating since it was dangerous. Face to face with a new experience, I said yes, almost unhesitatingly.

At five minutes past four he was waiting for me by the lycée's main entrance (we had not met in class that day), and in a way that made me feel rather shy he slipped his finger tips under my arm. How happy he seemed! He said a few words to me in Spanish, a language he spoke to perfection, and without quite understanding what he said, I was flattered. At that moment an incident occurred that I have always found inexplicable. We were almost in front of the little avenue when a schoolmate whom I scarcely knew and usually avoided, because he bored me, hurled himself at me, much as a dog hurls itself against one's legs. He was a short, rather ugly but sturdily built boy who always carried his satchel in both arms and *behind his back*. He leapt to my side, crying: "No! I'm the one who is going to see you home!" I moved aside and he pushed me toward the iron railings that bordered the lycée. Fury rose in Roger's face as he stood motionless on the curb. "I'm the one!" cried the boy. "I'm the one who'll see you home!" I thrust him away, and he began entreating me with extraordinary vehemence. What a strange sight he was: his arms behind his back, his violence, his anxious little face from which proceeded a sort of barking! It gave me a shock. Roger made an impatient gesture and crossed the street without me. I had a queer feeling of relief on seeing him move away. As to the intruder, he accompanied me in silence to the Rue Cortambert. I have often wondered what he had in mind. On reaching my door, he said good-by and left me.

230

◇ ◇ ◇

Was it around that time? I think so. That year, at any rate,
I received a visit that made a strange impression on me, although I only understood its full meaning too late. One evening
I was learning my lessons in the dining room, a lamp standing
by me on the big table. How well I see it all through the small
end of the telescope! My back was turned to both windows, the
curtains were drawn, the room seemed dark around me, but
on the table was that perfectly circular pool of light where my
hands turned the pages of books. Someone rang. I was alone in
the house with a maid who opened the front door. A moment
later, a woman came into the dining room.

I recognized her right away. It was Jeanne, Jeanne Lepêcheur,
my Jeanne. My heart leapt in my breast. I heard the dear, soft,
rather hoarse voice call me Joujou. Did I kiss Jeanne? Oh, I
hope so, without being too sure. I was morbidly shy. I remember her sitting at the table facing me and that she said: "So,
Joujou, you've become a young gentleman. . . ." She was the
same, she was exactly the same, with her pretty smile, a ribbon
around her neck, and her fetching plebeian accent—but she said
vous to me and not *tu*. . . . I looked at her lovingly and found
very little to say. Time stood between us. The breadth of the
table separated us, and that table was made up of all sorts of
things. Serious books, silence, the war all round us . . . Nothing remained of the Rue Raynouard world. The awkward, ignorant boy, the woman who had scarcely known what else to
do but love, now looked one another in the eye, vainly, having
met only to become strangers once more. "Your Mamma, Joujou . . ." I shook my head, Jeanne understood at once and
smiled sadly. How had she obtained our address? I do not
know. She stayed a few minutes and went away. I closed my
books, incapable of reading further. I never saw her again.

How many times in my life have I thought of her! I try to
see her as she was. She was very fond of love, perhaps exces-

sively so. Well, so much the worse, or so much the better, as you like. What counts is that there was not a trace of malice in her heart. She was good, and I loved her. If I had to begin all that again, if I could be sixteen once more and find myself with her, how I would take her in my arms and hug her!

What man of my generation can ever forget the spring of 1917? Russia's defection, then America's entrance into the war. Thoughtful Germans understood that they had lost the contest when they found white bread in French prisoners' haversacks, but I can only refer the reader to history books.

It was around the month of May that a peculiar idea sprang up in my father's brain. Far be it from me to criticize him. I immediately approved of everything he decided. In his quiet, rather muffled voice, he said to me one day that as I was getting on toward seventeen, it was time to think of doing something for the common cause. I did not understand. "The Allied cause," he specified. "To enlist in an ambulance service, for instance." He explained that America, without waiting to enter the war, had sent to France lots of boys who drove ambulances at the front. What he did not know was the established rule not to accept anyone under eighteen (and I was not yet seventeen). I did not know of the rule either and, anyway, never dreamt of kicking. Why should I not go to the front? I immediately lived the part. A hero. What was I frightened of? Of nothing. "Of nothing," I said aloud before my mirror. I thought myself sublime.

Today, I wonder why my father did not wait until I was seventeen and had finished my top classical form. No doubt he remembered the Civil War, when the South as well as the North sent boys of fifteen into action. And then, all I had to do was to drive an ambulance, and my father thought that the job entailed very few risks.

I kept to myself this decision of my father's. First of all, I liked having a secret, but no doubt self-pride prevented me from talking about it, because I was afraid people would make fun of me and also that they would think my father a little unreasonable. Yet, I felt obliged to say a word or two about it to Father X., who first showed some astonishment and then, his arms folded, looked at me skeptically: "You'll be a defeated man when you come back," he said. I did not reply, but it was easy to see that he considered the plan disastrous. By leaving so early, I lost a year of study, apart from being exposed to possible dangers, and it is true I have always felt the loss of a year in philosophy.

We were then in April and, with my usual unconcern, I ceased thinking about these things. One day, however, I whispered to Roger that I was going away and that he would not see me next year. "Ah?" he said. "Where are you going? To America?"—"No," I answered mysteriously, "farther away." He did not question me, because I no longer interested him much.

The truth is that I wished to announce my departure not to him, but to Frédéric. I had not yet spoken to him once, and this pained me so much that it finally became known. Perhaps Philippe had spoken. So people knew that I was in love, and with whom. No one made fun of me. On the contrary, I noticed kindness in all my comrades and their wish to be friendly. Not one of them alluded to what was common knowledge. Intolerance and cruelty, so frequent in men, were completely absent in the behavior of boys of sixteen, and they all smiled at me. It was probably at that period that I foolishly tried to imagine that by swallowing a handful of flour I would die, like Madame Bovary, who swallowed arsenic. I knew perfectly well that I was not going to die, but I wanted to die, on account of Frédéric.

One day I saw him come up to me and would have run away if I could, but amazement struck me motionless. With his usual grumpy air, he shook my hand and asked me to see him home; he lived at the Porte Maillot. Nodding yes, I followed him. It was plain that he had been told everything, and I felt myself dying with shameful joy. If my life depended on it, I could not remember our conversation. He was not talkative, and I was almost mute. I only recollect gazing intently at that pugnacious little profile during our whole walk. With a little more thought I would have understood that the boy acted out of pure generosity, for I did not attract him in any way. Yet every day until the summer holidays began, he allowed me to cover in his company the few hundred yards that separated us from his parents' house. I never said a word about my feelings for him, and our conversation was exemplary and moreover extremely dull, for we had no tastes in common. Once, I was bold enough to ask him if he liked ghost stories and he replied gently that such things did not interest him. He also told me, it would be more precise to say that his profile told me, for I hardly saw anything else, that where religion was concerned, he believed in God and that was that, and all the rest was bunk.

I looked at him with horror. He was not a Catholic! I was dealing with a deist, a disciple of Voltaire, perhaps. The blow was a violent one, then I fell back into a besotted contemplation of the fine blue eye that did not wish to see me and, suffering all the while, felt happy. That was what he unknowingly gave me, happiness in pain and, at the same time, a sort of peace. He ceased to be inaccessible. I called him and, oh joy, he answered. What more did I want? I do not know. I did not have what are termed evil desires for anyone, and not for him any more than for another. Had I been able to tell him I loved him, I think a great load would have been lifted from me, but it would have been necessary to make me understand that I was in love, a fact of which I was completely ignorant. He knew it, I did not. All the boys in my class understood, and I was the only one not to see what was the matter. However that may be, he restored peace in me, out of sheer kindness of heart. I still have the photograph he gave me of himself, the last time we saw each other that year. It shows me a charming face, less perfect no doubt that I imagined, but the expression is frank and happy.

It had been more than a year since Sidonie ceased working for us. Indeed, whom would she have worked for? Two of my sisters were nurses, the others aboard, we no longer needed her services, but, unless I am much mistaken, my father helped her as much as he could afford to do. I went to see her from time to time. She lived on the top floor of an old house on the Rue des Archives, and the window of her little room—which she compared in a way that was absurd and a little sinister to Mimi Pinson's room—looked out on an ocean of roofs. I leaned over the gutters and my insides tightened on seeing tiny pedestrians on sidewalks the size of a small ribbon, but I raised my head at once, my gaze lost in the sky. "How lovely it is, Mademoiselle!" I cried. And a rather mocking voice reached me from the other end of the room: "Ah, that's Paris, my lovely Paris!" When I turned around, everything seemed black for a few seconds, then I caught sight of the old spinster seated on a low chair, her lap covered with her work, a large piece of fabric. An iron bed, a few seats, a table with a basin behind a screen, that was about all that could be distinguished at first between walls whose paper had lost most of its design and color, but on the corner of a table refreshments were ready for me: two baker's cakes and a pallid cup of tea. In less than three minutes, cup and saucer were empty. We chatted and laughed about everything. I think she thought me a bit silly for my age, but she was fond of me and poked gentle fun as she plied her needle and raised it high above her gray head. "And so, Monsieur Julian, your Mamma bought you at the Maison de Blanc?" She removed her steel pince-nez in order to laugh more freely. "Anyway," she said, "you're not proud. You haven't forgotten your old friend." She would talk to me about the people. The word was always on her lips. "We're the people, here we're the people, the people of Paris, Monsieur Julian, you've only to look out of the window to see them, all that is the people." By talking thus she freed herself from some mysterious and unknown grievance, but I think that she had a universal grudge against those who did not live as she did, poorly and in a garret. I paid no attention to tirades whose meaning escaped me and asked her to allow me to play a tune, for she owned a phonograph whose immense horn, painted mauve, opened in the dim light like some monstrous flower. You adjusted the needle, put on the record, and the Republican Guard made the air ring with its resounding brasses. The *"Sambre-et-Meuse"* was followed by the *"Marche des Allobroges,"* but there was also a song all about love. The tune has remained in my head from start to finish, and I can still hear the tenor's voice, both nasal and languorous, giving its full value to the last line, spun out in a skillful decrescendo:

". . . Et confondre le rêve et la réalité!"

"It's pretty, don't you think?"—"Oh yes, Mademoiselle!"
Several times she talked about women. There again, she had some account or other to square with fate. Laying down her work, she settled her pince-nez and looked me straight in the eye. "Do you know how they make men stick to them, Monsieur Julian? I'll tell you. They are depraved." Not knowing what she meant, I kept silent. "Depraved," she repeated with a sort of fury, waving her skinny little arms. Poor old lady! What disappointments did you have to bear? I allowed her mysterious fit of rage to pass and then asked her to talk to me about her memories. She knew Holland, all the towns in Holland, but I preferred to hear about the Commune. The bright red sky, the Seine running between walls of fire. "Grapeshot fell in the

streets. We took shelter in a cellar all night, we heard the cannon. I was six." I left her reluctantly, I had spent a pleasant afternoon. In the street I tried to sing like the tenor and to mingle dreams with reality. When I come to think of it, have I ever done anything else?

At the lycée, we had a professor of whom everyone said that he had a mistress. He wore a black frock coat and striped trousers, and beyond any possible argument he was potbellied. I imagined that once a year he had tea with a woman in a little flat deep down in Auteuil and that afterwards they did the mysterious thing described by Giulio Romano. Once a year only. I do not know where this idea came from, one that Boccaccio had not been able to correct in me but over which, anyway, I no longer lingered much, because it did not interest me at that time. Yet what puzzled me a little was that the boys and girls in Mr. Kreyer's library were young, slim, and ideally beautiful. What was more, they assumed attitudes that were occasionally acrobatic. Was it possible to fancy the professor in question giving himself up to impurity in a manner that demanded litheness and agile arms and legs? Pooh, that was his business. As for me, I led a completely peaceful life, without desires, or almost.

I have never known exactly what my schoolmates thought of me. No doubt they judged me rather indulgently, for they did not torment me. They knew that I was a recent convert. One remarked in talking of me once: "He must not lose faith, for he would lose everything if he did." The boy's name was Juillard. Where is he now? He was my rival in French literature, but I was always ahead of him. On all other subjects, except mathematics, I was fair. I did not shine. I had some difficulty in memorizing texts. One day our professor suggested our learning a poem of our own choice and reciting it to him on the platform. I selected some twenty lines by Henri de Régnier, thinking that a reasonable length. Several pupils distinguished themselves, declaiming with expression, thus provoking unutterable embarrassment and a few fits of laughter. One treated us to the *"Cœur de Hialmar,"* with showy effects that made one long to hide under one's desk. My turn came. I mounted the platform and began:

"Cette colline est belle, inclinée et pensive . . ."

When I reached this point, I stopped. My memory refused to furnish me with a single word of what came next. "I've forgotten the whole thing," I said. "Yet I knew it a moment ago." Having pronounced this, I turned my eyes on my schoolmates, as though challenging them to laugh at me, but no one laughed. For the first time, and perhaps a little late, as we were on the eve of the summer holidays and I was not to see them again, I felt that they were fond of me. "Passing amnesia," grunted the professor, "a very well-known thing. I'll give you fifteen." (Out of twenty.) In the deepest silence, I returned to my seat. An absurd emotion made my heart pound, but to prevent this from being seen I crossed my arms on my breast and looked straight ahead of me. The idea that I was leaving in a few weeks filled me with sudden sadness.

Lord, I can clearly see the way You came toward me, but I cannot see the way that took me to You. Was it that I stood still? It seemed as though I forgot the evil I had learnt in Genoa, that a sort of ignorance was forming again over the little fragmentary notions that had only shown physical love under its most wretched aspect. That was where I placed sin, the whole of sin. Sin should be avoided under penalty of damnation, but I believed myself saved. Whence my unconcern. I was sure of my salvation. This assurance bore me up as the sea bears up a boat.

In the sort of dream that I lived, I went to the Sorbonne in

July 1917 to take my first *baccalauréat* (bachelor's degree). The fear of failing did not cross my mind, although I had every reason for anxiety, knowing nothing in physics, nothing in chemistry, less than nothing in mathematics. The questions I was asked were probably easy ones. However it was, I passed with "distinction," on account of my dissertations in French and English. That is, at least, what I suppose. I felt sure of passing, not because I imagined knowing more than another candidate, but because I was convinced that nothing unfortunate could happen to me. Whence this confidence? Nothing in all my life is more obscure. I had the idea that if I remained faithful to God, I was entitled to a full, total protection on the temporal plane. No one could touch or harm me, since I was wholly God's child. That was my secret, of which I think I never have breathed a word to a soul.

The day after my *baccalauréat,* my father took me to the Rue Raynouard, to a charming Directoire house that no longer exists and whose gardens sloped down to the Seine. Great trees leaned over long, winding paths that twined like so many arms around vast lawns where it would have been delightful to sit at the end of a fine day. Everything spoke of times happier than ours. I was sensitive to the melancholy of a place, traces of which would be sought vainly nowadays in Paris. At the bottom of the gardens, drawn up neatly in front of the iron gate that led to the Quai de Passy, I saw some twenty ambulances painted iron gray and adorned by a red cross. The last of these cars was mine. I had learnt to drive and my father had had a khaki uniform made for me. It was then only that I began to believe I was going away, that it was all true in a certain way— with many reservations, but here, memory fails me. I think that for the moment I was only obliged to present myself at the Rue Raynouard each day at a given time. Perhaps they were waiting for the section to have its full complement. I am unable to recollect how I spent my time, but something comes back to me that I think curious. There was a lot of coming and going in the Rue Raynouard house, and boys attached to other services than mine could be seen, all in uniform. One day, one of these boys came up to me and asked if I would have a drink with him at a neighboring café. I had never set foot in a café and hesitated a second or two before accepting, but the boy took me by the arm and we went down to the quay. It would be useless to look for the spot where the café stood. Everything has been turned topsy-turvy and that part of Paris no longer has the least relation to what it was before the 1914 war. The café looked like a provincial café, a dark, low-ceilinged room with leather banquettes. My companion made me sit facing the door and took a seat opposite mine at the table. The minutes that followed were strange and, so far as I am concerned, perfectly unforgettable. I sat very straight and kept silent. If I could, without being rude, I would have left, but the young American's eyes held me to my seat and, out of pride no doubt, I avoided turning mine away. He said nothing, pushed aside the drink that had been served him and, crossing his arms on the table, brought his face a trifle nearer mine. It was then that I began to feel greatly embarrassed and, not understanding our silence, tried to say something, but my commonplace remarks fell into empty air. The beauty of the silent face struck me. It seemed as though it wished to burn itself into my mind forever, for it remained perfectly still. What lived in this face were blue eyes where I suddenly read distress and a sort of appeal that filled me with deep uneasiness. Perhaps something of this was visible in my expression, for the young man got up, paid, and went out with me. On the quay, he cried: "So long!" and disappeared. I never saw him again, but have often thought of him.

One morning in July, at eight o'clock, my section started out for a destination known only to our chief, Mr. Ware. Mr. Ware was a slim, lively young man with the face of a tiger cat and a fierce little black mustache. On seeing me for the first time, he murmured something in the ear of his superior, Mr. Galatti, an olive-skinned, black-eyed American who simply answered: "I know, but you've *got* to take him." This allusion to my age disturbed me. However, that July morning, the whole section was present, the ambulances left one after the other, but not the last, which was mine.

I have said that I had learnt to drive. This is an overstatement. I knew how to make my car go forward, but how to direct it properly was another thing. Right and left of the great iron gates were two stone posts. I chose the one on the right to hit with my front wheel. Blushing did not straighten out matters. No one blamed me, but I was ordered to get down. I would have liked to get down to the center of the earth. After half an hour, the damage was repaired and I got into my ambulance, this time accompanied by a young soldier in horizon blue who knew how to drive, and some time later we joined the section at a village called Moulin-de-Meaux.

On several occasions in the course of time, I happened to think of the Quai de Passy stranger, because there was something in his eyes that I had never read in any other man's. I even wonder if, up to that period, I had ever paid any attention to what could be going on in the depths of a human being's eyes. It was a little as though a window opened in a dark room. I was in that room and could see outside it now, but all I could see was the sky of human distress. Why did the boy look so sad? That was a question I could not answer. I would have liked to talk to the mysterious being who had not said a word. Today, I am practically certain that he was the first to draw me out of myself and to teach me that the stranger, known as the *other*,

241

existed as much as I did. It was as though my *neighbor* appeared in my life. "Remember me!" said the silent, motionless face insistently. "Look at me, look at me!"

I said nothing about all this to anyone. Whom would I have told, anyway? My companions thought of nothing but laughter. They were like big, handsome children, a little given to scoffing, but always ready to help one another. We were settled in a huge farm where the attic had been transformed into a dormitory and each had his camp bed. In the daytime we were taken to the country in order to perfect us in the art of driving a Ford. The instructor in charge of me was a boy from New York; he observed me with a sarcastic eye as he chewed a blade of grass. He knew French, but was unaware that I knew it too. I came and went before him between two rows of vertical sticks that were not to be knocked over, and of course I never missed hitting a single one of them. Peasants watched this operation. "Do you think this one will learn?" asked one of them. "Never," answered my instructor with a cruel smile, "this one, never."

However, I had learnt enough to follow the car ahead of mine when we left Moulin-de-Meaux. Where were we going? Our chief did not tell us. The first day, we stopped at Vitry-le-François for the night, with our ambulances lined up in a street. It happened that a mass of metal stuff, which had been forgotten but should have been placed elsewhere, had been thrown into my car. I was so ignorant of what to do, so timid also and even so foolish, that instead of complaining, I simply covered the heaps of tools with a canvas and stretched on it to sleep. The wonder is that I almost immediately fell into a deep sleep only to waken the next morning at six o'clock.

Another rather long stage in our journey that day. I had learnt to drive, since all it meant was following the car in front of me without ever modifying the distance between us. We went slowly. Toward evening we reached Triaucourt. It was a charming little town, spared by the war, but apparently empty. True, we had been told not to walk beyond a certain street and the few inhabitants we met observed a distrustful silence. "Tomorrow we're leaving for the front," said my companions. . . .

Other books by Julian Green
from Marion Boyars Publishers

The Distant Lands

A novel of the antebellum South

Sixteen-year-old Elizabeth Escridge and her impoverished mother arrive in Georgia from England to seek refuge with wealthy relatives. Immersed in the South's aristocratic society — young men in morning coats duel for her favor at dawn — Elizabeth discovers a web of secrets, dark destinies and private tragedies concealed beneath the tranquil, genteel façade of Southern life. A compelling love story, *The Distant Lands* is also the story of political intrigue, of secession and above all of extravagant high society living: balls and banquets are described in minute and authentic detail.

'. . . a compelling drama of the 1850s South . . . colorful and careful historical fiction, Julian Green's opus is a delicious immersion into time and place, stylish and fluid, with an abundance of characters who attract with their humanness.'   *Booklist*

'The writing, the characterization and sensitivity all combine to foreshadow the doom of the elegant, aristocratic South in this epic and wonderful novel.'

The Sunday Independent

'Green indicates that the distant lands are sublime habitations. It is a triumphant novel of pilgrimage.'

The Literary Review

'Julian Green is . . . an astute observer of society and a subtle moralist. The prose of *The Distant Lands* is deceptively transparent, a lens, not a plane of glass.'

The Boston Globe

'A family saga full of dark and tormented characters, it is replete with Spanish moss, gloomy mansions and family ghosts, religious fervor and guilty conscience, passionate loves that may contain a wisp of incest.'

San Francisco Chronicle

'A tribute to the memory of his mother and to the defeated South, the lost paradise of his memories. Meticulously crafted and intensely readable.' *The Independent*

South

A Play

'Can you imagine a man lacking courage to the point of not being able to speak of his love?'(Act Three, Scene One)

In this drama of complex relationships and doomed love, Julian Green masterfully portrays the interaction of extremes in a significant historical setting. It is April 11, 1861, General Beauregard demands the capitulation of Ford Sumter in Charleston Harbor, and the American Civil War will begin the next day. But what does this matter to the people gathered on this torrid Sunday at the Bonaventure plantation?

The play is Green's vehicle for examining opposing elements in antebellum Southern society: the North versus the South; the white man against the black man; European values in contrast to those of youthful America; and how the sexually normal fail to understand the sexually deviant.

The Apprentice Writer

Essays

Julian Green is intensely aware of how language and personality can change together. It is an insight that leads this immensely creative intellect on to deeper questions that he explores in this unique collection of early essays. Written originally in English between 1920 and 1946, these essays reveal the extraordinary range of Julian Green's talent and passion, coupled with his deep curiosity, which is the hallmark of a natural writer.

He begins with some fundamental literary inquiries, but provides them with fresh insights: How does one write a novel? Who am I when I write? Where do the images come from that permit the writer to create an imagined world more real in many ways than everyday life? In pursuit of answers to these and other questions, Julian Green displays the subtle development of his thought and the depth of his interpretative powers.

This collection also includes the short story "The Apprentice Psychiatrist," Green's first work of fiction, written in English and published originally when he was 19 in the prestigious *Virginia Quarterly Review*, while the author was still a student at the University of Virginia.

The Apprentice Writer also provides portraits of the major figures in American and Continental letters whom he knew personally, as well as vivid glimpses of the fascinating social milieux associated with their life and work.

'Certainly no other living writer can boast a career studded with the names and honors that have surrounded Mr. Green: his friends included Gertrude Stein, André Gide and Jean Cocteau; his works were translated by T.S. Eliot and praised by Hermann Hesse, Carl Jung and George Orwell . . . (he is) the last survivor of this literary firmament.' *The New York Times Book Review*.

Paris

Bilingual Illustrated Edition
Translated by J.A. Underwood

Paris, Julian Green discovered very early on, when looked at on the map, takes on the shape of a human brain. This moment of recognition was an important step in the developing love affair between a man and a city. For the author, his adopted home is a street map of the human imagination. Green accompanies the reader on a stroll around this enchanted place — its secret stairways, court-yards and alleys — sharing his discoveries and sense of wonder at every turning. A stroll through a city becomes a journey through the sensitive mind of a writer and gifted craftsman. The book is illustrated with the author's own photographs of Paris.

'The tone is mainly elegiac, contrasting the charm of the old Paris of his childhood with the brashness of the new, and the style is exquisitely literary in a traditional French manner.'   *New York Review of Books*

'. . . the most bizare and delicious of all this winter's travel books . . . Green does not go far from home and how sharply he reminds one that the best travel writing has little to do with length or breadth of journey, everything to do with what the travellers have with them in the bulging backpack of the mind.'   *The Observer*

'The pictures are truthful, unpretentious and haunting, and Green's evocation of the city poetic and unsenti-mental.'   *Times Literary Supplement*

'If you care for good writing and are interested in seeing Paris from an unusual perspective, then try this lovely and elegant book.'   *Gay Times*

'. . . full of philosophical speculations, moody reveries, flights into the past and future.'
     The New York Times Book Review